PARALLAXIC PRAXIS

Multimodal Interdisciplinary Pedagogical Research Design

Pauline Sameshima
Lakehead University, Canada

Patricia Maarhuis
Washington State University

Sean Wiebe
University of Prince Edward Island, Canada

Series in Education

www.vernonpress.com

In the Americas:
Vernon Press
1000 N West Street,
Suite 1200, Wilmington,
Delaware 19801
United States

In the rest of the world:
Vernon Press
C/Sancti Espiritu 17,
Malaga, 29006
Spain

Series in Education

Library of Congress Control Number: 2018962664

ISBN: 978-1-62273-389-7

Cover design by Vernon Press.

Cover image by Pauline Sameshima.

Book Abstract

Parallaxic Praxis is a research framework utilized by teams to collect, interpret, transmediate, analyze, and mobilize data generatively. This methodology leverages the researchers' personal strengths and the collective expertise of the team including the participants and community when possible. Benefits include the use of multi-perspective analyses, multi-modal investigations, informal and directed dialogic conversations, innovative knowledge creation, and models of residual and reparative research. Relying on difference, dialogue, and creativity propulsion processes; and drawing on post-qualitative, new materiality, multiliteracies, and combinatorial, even juxtaposing theoretical frames; this model offers extensive research possibilities across disciplines and content areas to mobilize knowledge to broad audiences.

This book explains methods, theories, and perspectives, and provides examples for developing creative research design in order to innovate new understandings. This model is especially useful for interdisciplinary partnerships or cross-sector collaborations. This book specifically addresses issues of research design, methodology, knowledge generation, knowledge mobilization, and dissemination for academics, students, and community partners. Examples include possibilities for scholars interested in doing projects in social justice, community engagement, teacher education, Indigenous research, and health and wellness.

Reprint Acknowledgements

Grateful acknowledgement is made for permission to reprint the following article:

Sameshima, P., Vandermause, R., Chalmers, S., & Gabriel. (2009). Introduction. *Climbing the ladder with Gabriel: Poetic inquiry of a methamphetamine addict in recovery* (pp. 3-16). Rotterdam, The Netherlands: Sense.

Reprints under the Creative Commons Agreement:

Attribution-NonCommercial-NoDerivatives 4.0 International (CC BY-NC-ND 4.0) (http://creativecommons.org/licenses/by-nc-nd/4.0/)

Sameshima, P., Miyakawa, M., & Lockett, M. (2017, Dec.). Scholarly engagement through making: A response to arts-based and contemplative practices in research and teaching. *Revista VIS, 16*(2), 45-67. Accessed at: http://periodicos.unb.br/index.php/revistavis/article/view/25466

Stock, R. V., Sameshima, P., & Slingerland, D. (2016, July). Constructing pre-service teacher identities through processes of parallax. *LEARNing Landscapes, 9*(2), 489-512. Accessed at: http://www.learninglandscapes.ca/index.php/learnland/article/view/Constructing-Pre-Service-Teacher-Identities-Through-Processes-of-Parallax

Wiebe, S., & Caseley Smith, C. (2016). A/r/t/ography and teacher education in the 21st century. *McGill Journal of Education, 51*(3). 1163-1178. Accessed at: http://mje.mcgill.ca/article/view/9312

Wiebe, S., & Sameshima, P. (2017, Dec.). Generating self: Catechizations in poetry. *Revista VIS, 16*(2). 140-155. Accessed at: http://periodicos.unb.br/index.php/revistavis/article/view/25465

Wiebe, S., & Sameshima, P. (2018, January). Sympathizing with social justice, poetry of invitation and generation. *Art/Research International, 3*(1)7-29. Accessed at: https://journals.library.ualberta.ca/ari/index.php/ari/index

Table of Contents

List of Figures

List of Tables

Foreword

Eleven Perspectives on Parallaxic Praxis

Carl Leggo

University of British Columbia

carl.leggo@ubc.ca

1

Parallaxic praxis is a celebration of the hard work that is heart work. In *University commons divided: Exploring debate & dissent on campus*, Peter MacKinnon (2018) notes that "intellectual work is hard work, and those committed to it must take the time to inform themselves carefully, to think their way through complicated questions, and to test their thinking in the marketplace of ideas" (p. 57). In *Parallaxic praxis* Pauline Sameshima, Patricia Maarhuis, and Sean Wiebe understand MacKinnon's perspective on intellectual work as hard work. They take up MacKinnon's call for scholarship and practice that "requires disciplined, patient effort, and a determination to engage and listen to others" (p. 57). Moreover, they agree with MacKinnon's claim that "universities exist to develop the human intellect, to enable discernment and the search for truth, and to resist ignorance, intellectual laziness, and coercion" (p. 104). *Parallaxic praxis* is a sophisticated book that presents a comprehensive overview of the concepts and principles of parallaxic praxis as well as engaging exemplars of research design that address urgent issues and questions including methamphetamine addiction, interpersonal violence, Indigenous mental health care, learner-centered pedagogy, cervical cancer screening, dementia studies, teacher education, technology and inclusive education, literacy, knowledge generation, and veteran post-traumatic stress syndrome.

2

Perplexing Pedagogy: Pensées

> if lost in mystery
>
> something emerges

a time you learned something almost
always begins with letting go

at the end of the day, writing is about desire,
the heart, breathing and not breathing

I will learn to live attentively in tentative times
I will learn to live the tenuous in tensile times

under the sky where possibilities defy calculus
I am a radical rooted in earth, heart, and wind

I attend to the familiar with unfamiliar words
I attend to the unfamiliar with familiar words

if we don't see the value in our lived stories,
we won't see the value in others' stories

seek words infused with the heart's rhythms
efficacious, capacious, effervescent words

I come alive in my writing where
I see, hear, know promises

no day is complete without
reading and writing poetry!

I am in process,
I am content

3

Parallaxic praxis is a memo to the world to remember to listen, to hear one another. In her poignant novel about racism, immigration, and colonialism, *In another place, not here,* Dionne Brand (1997) writes: "Already their stories were becoming lies because nobody wanted to listen, nobody had the time. That's what happens to a story if nobody listens and nobody has the time, it flies off and your mouth stays open" (p. 60). According to Brand, "you end up being a liar because what you say doesn't matter. And there's no tracing or lasting to your stories" (p. 60). Parallaxic praxis is about learning how to listen to the stories of others, so those stories sing with truthfulness about lived and living experiences.

4

It's All Greek to Me

antiphona

aporia

catechization

dialogue

ekphrasis

ethics

evanagnostos

métissage

mimesis

palimpsest

parallax

poiesis

praxis

sorites

trauma

And that is a significant strength of *Parallaxic praxis*—it offers richly evocative concepts that are full of possibilities for revisiting traditional practices, and shaping innovative approaches, and honouring the intricacies of interconnections among distinct disciplines that should never be held separate.

5

Parallaxic praxis is a confession of desire. In *Ecology of everyday life: Rethinking the desire for nature*, Chaia Heller (1999) notes that "informed by a capitalist sensibility, desire is often reduced to yearnings for an accumulation of private property, both material and symbolic" (p. 5). Therefore, "rarely do we view desire as a yearning to enhance a social whole greater than our selves, a desire to enrich the larger community" (p. 5). Heller calls for "a desire for a more healthful and sensual expression of everyday life" (p. 6) as we nurture "the ability to synthesize reason and passion" (p. 9). Heller wants to create "a new relationality, an empathetic, sensual, and rational way of relating that is deeply cooperative, pleasurable, and meaningful" (p. 93).

Parallaxic praxis resonates with Heller's hopeful understanding of desire and love: "It is in the space between individuals, within the hearts of individuals, that Eros flourishes. Eros, then, represents an *embodied* quality of social relationships—an attraction, passion, and yearning of one self for other selves" (p. 94).

6

A Poem Is

a heart beat   a light breath
a dream hanging on the line
stretched between poles we cannot see
falling in love with the alphabet
growing intimate with grammar and syntax
a game of peek-a-boo   scribbles in snow
a call, filled with hope somebody will hear
a message in a bottle dropped in the sea
attending to the familiar with unfamiliar words
a love note sent to creatures light years away
words infused with the heart's rhythms
words, efficacious, capacious, effervescent words
enjoying the sunlight through the study blinds
learning to live attentively in tentative times
cedars dancing in my neighbor's backyard

7

Parallaxic praxis is a sacred testimony. In her moving memoir *Gently to Nagasaki.* Joy Kogawa (2016) asks, “Do we write to be free of our ghosts or to welcome them?” (p. 190) For Kogawa, the world is “an open book embedded with stories. We hear them if we have ears to hear” (p. 149). She knows that her “story is from the belly of the dark” (p. 47). She is both “forbidden to tell it and commanded to tell it” because she knows “that to speak is to slay and not to speak is to slay. What is needed is right action” (p. 47). Therefore, she concludes that “for my part, I hold with a fierce and painful joy my trust in a Love that is more real than we are” (p. 42). This is the spirit of parallaxic praxis.

8

Parallaxic praxis is a political manifesto that champions interdisciplinarity in scholarship and social activism . . . . Parallaxic praxis is a love song! In “Everyday life at the corporate university,” Jane Juffer (2009) refutes binary oppositions in order to promote “the *intersections* of globalization, job training, cultural production, and ethical engagement” (p. 147). According to Juffer, “the challenge is to truly think in interdisciplinary terms . . . , which requires one to think about the ethical possibilities *in the relationship between* the humanities, business, education, engineering, information sciences, health services, and other fields” (p. 153). In a likeminded way, Andrew Ross recommends that “we are living through the formative stages of a mode of production marked by a quasiconvergence of the academy and the knowledge corporation” as they mutate into “new species that share and trade many characteristics” (p. 182). Parallaxic praxis sings with enthusiasm for social activism and change.

9

While I read *Parallaxic praxis* I lingered with many questions including:

1. In parallaxic praxis, what are the differences between collecting, representing, interpreting, and disseminating research?
2. What is the difference between using the arts to make sense of research conducted using traditional social science methods, and using the arts to research traditional social science issues and questions?
3. What is the relationship between ethics and aesthetics?
4. What is data?

5. What is the difference between rendering and surrendering?
6. What are the criteria for assessing Arts Integrated Research?
7. How can we make Arts Integrated Research more persuasive and useful?
8. What about: validity? vigour? vitality? vivaciousness? vibrancy? verity? trustworthiness? reliability? rigour?
9. Should we develop criteria for assessment from social science methodologies and practices, or from artists' methodologies and practices?
10. What is Arts Integrated Research good for?

10

Lunatic Scholars

education research and practice
should always charge us with insights
(in legal electrical business military ways)

living with the flux, listening to ducks
laughing on the dike, an encouragement
not to duck the flux, to laugh too

dance a highland jig, even if we don't
know how, right in the middle of
the flowing, furling, flashing flux

leave the models and wall charts
and kits and formulas to others
who wear suits or pretend they do

we become masters like Ted T. Aoki
is a master, always pushing boundaries
we have not yet seen or been

to inscribe our own insights
we do not need to repeat
everything others have done

our hang-ups are the stories
we seldom tell, the handicaps
that trip up our successes

the hang-ups are our humanity,
at least as integrally who we are
and are becoming, as any gifts

perhaps the classroom needs
to be a place where human beings
hang out with their hang-ups

instigating a revolution,
a twisting turning, to and fro,
in the heart of pedagogy

why do scholars speak so quietly?
why do scholars mumble rumble stumble?
why do scholars amble in their preambles?

if you are going to be witty, ironic, comical,
be prepared (in the best Boy Scout ethic) to be
misunderstood, misinterpreted, misrepresented

write with a kind of reckless, ruthless,
ruminative, revelling resolve
to defer solution and resolution

11

Parallaxic praxis is a love song! In a remarkable book titled *Three moments of love in Leonard Cohen & Bruce Cockburn*, Paul Nonnekes (2001) spells out a profound definition of love:

> Structures of love are created not through the fixing of desire in secure borders and boundaries, but through establishing frameworks of intersubjectivity, the activity of subjects reciprocally recognizing each other's independence and freedom, recognizing each other's difference, establishing a big space for the entertaining of diversity. (pp. 174-175)

Like the authors of *Parallaxic praxis*, Nonnekes understands "love as movement forward, not staying in one place, not being stuck or fixed" (p. 56). For Nonnekes, "love must move outward into the complicated world of social relations, of politics and power, of intersubjective conflict" (p. 66). Nonnekes calls for "the prophet-poet" (p. 178) because "the prophetic voice of the poet is outside the established system" (p. 129). Nonnekes calls for "an activist community fighting for change, for a better world" (p. 94); he calls for "a community of love" (p. 93). Even if "everything is falling apart, yet love rules" (p. 178) because love "is the active agent in human desire. It is what keeps us burning for something more than what presently exists. Burning for love, for justice and the overcoming of evil" (p. 60). The authors of *Parallaxic praxis* are all committed to "burning for love." And we are all bountifully blessed by their commitments!

References

Brand, D. (1997). *In another place, not here.* Toronto, ON: Vintage Canada.

Heller, C. (1999). *Ecology of everyday life: Rethinking the desire for nature.* Montreal, PQ: Black Rose Books.

Juffer, J. (2009). Everyday life at the corporate university. In M. Rothberg & P. K. Garrett (Eds.), *Cary Nelson and the struggle for the university: Poetry, politics, and the profession* (pp. 141-157). Albany, NY: State University of New York Press.

Kogawa, J. (2016). *Gently to Nagasaki.* Halfmoon Bay, BC: Caitlin Press.

MacKinnon, P. (2018). *University commons divided: Exploring debate & dissent on campus.* Toronto, ON: University of Toronto Press.

Nonnekes, P. (2001). *Three moments of love in Leonard Cohen & Bruce Cockburn.* Montreal, PQ: Black Rose Books.

Ross, A. (2009). The rise of the global university. In M. Rothberg & P. K. Garrett (Eds.), *Cary Nelson and the struggle for the university: Poetry, politics, and the profession* (pp. 167-184). Albany, NY: State University of New York Press.

Chapter 1

Introduction

How the book is organized:

- Model Overview
- The Catechization Process
- Theoretical Foundations
- Ethics
- Examples

Parallaxic Praxis is a multi-modal, transmethodological research framework utilized by interdisciplinary teams to collect, interpret, transmediate, analyze, and mobilize data generatively. Parallaxic praxis is used as a noun to refer to the model and also as a verb to describe the research practice. The methodology leverages the researchers' personal strengths and the collective expertise of the team including the participants and community when possible. The reparative and residual research design benefits include the use of multi-perspective analysis, multi-modal investigations, informal and directed dialogic conversations, innovative knowledge creation, and models of residual and reparative research. Relying on difference, dialogue, and creativity propulsion processes; and drawing on post-qualitative, new materiality, multiliteracies, and combinatorial, even juxtaposing theoretical frames; this model offers extensive research possibilities across disciplines and content areas to mobilize knowledge to broad audiences.

The model originated in a methamphetamine addiction and recovery project in 2007. The first iteration of the model (Sameshima & Vandermause, 2008) was developed in collaboration with a team from multiple departments spearheaded by Dr. Roxanne Vandermause in the Nursing Department at Washington State University (see Women and Meth Project example, this volume). The model's intent is to stimulate a fuller and richer understanding of the research project and to advance clinical, methodological, and social change. The model has since been used in various disciplines and for a range of research projects. For example: human immunodeficiency virus research (Defechereux, 2017), responses to experiences of interpersonal violence (Maarhuis, 2016), Indigenous mental health care (Saunders, 2015); learner-centred pedagogy (Ingalls Vanada, 2017); cervical cancer screening (Sameshima et al., 2017); dementia studies (Wiersma et al., 2015); teacher education identity studies

(Stock, et al., 2016, reprinted in this volume), technology and inclusive education (Marino et al., 2009), knowledge generation (Wiebe & Sameshima, 2017, reprinted in this volume), veteran post-traumatic stress syndrome (Upshaw, 2018), literacy (MacLaren & Becker, 2018), and more.

The research framework of Parallaxic Praxis grew out of the work from the book *Seeing Red, A Pedagogy of Parallax* (Sameshima, 2007a) and draws from a variety of traditions, some, often believed to be disparate. The tenets of arts integrated research utilized in this model are rhizomatic extensions of arts informed inquiry (Cole & Knowles, 2000, 2008); arts-based educational research (Eisner, 1991; Barone & Eisner, 1997; 2012) and a/r/tography (Irwin, 2004). These three methodological approaches each include creative tenets and yet differing epistemologies (Tsun Haggarty, 2017). Thus, we use the term arts integrated research to refer to research design that includes creative or generative construction as part of the research design without implied attachment to disciplinary or epistemological alignments.

Arts Integrated Research

We use the term Arts Integrated Studies to refer to research projects in which the arts are used specifically as a generative mechanism in the research design process. The arts can be used to advance scholarship by a researcher working independently, by an artist-researcher working with a team, by a research team collaborating with an artist, or any combinatory practice.

Integrating the arts in research methodology affords scholars new lenses for viewing, analyzing, representing, and disseminating research (Sameshima, 2007a). As marketers and mathematicians use bar graphs, infographics and schematics to demonstrate relationships between numeric data, artist-researchers render research data into stories, plays, documentaries, movies, paintings, posters, poetry, and so forth to better discern and represent relational connections. Art-making can happen at any point in the research process and produces artefacts to purposefully generate data and further analyze data, offer new perspectives, generate models of theories, and so on. During the research process art-making is also used to mobilize knowledge across the audience spectrum and to use as teaching tools for students in formal and informal educational settings (Cole & Knowles, 2001). Using the arts to research and disseminate results is synergistic—humans make sense of the world through their writings, music, artworks, and various forms of representation (Barone & Eisner, 1997).

Integrating the arts as a teaching method in educational settings has demonstrated increased learning engagement and content knowledge (Burnaford, April & Weiss, 2000; Gelineau, 2004). Arts integrated studies require:

1) theorizing through metaphors using theoretical frameworks in education, cultural studies, philosophy, psychology, history, and other disciplines; 2) strong foundational understandings of various traditional qualitative methods; and 3) personal study in art skill development or collaboration with arts experts. This theoretical framework is grounded in multiple perspectives including Stuart Hall's (1973) notions on coding and encoding; Roland Barthes' (1996) polysemic readings (having different meanings) of texts—including non-word-based texts; and Mikhail Bakhtin's (1981) ideas on utterance, heteroglossia, and carnival. Arts integrated studies use a constructivist and post-qualitative theoretical framework with a dynamic and multi-viewed approach. Constructivist epistemologies focus on schemata or knowledge systems that position knowledge generation as relational—that meaning occurs through interaction between experience and thought and that meaningful reality is socially constructed (Crotty, 2003). Thus, knowledge generation and meaning-making are always continual, ontological, and incomplete.

Interdisciplinary Research

Interdisciplinary research accesses vocabulary, tools, techniques, methodologies, and theoretical frameworks from two or more specialized knowledge fields. As various academic disciplines each have their own ways of organizing and framing meaning, artistic disciplines (creative writing, visual arts, performing arts, film, new artistic practices, and more) also each have their own 'language.' Interdisciplinary arts integrated work can expand innovation capacity by encouraging dialogues to develop among scholars with different lexicons, semantic fields, disciplinary expertise, epistemologies and ontological framings of the world (Sameshima, 2007a; Sameshima, Vandermause, Chalmers & Gabriel, 2009).

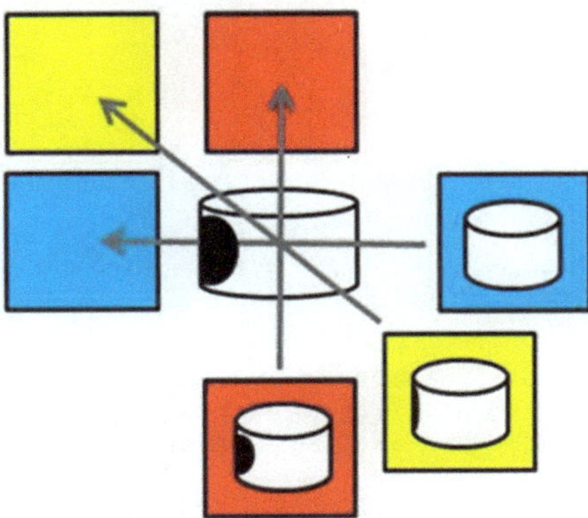

Figure 1.1. Parallax.

The Concept of Parallax

Parallasséin, the Greek word for parallax, means to change, to cause to alternate, to vary (dictionary.com, 2018). The noun refers to "*the apparent displacement of an observed object due to a change in the position of the observer.*" For example, in Figure 1.1, the three perceived views (lower right) of the same object produce a different looking object embedded within three different contexts. This notion of perspective as determined by discipline, modality, language, time, space, light, and a multitude of other variables is significant in conceptualizing understanding. "The concept of parallax encourages researchers and teachers to acknowledge and value their own and their readers' and students' shifting subjectivities and situatedness which directly influence the construct of perception, interpretation, and learning" (Sameshima, 2007a, p. 2).

The Model

The model's name is drawn from a *pedagogy of parallax* (Sameshima, 2007a), that all that is known is partial and the known is always in relation; and the notion of *praxis*, the embodied form of engaging, realizing, and applying theory in practice.

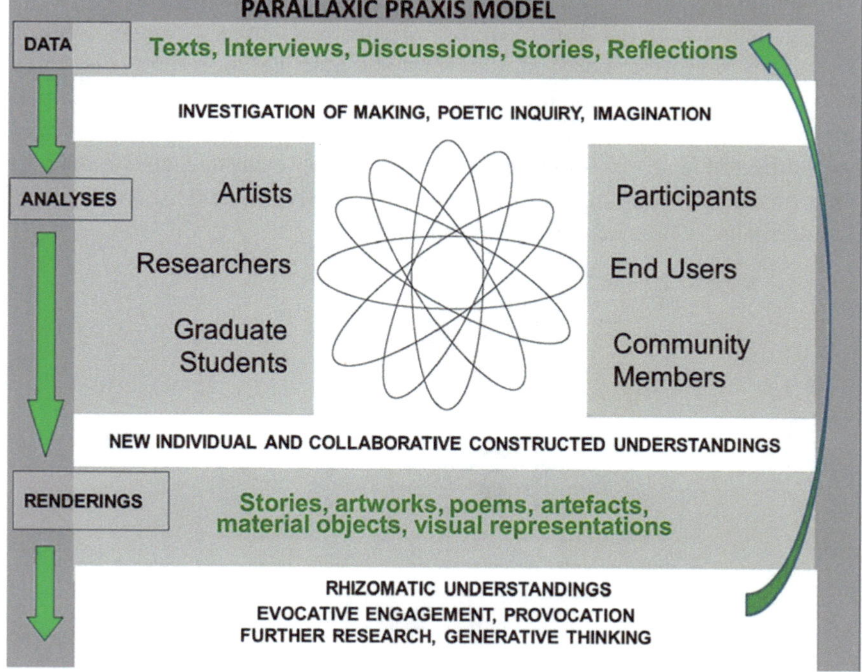

Figure 1.2. Parallaxic Praxis, Generic Model.

The Parallaxic Praxis model (see Figure 1.2) can be used both as a research conceptual framework and an educational model to structure inquiry through relation, dialogics, and multi-modal means of generating data, accessing and engaging with data, analyzing thinkings, materializing and representing learning, provoking imagination, and disseminating research. While the framework/model appears linear here (beginning at the top of the graphic), the model is cyclical, moving from top to bottom and returning to the top as new questions are generated. It is important to note that the model is not prescriptive. To be effective, parallax relies on multiple viewpoints that are genuinely personalized and designed with consideration for the researchers, the participants, and the local needs and goals of the study. There are three organizational phases in the model framework: Data, Analyses and Renderings.

Chapter 2

Phases of the Model

- In the DATA PHASE, researchers collect data in traditional and non-traditional ways.
- In the ANALYSES PHASE, researchers from different fields interpret the data through their disciplinary expertise.
- In the RENDERING PHASE, the completed artifacts created during the previous phase are used as touchstones to provoke thinking and generate discussion.

Phase I – Data Collection

A wide range of data collections can be utilized in this phase. Data may consist of raw numerical data, audio or transcribed interview transcripts with individuals or focus groups, collections of texts, collections of artefacts, and more. Because this is a cyclical model, the first analyses of original data can itself become the focal data in the next cycle.

Examples of original data included in examples in this book include: a participant's interview transcripts (Women and Meth Project); 90 cloaks made by pre-service teachers (Teacher Identity Project); participant decorated t-shirts (Clothesline Project); or an author's select writings (Nuno Scarf Project).

In this model, the arts can also be used in the data collection process to improve the quality of the data. For example, in a project addressing barriers to cervical cancer screening, the use of crafting during the research focus sessions created improved dialogic conversation by displacing positionalities of researchers and participants (Sameshima et al., 2017).

Phase II – Analyses

In the Analyses Phase or artefact-making stage, researchers through different fields, lenses, methodologies, or modalities interpret the data through their independent disciplinary lenses. The analyses phase may include coding the raw data, grouping co-occurring themes, and looking for connections and commonalities. In this phase, analysis refers to indwelling, deep engagement, the study of the data and the creation of artefacts based on the original data. An artefact could be a graph, a chart, a narrative timeline, a painting, or more.

Quantitative, qualitative, and post-qualitative analyses take place in this phase of the model. As mentioned above, in this phase, data is distilled, reiterated, or translated into other forms. The Analyses Phase is the creation of artefacts based on the data set.

In the translation/making process, a researcher is inherently fully engaged in the nuances and meanings of that data. For example, an audio interview with a participant is layer one. Transcription of the interview is layer two. While some researchers hire transcriptionists, the act of translating the oral to text is a form of analysis and indwelling. The transcriptionist will inadvertently fill in minor words that may be inaudible but which complete expected sentence construction. In this process of creating the artefact of the interview text from the recording, the transcriptionist provides one perspective of the original data. In this model, there is not only one meaning or one truth. The artefacts are creations of how the data is experienced through a particular modality in relation to the researcher in time and space. Layer three could be a graphic chart demarking key co-occuring themes from the data set. Layer three could be a metaphoric or literal snapshot painting from the interview transcripts. Layer three could be a found poem based on key events in the transcript.

The express intent of artefact making is a translation of a snapshot of part of the data. Likened to a therapist summarizing a client's concerns, the artefact is a mirror of part of the data through a different modality. This translation becomes another way of understanding the data. Wiebe and Morrison-Robinson (2013) suggest that expanding imaginations across multiple domains enables social tendencies that privilege economic valuing to be redressed. Through transmediative processes wider semantic fields of language are engaged and generative possibilities for knowledge creation are enhanced.

The making of the artefact creates new understanding for the researcher, the team, and the audience, resulting in co-learning, knowledge production, and later, research dissemination. The aim is to look at the data from various disciplines, lenses, and modalities as a means to complexify the interpretive possibilities and to generate collaborative dialogic analyses in the next phase of this model. Teams may utilize arts-based research (Barone & Eisner, 2012); arts-informed inquiry methods (Cole & Knowles, 2001); poetic inquiry (Prendergast, Leggo & Sameshima, 2009); a/r/tography (Irwin, 2004); heuristic inquiry (Djuraskovic & Arthur, 2010), or other processes to create interpretive renderings in response to the data collected. These multiple perspectives are created as a means to generate an enlarged investigative field.

The Analyses Phase is a method of fractalling the boundaries of the original data collection. The process offers traditional and metaphoric ways to view the data, thus opening up larger semantic fields for discussion particularly among broad community audiences and various stakeholders. Metaphors work by reordering the relations of a semantic field by mapping them onto the existing relations of another semantic field (Stern, 2000). Translating data into other modalities invokes polysemy (phrases and words having multiple meanings) and pluralism (multiple interpretive views). The making of the artefact is a reparative gesture in that the artefact demonstrates to the participants that their stories are heard and acknowledged. These artefacts aim to provoke further rhizomatic understandings, challenge conceptions, and generate the emergence of more questions (Sameshima, Vandermause, Chalmers & Gabriel, 2009).

Eisner (2008) suggests that "*something that mediates the researchers' observations and culminates in a form that provides the analogous structure*" (p. 7) can be a means to generating the articulation of the unsaid.

Phase III – Renderings

In the Rendering Phase, the various artefacts created during the Analyses Phase are used as juxtaposed touchstones for the research team to discuss their personal experiences of the data, the methodological processes, the metaphoric and symbolic references, and the creative practices utilized. These independent renderings of the data are discussed with the team informally or more formally using a dialogic process called The Catechization Process. The renderings can also be used as pedagogic tools in formal and informal settings to mobilize knowledge and generate discussion.

Individual renderings (i.e., a paper, a poem, a poster, a graphic from survey data, an artwork, and more) can be very useful in generating discussion; however, when there are several types of artefacts, the juxtaposition and correlation of ideas between and across artefacts and the modes of creation extend the semantic and imaginative fields for further reflective analysis. This dialogic area is where the colliding chronotopes (time-space) of discourse and modality generate new forms, frames, assumptions, categories, and patterns. Bakhtin (1981) explains the chronotope as "*the place where knots of narrative are tied and untied*" (p. 250).

The renderings are used by the team, participants, and wider community as catalysts to stir conversations on the issues surfaced in the Analyses Phase. While the Rendering Phase could simply be an informal sharing and discussion of the artefacts created from the analysis with the research team; it could be a Philosopher's Cafe where there is sharing with a focus group; it could be a meeting with participants as a type of member check; it could be an exhibition of the works; or it could be a very specific process of dialogue called the Catechization Process explained in the next chapter (also see examples in this volume: Stock, Sameshima, Slingerland, 2016; Wiebe & Sameshima, 2017).

The Catechization Process is a synthesizing analysis of the various renderings made. The Catechization Process uses questions to move the dialogue and learning forward and is a formal systematic approach of discussing the renderings. Invariably, the Catechization Process creates new questions and wonderings, leading the researchers back to the data in a recursive research loop.

Chapter 3

The Catechization Process

In a parallaxic praxis, following the creation of 'renderings,' researchers visually juxtapose and analyze the various multi-modal artefacts through dialogic practices called catechizations. The catechization process is a specific methodological process that supports synthesis and evaluation. Catechizations are tools to guide visual analysis. The word catechize, comes from the Greek word katēkhein: *kata*, meaning down, off, out and *cata* to sound, and means to question or examine closely or methodically (free dictionary.com, 2018); and to move knowledge forward through questioning systematically or searchingly (Merriam-Webster, 2018).

Throughout the analysis, interpretation, and rendering processes, specific catechizations were found to be beneficial to meaning-making and focusing research questions. Using specific categories of questions, the team/participants can catapult dialogue in new directions. To better understand catechizations as a creativity propulsion strategy, please see Chapter 7.4 in this volume.

Catechizations use questions and inquiries to propel dialogue forward, inward, and into new understanding. Catechizations can strengthen and enrich any number of dialogic practices and integrative methods, such as duoethnography (Norris & Sawyer, 2016; Norris, Sawyer & Wiebe, 2016; Sawyer & Norris, 2013; Norris, Sawyer & Lund, 2012, Sameshima, 2013) or métissage (Chambers, Hasebe-Ludt, Leggo & Sinner, 2012; Hasebe-Ludt, Chambers & Leggo, 2009; Hasebe-Ludt & Leggo, 2018). The dialogue focuses on the artefacts and since the interpretations often work through metaphor—and metaphors depend on there being a common referent for both maker and viewer in their associative and established meanings—the "metaphors both presented by the user and interpreted by the reader always present ambiguity and thus provide openings for learning" (Sameshima & Irwin, 2006, p. 51).

The Catechizations

- Mimesis (relational)
- Poesis (realization in time)
- Palimpsest (depth)
- Intertextuality (breadth)
- Antiphona (harmonies)
- Sorites (cumulative)
- Aporia (conditions)
- Evanagnostos (readability)

The catechizations work to create relational aesthetics through *visual re-formations*. Recombining discernible moments in the data set creates structured conditions for an exchange or encounter between different narratives and dialogic interpretations. These reconstructions are also dynamic between the researcher, participant/subject, and audience (Bourriaud, 2002). Through modal deconstruction of the data set into 'snapshots' the team is then able to bricolage new possibilities for meaning making.

How do Catechizations Enable Synthesis and Evaluation?

The Catechization Process

- provides avenues toward 'common reflection' in interpretive work and dissemination (Barone & Eisner, 2012)
- provides explicit, though not standardized, vocabulary and practices helpful in attaining significance, value, and meaning
- actively expands the semantic and perceptual field and assists in analysis and interpretation
- offers pragmatic 'how to' approaches in evaluation and artful interpretation, especially for those new to arts integrated research
- enhances transformative communication between researcher(s) and with participants and audiences in dissemination processes
- provides a means for multiple researchers to present their work in an integrated, accessible, and cohesive manner

Over the last decade, as the model has been used across disciplines and applied in various contexts with wide-ranging content, ongoing study and understandings related to evaluative processes for cross-disciplinary and multi-modal research have been studied. The Catechizations enable research teams to think about:

- what constitutes an interpretation
- the meaning of an interpretation from a participant experience
- how the artefact interprets
- how the artefacts interact
- how the interpretations might communicate within a particular environment (not all artefacts are appropriate for all environments)

- how and why interpretations engage with one another
- what and how the interpretations communicate to an audience
- how the multi-modal aspect of the research framework fractals complexity into the data
- if the artefacts interpret and re-present the narrative in a meaningful way that enhances empathy and understanding
- the specific arts integrated practices that are employed to assist in analysis, interpretation and dissemination
- how the catechizations enhance the process of research analysis, interpretation, evaluation, and dissemination
- the tools we are using to analyze interpretations

Catechization Café

Worksheet How-To

Instructions for the facilitator: When artefacts or more than one translation has been made of the data, a Catechization Café can be set up. A café is a special invited meeting where there are often refreshments and hospitality is deliberately planned. The artefacts are displayed in the room, via a shared photo album (if researchers are not local), or on screen. Depending on the artefact, the interpretations can be shared in advance or for the first time at the meeting. For example, a fictionalized novella based on the participant data would be shared at least two weeks before the café.

The questions in each catechization can be modified in advance to be specific to each project. A copy of the worksheet is printed for each person involved in the meeting.

The language of the catechizations can be intimidating and is best used with directed dialogue. The use of the specific terms is intentional as the meanings of the categories have ambiguous interpretations and thus offer more possibilities for participants to make meaning for themselves. The facilitator leads the group through one Catechization at a time, inviting dialogue. The café focus group is recorded, transcribed, and coded for summarizing findings. The following text may be printed on a sheet of paper with space to write below each Catechization. The open space is for café participants to jot down relational ideas as the dialogue takes place. A digital download is available at: http://www.solspire.com/research-model.html

The Catechization Worksheet

Mimesis

imitation; reproduction; representation by means of art (Online Liddell-Scott-Jones Greek-English Lexicon, 2018)

imitation or making a likeness (http://logeion.uchicago.edu/index.html#mimesis)

- refers to a reproduction or a mirroring. In looking at the artworks, how are ideas or authors' works re-created or mirrored? In what ways are the artefacts mirrors/echoes of your thinking? What do you see in the various works that echo themes in your project or across the larger project?

Poiesis

make, produce; create, bring into existence (Online Liddell-Scott-Jones Greek-English Lexicon, 2018)

- refers to a moment in time, where the mimetic work rises up into a realization through interpretation, dialogue, bearing witness, and reflection. The mimetic work provides the opportunity for an interaction, or an event, for the researcher and participants. How do we, as teachers, researchers, learners and creatives respond to these artefacts now, in this moment? What do we take from the work that was created? What do we notice about the artefacts here, now, in relation? What has changed in speaking together now compared to individual experience or looking back to ideas in the past?

Palimpsest

Scraped again. (Online Liddell-Scott-Jones Greek-English Lexicon, 2018)

The name given to a manuscript from which the original writing has been rubbed off, in order that the leaves may be used again for fresh writing. This process is occasionally repeated, so that the leaves receive a third text. From vellum and strong substances the writing was removed by scraping or rubbing, but from the delicate papyrus leaves by washing, usually with a sponge (http://logeion.uchicago.edu/index.html#palimpsest)

- refers to trace—that over time, whatever is below sometimes seeps through. There is a trace of what was below (an example is a painting that has been painted over). Palimpsest provides depth and layering. Another view is to consider how both the participant/researcher or student/teacher or researcher/researcher can be present at once. How or when were you present as a researcher or the self in a focus group? What traces are coming through from the artefacts in your lives as teachers, researchers, learners and creatives? What are the under layers that are more complex beyond the surface of what has been made? How does the particular material/modality/medium speak to you? In what way does your artefact echo or trace the data?

Intertextuality

That which is woven; textum (Perseus-Tufts Latin Dictionary, 2018)

- is the relationships between texts. In this case, we might consider ideas across the artworks/artefact, or between the researchers here. How do the artefacts work in combination with each other? What commonalities do they have? How do the artefacts work in combination to teach us something anew?

Antiphona

sounding in answer, concordant; responsive to (Online Liddell-Scott-Jones Greek-English Lexicon, 2018)

- expands on intertextuality. The Greek term antiphōna refers to "'harmonies." We might ask in this research, now that we have named some commonalities, how *do* they work together to teach us something new? What can we learn from these commonalities? In what ways do the materials, the model, or our discussions teach us?

Sorites

heap; summation (Online Liddell-Scott-Jones Greek-English Lexicon, 2018)

- refers to the marking of a threshold. When does a heap become a heap? If you have a handful of sand in your hand you can say that is a heap of sand but if you saw a big pile of dirt on your driveway that is also a heap of sand. So the heap isn't based on an amount, it just becomes a heap because we think it is. If we can think how certain things became significant "heaps," we might be able to discuss how we frame or value particular aspects of the phenomenon that create thresholds for significance. What themes appear to be significant? Why? What specific quotes or ideas from the data do you see expressed in the artefacts?

Aporia

being at a loss, embarrassment, perplexity; question for discussion, difficulty, puzzle (Online Liddell-Scott-Jones Greek-English Lexicon, 2018)

- refers to "an impasse or puzzlement" and philosophically is a "puzzle or a seemingly insoluble impasse in an inquiry, often arising as a result of equally plausible yet inconsistent premises . . . the state of being perplexed or at a loss" (Collins English Dictionary, 2011). A question we may want to consider is, what puzzles us, or challenges us when thinking about the artefacts created? How do the artefacts play with or against one another?

Evanagnostos

easy to read; easy to expectorate, pronounce (Online Liddell-Scott-Jones Greek-English Lexicon, 2018)

- refers to the Greek word for something being legible and easy to read (Wordreference.com, 2018). When artful works are congruent in readability with the audience, capacity for transactional dialogue and understanding are enabled and the impetus for rippling effects initiated. Questions to ask may be: What is it in the artwork that speaks to you? What do you notice in the artefact that speaks a truth about a particular experience?

Theoretical Foundations of the Catechizations

To further detail the theoretical foundations of the Catechizations, Maarhuis and Sameshima offer perspective in the context of one of their research projects. The Women and Meth study is detailed as an example in Chapter 7.2. Here, a selection of that project is used to help the reader situate how four ekphrastic interpretations of the same data can yield generative possibilities for studying participant experience, researcher interpretation, and research knowledge mobilization through a Catechization Process (see Figure 3.1). The artefacts were created from three interviews conducted with Jill (pseudonym), a methamphetamine addict in recovery. The artefacts can also be viewed here: https://www.womenandmeth.com/arts-integrated-studies.html

Patricia Maarhuis	**Victoria Bolduc**	**John-Paul Chalykoff**	**Pauline Sameshima**
So NOT Hollywood Series	*Frosted Glass Series*	*Music Series*	*Constructing Control Series*
10 Digital faux movie posters with artist statements. Found poetry accompanying 7 of the posters	6 Watercolor and ink on paper paintings	8 Live-based recordings	4 Plexiglass and fishing line framed works accompanied with transcript text
Deliberate overstatement, movie industry representations	Representation of specific events and interpretive symbolism	Interpretive soundscapes, atmospheres and feelings	Interpretive metaphoric themes and imagery
http://www.womenandmeth.com/maarhuis-response1.html	http://www.womenandmeth.com/bolduc-response.html	http://www.womenandmeth.com/chalykoff-response.html	http://www.womenandmeth.com/sameshima-response1.html
Example	Example	Example "Bargaining" QR link	Example

Table 3.1. Four Ekphrastic Interpretations of Jill's Interviews.

During the Catechization Process, using a questioning technique, the creation of aesthetic relationship and "*social interstices*" acquire existence and form and become evident (Bourriaud, 2002, p. 14, 22). The Catechizations support phenomenological meaning-making. 'The new' is the aha, the gestalt, and the essence which amplify themselves across and through material processes in this research. The catechization practice develops dialogic inter-subjectivity. The artefacts are not simply artful depictions of retroactive trace but act as generative aesthetic forms of layered time-space-images that gesture toward the conditions of production and the social relations brought on by them. Dewey (1934/2005) describes aesthetic experience as "*a body of matters and meanings, not in themselves esthetic, [yet they] become esthetic as they enter into an ordered rhythmic movement toward consummation*" (p. 339).

Mimesis. Mimesis is an imitation, reproduction, or copy (Online Liddell-Scott-Jones Greek-English Lexicon, 2018). In this work, the practice of mimesis is used to excavate the idea of response-translation. Theoretically, Gadamer (1975/2004) describes a practice of mimesis that goes beyond semiotics, representation, and imitation toward the interrelationship between representation and the represented within a particular performed event or presentation (Lotz, 2012). In *Truth and Method* Gadamer explains:

> *Thus the situation basic to imitation that we are discussing not only implies that what is represented is there, . . . but also that it has come into the* There *[emphasis added] more authentically. . . Imitation and representation are not merely a repetition, a copy, but knowledge of the essence. Because they are not merely repetition, but a "bringing forth," they imply a spectator as well. They contain in themselves an essential relation to everyone for whom the representation exists.* (p. 114)

Understood in this way, mimetic works are not simply static copies or an imitation but rather ecstatic formations that unfold ontologically, fluidly, temporally, and referentially. "*The formed image is to be understood as an active and dialectical notion, and leads throughout its constitution to a clarification of itself*" (Lotz, 2012, p. 93). Consequently, within parallaxic research, relational mimesis is a type of response translation, in this case, a relational re-presentation of phenomenological narrative that openly accrues more perspectives and, in so doing, allows that the subject matter becomes more fully what it is. "*By being presented it experiences, as it were, an increase in being. The content of the picture itself is ontologically defined as an emanation of the original*" (Gadamer, 1975/2004, p. 135).

Additionally, within the Catechizations, mimesis is a practice of remembrance and bearing witness through multiple interpretive works. In this project, Gilda bears witness to her own experience with addiction and recovery and we, the researcher-artists, bear witness to Jill's experience as well as our own. Together these reflexive works "*open in the interstitial boundary space, the intersubjective time of testimony-witnessing. . . [as] a renewal of the possibility of the past, which may innovate and interrupt the performance of the present*" (Simon, 2000, p. 23). A relational mimesis of experience and events offers a connection between re-presented works in the interstices of documentation, interpretation, witness, and the impossibility of claiming truth or full knowledge.

And last, relational mimesis gives rise to ethical interruptions and invites reflection on simple subject-object binaries and dominant cultural discourse, especially in regard to difficult, even traumatizing, experiences such as methamphetamine addiction and recovery. This pushes mimesis beyond reductional identification to embed it directly within poiesis (Levine, 2009).

Poiesis. Etymologically derived from ancient Greek, poiesis means 'to make' (Online Liddell-Scott-Jones Greek-English Lexicon, 2018); however, in a Deweyan sense, it also is an ontological state, a moment of ecstasis, when, over time, there is movement away from 'being' as one thing to become another: "*Like the soil, mind is fertilized while it lies fallow, until a new burst of bloom ensues*" (Dewey, 1934/2005, p. 24).

Engaging poiesis in parallaxic praxis research shifts the metaphoric work of art from a static object of representation to an "*ec-static*" interpretive event, fully embracing an affected, vitalistic, and ontological becoming (Lash & Lury, 2007). For example, relational mimesis is made manifest in the circuitous but responsive poiesis of artful interpretation, dialogue, bearing witness and reflection. Poiesis opens the capacities of the researcher-artist, participant, and the audience to be present with, to be changed by, and to compassionately respond to the convoluted experiences of another. Works of art and the work of art is "*recreated every time it is esthetically experienced*" (Dewey, 1934/2005, p. 113).

Palimpsest. In creating arts-informed representations, layers of meaning are affixed to the original narratives but in such a way that no new layer completely obscures the previous one. The work is re-contextualization into another medium (For example, participant narrative to sculpture) but doesn't completely lose the original meaning. It is ontologically re-articulated into a translucent and overlapping palimpsest where new layers of meaning overlie older ones, once the phenomena or object is placed in a different medium or context (Lidchi, 1997). Viewing arts-informed representation as a palimpsest of meaning allows researchers to coalesce complex cultural contexts into deep interpretive analysis of phenomena.

Palimpsest allows the multiple voices to be concurrently present—foregrounded and backgrounded—in the layering of interpretation. Directly including the participant voice within analysis and interpretation is an empowering research practice and enhances agency by challenging the dominance of the researcher/artist and using multiple subject/object positionality. Through palimpsest, the participants are able to constitute their own experiences when they participate (or are included) in the formation of the cultural construction of meaning through representations about their experience and self. Foucault describes this as "*techniques or practices of the self*", through which subject-position are held by individuals:

> *. . . it is not enough to say that the subject is constituted in a symbolic system. It is not just in the play of symbols that the subject is constituted. It is constituted in real practices. There is a technology of the constitution of self which cuts across symbolic systems while using them.* (in Hall, Rabinow interview of Foucault, 1997, p. 322)

Additionally, Barone and Eisner (2012) note that the inclusion of the participant's perspectives is "*critical in an arts-based text*" when attending to ethical practice in research methods (p.134). Research analysis, artful interpretations and knowledge generation that are steeped in deep layers of multiple perspectives provide guidance for an ethical and empathetic imagination about unique life situations, like methamphetamine addiction, that are full of incompatible moral demands, uncertainty, and personal hazard (Fesmire, 2003). Dewey (1934/2005) offers pragmatic grounding for the capacity of conscious moral and ethical practice as arts informed researchers and educators: "*The moral function of art itself is to remove prejudice, do away with the scales that keep the eye from seeing, tear away the veils due to wont and custom, perfect the power to perceive*" (p. 338).

Intertextuality. While the practice of palimpsest provides depth, it is the practice of intertextuality that provides the breadth in parallaxic interpretation and re-presentation (Hall, 1997). Intertextuality occurs when representations accumulate meaning across multiple texts—where one artful work refers to another. It also occurs when meaning is altered, when interpretations are placed next to each other across a variety of media and 'read' differently depending on the placement. In this way, the representations do not hold onto specific and fixed meanings. To carry this notion a step further, a parallaxic research project is 'doubled' through its intertextuality in that it depends on its meaning being 'read' in relation to the original interpretive work (transcriptions from the participants) and in comparative relation to each of the researcher's interpretations.

The breadth of intertextuality is one way the researcher is able to move away from stereotypical representations of difference and, instead, emphasize common humanity and common experiences. The cultural stereotypes of meth addiction have been portrayed in the popular media through graphic images of emaciated and empty-eyed individuals with rotting teeth and blistered skin, which are specifically designed to influence substance use behavior through eliciting fear and disgust in the viewer (Meth Project Foundation Inc., 2012). These types of portrayals purposefully work to position the addict/participant as the distant Other—strange and deeply undesirable. The singular portrayal of meth addiction through images and stories of the brutal and ugly physical consequences in the later stages of the addiction process is a reductionist and voyeuristic form of 'typing' (Hall, 1997). It comfortably embraces a cultural verisimilitude about who is an addict and how addiction is expressed. Nevertheless, the researcher can portray phenomenological realism within intertextuality and other parallaxic practices as a means to develop an empathic understanding of the full contexts and experience of meth addiction. This research practice creates tension between the cultural verisimilitude and phenomenological realism as well as the potential for ongoing shifts in cultural representations and the production of meaning (Hall, 1997). It is a means to root out the "*nested dualisms*" and intertwined binaries in our limited socio-cultural understandings and practices (Fishman & McCarthy, 1998, p. 16-17).

Antiphon. Expanding the practice of intertextuality in and between interpretive works is the creation of antiphon (Online Liddell-Scott-Jones Greek-English Lexicon, 2018)—used in the catechization practices as a choir—or in this project, a collection of independent voices that allows the interpretive call and response of researchers' works to 'sing into the latency' of collaborative research and dissemination (Whitacre, 2013). Throughout engagement in parallaxic praxis and the display of multiple artful interpretations, researchers don't work to be perfectly together and exact or in sync with a single 'truth' or perspective. Consequently, there is latency or starts, stops, pauses, listening, and delays when multiple people collaborate on analysis and interpretation from a distance or in close proximity. Ranging from discordant to harmonic refrain, a group of researchers can engage analysis, interpretation, and dissemination that simultaneously create solo works as well as an ensemble of interpretations. To build upon this the metaphor, Dewey (1934/2005) notes, "*Music . . . is a vehicle which becomes one with what it carries; it coalesces with what it conveys*" (p. 207).

Antiphon furthers the breadth of intertextuality, accumulating and altering meanings across multiple texts, to that of a merged production or poiesis of interpretation the audience can take in as a whole. These interactive concepts of space, latency, voice, pace, and ensemble go beyond the contemporary understanding of research dissemination as a linear information exchange and fosters a more dynamic and contextualized practice. Jazz-like improvisation in the moment to moment of research, clinical, and educational encounters produce presence and creativity through technique and communication as an act, as a trait, and as an event (Haidet, 2007). Whether displayed side-by-side in a gallery setting, digitally on a webpage, discussed in phone conference, or printed in a peer-reviewed journal, the antiphon or ensemble of analysis and interpretations make manifest the parallaxic research process of meaning making as collaborative, generative, relational, and interactive.

Sorites. Building from the notion of antiphony is a practice that keeps the research process and aesthetic experience both elastic and coherent—a sorites phenomenon that is culture-bound and cumulative. This type of knowledge is beyond specialized information; rather it is a skill used within an aesthetic encounter that attends to tensionality and interplay, institutional frame and individual freedom, between phenomenological surface and depth (Eaton & Moore, 2002).

> *Aesthetic experience should not be understood as emotive and conative to the exclusion of its cognitive aspects . . . . Artworks invite us to deploy our skills in interpreting and reinterpreting our world. And in this way they stimulate our capacities to make comparisons and discriminations to make judgments about categorical membership, and to appreciate various (often nonverbal) ways in which one thing may represent or exemplify another.* (Eaton & Moore, 2002, p. 15)

There are two important points to consider when addressing the aesthetic experience within parallaxic praxis. First, the aesthetic experience is a culture-bound concept and works to comprehend the emotional elements of particular phenomena. As such, it is dependent on the language—a network of signs and signifiers—of a community for recognition by the audience. One cannot expect that the "*conceptual cluster*" composed by researcher and participant be neatly resolved into a simple formula (Eaton & Moore, 2002, p. 16). Case in point, both qualitative and quantitative research provide a broad, complex, and yet incomplete description and investigation of women and meth addiction (Boeri, 2013; Brecht, O'Brian, von Mayrhauser, & Anglin, 2004; Cohen, Greenberg, Uri, Halpin, & Zweben, 2007; Sameshima, Vandermause, & Santucci, 2012; Sameshima & Vandermause, 2008 & 2009; Semple, Grant, & Patterson, 2004; Semple, Strathdee, Zians, & Patterson, 2011; Vic & Ross, 2003).

Second, when addressing complex cultural contexts through the aesthetic experience and arts integrated research, one is confronted with the sorites phenomenon or cumulation. The word sorites originates from Greek and means 'heaped' (Collins English Dictionary, 2012). It is a premise that addresses the paradox of form: What constitutes a heap? For example, if you put a grain of sand on the ground and ask observers whether it is a pile, they will surely say no. When you add a second grain, the answer will be the same. This will go on for the third and fourth and fifth grains. Yet at a certain point, the observers will agree that there is a pile of sand on the ground. But when? There is simply no way of knowing. It is a matter of a cumulation of grains without any decisive line of qualification regarding what constitutes a heap.

Multi-interpretive research practices within parallaxic practice are sorites phenomena in that "it comes into being when a number of contributory elements add up to a sufficient sum" (Eaton & Moore, 2002, p. 16). This is not a conceptual jumble. It is an act of cumulation or a heaping of pertinent phenomenal elements, language, and interpretations before one crosses a decision line or threshold that may be indistinct but, in the final analysis, is recognized as a process that answers research questions within parallaxic praxis. As well, this threshold implies that the research interpretation is not conferred, but rather achieved by the researcher, participants, and the audience. It requires acceptance by and interaction with the audience as well as participants and the community of those who have a stake in the particular cultural phenomena, in this case, women in recovery from meth use.

Clearly, when both of these aspects of sorites are brought together, the idea of (ac)cumulation of knowledge and understanding goes far deeper than static storage and "*acquisition of information for purposes of reproduction in recitation and examination*" (Dewey, 1916/2011, p. 77). In sum, the parallaxic research process is kept both elastic and coherent through the acknowledgment and practice of sorites in phenomenological research as culture-bound and cumulative through interactions between researcher, participant, and audience.

Aporia. Within the catechization practices a displacement is created, which brings the artist researcher, participant, and viewer into a deep examination of the contexts and conditions of the phenomena. What does this mean, beyond naming and representing the specific demographics and circumstances of the participant? It means bringing aporia directly into the research process. Aporia means "an impasse or puzzlement" and philosophically is a "*puzzle or a seemingly insoluble impasse in an inquiry, often arising as a result of equally plausible yet inconsistent premises. . . the state of being perplexed or at a loss*" (Collins English Dictionary, 2012).

To embrace aporia the researcher, viewer, and participant must sit in the dissonance of simultaneous and seemingly contradictory life circumstances, that doesn't fit into familiar cultural narratives and 'truths' (Dewey,

1934/2005; Spivak, 2012). For example, when looking deeply at Jill's life, we acknowledge that she lived a middle-class suburban lifestyle AND was a meth addict. We know that she was a mother who loved her children very much AND, as an addict, chose meth over her children. We understand that Jill made choices as an individual that led to addiction AND that drug use—from a very young age—was part of the power relationships enacted by family members and the larger community.

Engaging aporia in the research and dissemination process is the purposeful acknowledgement of duality, the tight binaries of the shamed, the addicted, and the subjugated, in representational cultural structures (Hall, 1997). Spivak (2012) proposes that

> *only an aesthetic education can continue to prepare us for this, thinking an uneven and only apparently accessible contemporaneity that can no longer be interpreted by such nice polarities. . . Everything else begins there, in that space that allows us to survive the singular and unverifiable, surrounded by the lethal and lugubrious consolation of rational choice.* (p. 2)

Through parallaxic praxis and catechization methods, a state of aporia can be aroused artfully through a dialogue between researchers, artwork, participants, and the audience. Interpretations within parallaxic praxis become dialogic when placed alongside other interpretations to form a particular reconstructive and potentially uncomfortable experience: "*For 'taking in' in any vital experience is something more than placing something on the top of consciousness over what was previously known. It involves reconstruction which may be painful*" (Dewey, 1934/2005, p. 42). This interactive dialogue draws attention to particular phenomenological contradictions, problems, and conditions and instills within the viewer the desire to question and inquire more deeply. "*Rendering content through new lenses affords the audience to think more critically about the content from a personal meaning-making perspective*" (Sameshima et al., 2009, p. 10). Parallaxic praxis and the resulting aesthetic education is not a solution to the dissonance of aporia but, rather, an experience of relating to and imagining of others—in this case, a means to negotiate and understand the complexities and contradictions of a phenomena. (Dewey, 1934/2005; Spivak, 2012).

Similar to other traditional research methodologies, parallaxic praxis research is initiated with questions but focuses analysis on the "*open confluence of multiple interpretations*" and systems for meaning-making (Sameshima et al., 2009, p. 8). To use a transliteration of aporia, it is a dissonant state of making "meaning without passage" into the comfort of rational and logical conclusions (Spivak, 2012).

> *To paraphrase Heidegger, when we set out "to reveal the real," if we were to change "our mode of ordering," the real reveals itself to us (Heidegger, 1977, p. 20). The openness to revelation is simply the acknowledgment that there are possibilities that exist beyond our current frameworks. Such acknowledgment is the basis of research, that there is knowledge yet to be discovered, that we do not and cannot yet completely and fully understand. We add too, that this aporic view leaves all revelations, findings, and knowings ongoingly incomplete.* (Wiebe & Sameshima, 2018, p. 11)

Evanagnostos. In order for the artefacts to be successful in dialogue, the research design relies on the evaluative methodological process of evanagnostos, the Greek word for something being easy to read and legible (Online Liddell-Scott-Jones Greek-English Lexicon, 2018). Readability creates transformation capacity and impetus for the generation of ripple effects that instigate potential for change, agency, and meaning making. Not only do the researchers seek readability but also a legibility, which makes the dialogue accessible (reachable, able to enter into) for those participating in the research dialogue and to those 'listening or reading or looking' in the audience.

Within the ekphrastic process, interpretive artful works must be legible to audiences, which can then bring about transactional dialogue and understanding. The semantic labour (Kester & Strayer, 2005) in the meaning-making process takes place over time and upon reflection by the artist and audience. If an interpretive work of art is highly readable and legible, then there is an opportunity for the audience to look beyond the medium of the artwork toward broader meaning making. Readability and legibility of artful interpretations are directly linked to the research question and animate the research design, which is concerned with the transactional dialogue between the ekphrastic works. Comprehension and understanding gained by the audience through evanagnostos can depend on the level of direct representation and the use of responsive images, graphics, or narrative text between the multiple interpretive works and during the linked ekphrastic dialogue.

When rippling traces of common themes and recognizable tropes or aesthetic dimensions within ekphrastic dialogue can be followed across and between multiple artful works, and the participant-created artefacts and artist-researchers' ekphrastic works clearly interact with each other with a high level of readability and legibility, researchers can contend that intercoder reliability (Lavrakas, 2008) is strong—independent coders recognize similar patterns.

Research teams can celebrate the common themes; however, it has been our experience that when readability of artworks are strong individually, but that the codes and themes differ, this allows the team to focus on the juxtaposition of the various works, the new directions or evolutions in the ekphrastic dialogue, and to pay attention to the spaces between the artworks. In other words, in a parallaxic praxis, in order to more deeply interrogate meaning, the artefacts must first become the negative space (what is common is already known and is of less importance), and the once negative space, the areas once unnoticed, come forward as the new positive. The artefacts thus, have become the view finding framing devices of the ma, the unconscious, unattended, or overlooked interval between two markers. See Chapter 4 on "ma" for a deeper discussion on the generation of meaning from the void spaces.

We use the word readability not simply as a reference to a literary reading but literacy for understanding the narrative of the artefacts. Readability is a critical catechization because the capacity for improving dialogic transformation rests in the agency of the artefact. Roland Barthes (1977) writes about three kinds of texts: The first, the readerly text, while not reproducible at the reader's skill, is easily legible and understood by the reader—this is an artefact the viewer easily consumes. It is likely following acceptable aesthetic forms and uses recognizable metaphors or texts. The readerly text has a strong impact on transformation capacity for wide audiences.

The second text Barthes (1977) describes is the writerly text. It is a text that requires engagement in conversation between the artist and reader to make meaning of the text or meaning can be had with exhibits accompanied by a research talk or an information pamphlet. While impact-capacity will appear to be contingent on the presence of the explanation, it is oftentimes this type of text that has the most personal impact on the participants. For example, in a dementia study (Sameshima & Slingerland, 2016), where the artefact, a penny rug, was created from the participant's quilting remnants, and the motifs representations from an ATLAS.ti coding of the interview transcripts, the artefact played a significant role in meaning making for the family. The penny-rug itself still maintained its capacity for change by way of its material marking of the research project in public displays.

The third type of text is the receivable text or sometimes translated as unreaderly text (Barthes, 1977) which "*catches hold, the red-hot text, a product continuously outside any likelihood, whose function—visibly assumed by its scripter—would be to contest the mercantile constraint of what is written. . . It is received like a fire, a drug, an enigmatic disorganization*" (p. 118). This text is that artefact that shocks, or is aesthetically engrossing but holds no initial perceived connectivity to the research project. These types of artefacts can have a significant impact because the punctum of the art, the thing that leaps out to pierce the heart, is strong enough to force the viewer into receiving it or for the project to become memorable.

Toward Polysemic Frames

Questions Studied in this Section:

- How is integrity maintained in interpretation and analysis?
- How are the qualitative researchers interpreting the data?
- How do qualitative researchers avoid assumptions?
- How does a team move beyond their disciplinary lenses?
- Do the interpretations authentically represent the participant story?
- What story are the researchers unintentionally re-inscribing or moving forward?
- What narratives have already framed ways of interpreting?
- How does the multi-modal aspect of this framework open conversations into the data?
- What enables a research team to more deeply fractal the data and to see clarity in complexity and complication?
- How do the catechizations further the analysis and evaluation process as well as enhance the understanding of form in arts integrated research?

While the theoretical foundations of the Catechization Process were contextualized in the Women and Meth study with four artists analyzing Jill's interview transcripts, the following discussion looks at the **processes of collaborative dialogic analyses of the renderings.** This inquiry is based on artefacts produced from Gilda's story, a different participant in the Women and Meth Study. We explain the process through praxis because there is not a singular procedural pathway in synthesizing across multi-modal data. ATLAS.ti, traditional coding systems, hermeneutic phenomenological processes or heuristic research tools offer forms of synthesis which they themselves can be compared and overlain with one another. The synthesis of a parallaxic praxis always generates more questions for study, thereby deferring the full completion or completeness of research.

Dewey's (1916/2011) reflections on knowledge generation, socio-cultural experiences, and connection guides us forward:

> *To 'learn from experience' is to make a backward and forward connection between what we do to things and what we enjoy or suffer from things in consequence. Under such conditions, doing becomes a trying; an experiment with the world to find out what it is like; the undergoing becomes instruction—discovery of the connection of things.* (p. 78)

To that end and with deliberation, we extend the call to move forward in dynamic methods of arts integrated research with constructive imagination and heuristic compassion.

Polysemic Framing

Cultural theorist and sociologist Stuart Hall's (2007/1973) communication theories on encoding and decoding were utilized to more deeply examine the artful process and products of multiple simultaneous analyses and interpretations. Hall's work opens spaces for rethinking assumptions on producing, circulating, distributing/consuming, and reproducing messages. His work is particularly useful in thinking about multi-disciplinary and multi-modal interpretations of the same data set. Hall argues that polysemy and pluralism are not one and the same. *Polysemy* refers to phrases and words having multiple meanings while *pluralism* denotes multiple interpretive views. Hall suggests that similar repeated performative retellings of particular narratives create culturally specific interpretations which move these interpretations to 'common-sense' plausible truths. How are the qualitative researchers interpreting the data? How does the multi-modal aspect of this framework open conversations into the data? What enables a research team to more deeply fractal the data and to see clarity in complexity and complication? How does a team move beyond their disciplinary lenses? Consequently, the construction of meaning in this model through collaborative dialogic analyses and the catechizations promotes cultural communication and representations which evolve into polysemic frames, not remaining simply pluralistic.

The Women and Methamphetamine Addiction and Recovery Study

The parallaxic praxis model and an ekphrastic research framework are particularly useful when research questions are focused on discovery, rich context, and the meaning of phenomena such as the development of addiction, which are complicated, encountered across multiple relationships and identities and can elicit dissonance when addressed. Additionally, in an effort to deeply examine complex phenomenon and the interpretation of meaning through multi-modal layering, an ekphrastic research framework approach is utilized (Sameshima, Vandermause, & Santucci, 2012; Prendergast, 2004). Specifically, ekphrastic methods and artful interpretations are engaged to reveal meaning through deep analysis of the participants' narrative transcripts. As well, this study draws upon an ecological or systems model of addiction. This model posits that addiction is multiply determined and includes biological, psychological, sociological, and cultural factors as contributors to the development and maintenance of addiction (Donovan & Marlatt, 2005).

Past research on women and methamphetamine use is plentiful and primarily quantitative in design (Brecht, et al., 2004; Cohen et al., 2007; Semple et al., 2004; Semple et al., 2011; Vic & Ross, 2003). A review of the literature revealed that previous studies, outside of the Women & Meth project, had not examined the "experience" of addiction and recovery through arts integrated research methods.

The data sources included one participant's interview transcripts (pseudonym Gilda) and the two researcher-created 'translations' and renderings. Artful ekphrastic works were created throughout the qualitative data cataloging and analysis. Prior researcher renderings and hermeneutic analysis in the Women & Meth Project (Sameshima, Vandermause, Chalmers, & Gabriel, 2009) revealed constitutive patterns previously presented and answers in part, society's questions of how women with children get involved with drugs and what happens. This project addressed new questions regarding analyses of the researchers' interpretations, their assumptions, and a critique of the limitations and positive aspects of this interdisciplinary model.

Creation of ekphrastic interpretations and the process of analysis were conducted in two steps. First, Maarhuis and Sameshima worked from the same Gilda interview transcripts but fully independent and separate from each other. The resulting artful interpretations re-present and translate emergent themes found through qualitative analysis. Second, after the separate analysis and interpretation were completed, Maarhuis and Sameshima viewed each other's work, engaged in dialogue and conducted further collaborative analysis on interpretive art works, transcript themes, the use of research practices specific to the ekphrastic methods, as well as an analytical comparison between the works. Out of the ongoing dialogues a comparison chart (see Figure 3.2) was created that closely examines intersections and divergence between the two bodies of work.

Evaluation

The inclusion of multiple open interpretations can raise questions about the analysis and rigor of arts integrated research. Certainly, one can regard an open research process as a needed departure from positivistic orderliness, dualisms, and definistic restraint. Then again, if the research and interpretation process is completely open, how can one resolve basic issues about the integrity of the arts integrated research process, analysis, and interpretation? Do the interpretations authentically represent the participant story? What story are we, as researchers, moving forward? What stories have already framed our ways of interpreting?

First, we experienced excitement at the nexus of the various modalities and disciplines coming together within a transdisciplinary model where two artist-researchers created artifact series independently with one participant's transcripts. To work on various teams with colleagues in disparate disciplines, creates rich and invigorating dialogue.

Later, we noted that, although we each used very different modalities to render the transcript-inspirited artefacts, we found that our senses were drawn to similar interpretations. For instance, out of the hundreds of lines of transcribed interviews, we both alighted on particular phrases that drew our attention. We found that despite the representative differences, our initial attentions were given to similar and sometimes, exact phrases in the transcript. These notions about the kinds of frameworks we are attuned and acculturated to view through, are significant limitations to broadening and seeing data anew. Our continued work with this model sought ways to further challenge us to 'see' beyond the lenses, to which we are accustomed.

Arts integrated methods—grounded in the integrated unity of lived experience—begin "*with things in their complex entanglements rather than with simplifications made for the purpose of effective judgment and action*" (Dewey in Boisvert, 1998, p. 16). Particularly, questions regarding evaluation in arts-based research are addressed through the use of criteria regarding significance or value of the work, such as: incisiveness, concision, coherence, generativity, social significance, evocation and illumination and "*function as a cue for perception*" (Barone & Eisner, 2012, p. 154). Barone and Eisner note that these six criteria are a starting point and call for further inquiry into the application of evaluative practices. Development of the catechization practices came, in part, as an answer to this call for further inquiry and to attempt to develop a more dynamic situated evaluation criterion.

Form

Catechizations do not replace evaluative criteria but act as an incomplete index of methodological practices for use in the analysis and evaluation process. The catechizations deepen the understanding and exploration of the concept of form within arts integrated research. Eisner (1991) aptly notes that "*the forms through which humans represent their conception of the world have a major influence on what they are able to say about it*" (p. 7). Cole and Knowles (2001b) contend that "*when researchers have a particular commitment to pushing the boundaries of method and audience, representational form is central to the achievement of research goals*" (p. 213). Form is the defining element of arts-informed research (Cole & Knowles, 2008), guiding the inquiry as well as dissemination process and is manifested as: genre and/or medium, method, as structural element, technical element, communication element, aesthetic element, procedural elements in emergent phenomenon, and as reflection of the qualities of goodness of inquiry (see p. 62). We suggest, as further discussed in Chapter 5 that form materializes the possibility for new identities and understandings to be seen. Figure 3.2 provides an overview of the two different artefact series Maarhuis and Sameshima created in this study based on Gilda's transcripts.

Maarhuis	**Sameshima**
Doors & Windows Installation Series	*Vessels Series*
Collage on doors and windows	22 Raku clay bowls
http://www.womenandmeth.com/maarhuis-response.html	http://www.womenandmeth.com/sameshima-response.html
Example	Example
Installation: Found objects, everyday cultural images from 1970's	Raku ware pottery: 16th Century, culturally integrated
Universal: Objects, experiences, relationships common to most people	Alone: Singular, garish, embarrassed, ashamed, hiding
Big, chunky, and heavy with delicate details	Heavy and light, fragile, implosive
Gateways, transitions, and movement	Vessels—circulation and travelling above
Means of management, control and coping in difficult circumstances	"Stops" as a controlling measure to hold life in check
Response to relationships and emotions within a particular place	Surreal view—distanced management of her life

Table 3.2. Intersections and Divergence.

How do the catechizations further the analysis and evaluation process as well as enhance the understanding of form in arts informed research? First, the catechizations can provide avenues toward "*common reflection over what might be attended to in looking*" at interpretive work and dissemination practices (Barone & Eisner, 2012, p.155). Second, the catechizations can provide explicit—though not standardized—vocabulary and practices helpful in attaining significance, value, and meaning in arts integrated research. Like the criteria listed by Barone and Eisner (2012), the catechizations are "*idiosyncratic to the work*" of artful inquiry itself: innovative, informed, and imaginative (p. 155). As such, the practices can actively expand the semantic and perceptual field and assist in the evaluation of the analysis and interpretation. Third, the catechizations can offer pragmatic 'how to' approaches in evaluation and artful interpretation, especially for those new to arts informed inquiry. Fourth, catechizations practices inherently provide multiple perspectives and can enhance transformative communication between researcher(s) and within the audience in dissemination. Fifth, catechizations can provide a means for multiple researchers, who utilize a variety of media and dissemination strategies, a way to present their work in an integrated, accessible, and cohesive manner. In sum, the catechization practices—specific and important to parallaxic praxis methods—have been developed and utilized to strengthen and deepen evaluative rigor in the exploration of form and communication within collaborative research and dissemination. The catechization practices also expand the dialogic or semantic field, providing a method for interdisciplinary teams to converse across discourse.

Findings

Concurrent and collaborative use of analysis and interpretation, evaluation, as well as the inclusion of specific ekphrastic research practices worked to provide answers, at least in part, to our research questions: How do qualitative researchers avoid assumptions? How does the multi-modal aspect of this framework fractal complexity in the data? How does a team move beyond their disciplinary lenses? Naturally, as parallaxic praxis and ekphrastic methods are an open and ongoing process, more ideas and questions are generated about the experiences of women and methamphetamine use through the process of research.

Catechization practices used within parallaxic praxis research methods work to provide answers, at least in part, to our research questions. This study reveals, not just the need to, but avenues for the artist-researcher to move outside of the self with a focus on the Other (Levinas, 1981) during interpretive art-making. The combination of catechization practices within a parallaxic research model demonstrates how the multi-modal aspect of this framework fractals complex participant experiences and allows the research team to move beyond their disciplinary lenses and surface understanding. Likewise, the catechizations pragmatically and efficiently 'double' as instruments in the dissemination and education process. Using the catechization practices actively expands the semantic and perceptual field and assists in the evaluation of the analysis and interpretation.

Specifically, the research on Gilda's narratives revealed constitutive socio-cultural patterns in the development of methamphetamine addiction and answer, in part, society's questions of how women become involved with drugs, how health behaviors such as addiction are linked to everyday experiences, not the failure of will-power or morality, and how these common everyday experiences can separate and bind us together. This project materialized what is experienced but often unnamed through making art and text.

Findings suggest further research is necessary on researcher/participant/viewer lens and position, ethical considerations in interpretation/translation, the ongoing development of ekphrastic research practices, and effective dissemination and education strategies regarding complex and entrenched socio-cultural problems and concerns.

Chapter 4

Theoretical Underpinnings of the Model

The research model uses a hermeneutic lens and forefronts lived experiences through various methodological perspectives. Questions of meaning are fractalled through the expansion of analyses across discipline, perspective, and modality. The use of arts integrated research methods and traditional and innovative methodologies are layered in this framework. The strength of this model relies on difference—that though combinatorial, even juxtaposing theoretical frames, the generation of new knowledge is possible in the interstices of the known. The following section offers thoughts on theorists, theories, and tenets that underpin this research framework.

Locating Imagination

This section draws from ideas and excerpted texts on *imagination as methodology* from:

- Sameshima, P., Wiebe, S., & Hayes, M. (in press). Imagination: The generation of possibility. In B. Andrews (Ed.), *Perspectives on arts education research in Canada.*

- Hayes, M. T., Sameshima, P., & Watson, F. (2015, February). Imagination as method. *International Journal of Qualitative Methods, 14*(1), 36-52.

We locate parallaxic praxis in the theoretically post qualitative, affirming imagination as method (Hayes, Sameshima & Watson, 2015). Imagination is much more than the creative workings of the mind and includes the ways consciousness, self, and world merge and emerge together. Through imagination we are constantly making and remaking ourselves and the world. Imagination is the creative impulse through which we co-emerge with the world.

St. Pierre (1997) describes post qualitative methods as the employment of methods that "*use post theories to critique and/or to deconstruct in order to make data unintelligible* "(p. 175). The intent is to "*produce different knowledge and produce knowledge differently*" (p. 175). In this sense, post qualitative methods are positioned well historically as a coming after and an important problematizing of part/whole or self/society or subjective/objective dialectics.

The notion of assemblage has been a generative metaphor for post-qualitative methods. It has helped qualitative researchers move from dialectical theorizing to consider the "*assemblage of heterogeneous components*" (Lee & Denshire, 2013, p. 222). Deleuze and Guattari (1987) use the idea of *assemblage* of thoughts while Barad (2007) speaks of *entanglements* and O'Sullivan (2006) uses the term *encounterings*. The "*emergence of the new*" (MacLure, 2013, p. 659) is built on a base foundation that is not sequential unidirectional constructivism but multi-level, multi-planed, dimensional, and contingent on place, time, and histories.

As a phenomenon is studied, a foundational premise we support is that there are always multiple truths that span time horizontally and vertically. So, for example, while we acknowledge parallactic perspectives in the current present—the notion that one cannot see more than one can see and that each person is seeing the same phenomenon or event differently at the same moment—we also note that the truth of an event changes over time. Greene (2006) urges,

> *There must be an ability to anticipate and accept incompleteness. Even when a controversy appears to be resolved, gaps and spaces remain, and the need for open questions. And where there is a space, a gap, there is the possibility of new choices, renewed reflection.* (p. 1)

Bruno Latour (2005) asks if the social can be reassembled—how do we change how we see? He explains that the social is constructed through associations that if followed systematically, can create a "*shared definition of a common world*" (p. 257). To render the established norm, the assemblage of associations must have a procedure that allows a systematic mapping. This reproducible tracing creates a shared definition. Latour (2005). He explains that "*if there are no procedures to render it common, it may fail to be assembled.*" He goes on,

> *we have to restudy what we are made of and extend the repertoire of ties and the number of associations way beyond the repertoire proposed by social explanations. At every corner science, religion, politics, law, economics, organizations, etc. offer phenomena that we have to find puzzling again if we want to understand the types of entities collectives may be composed of in the future.* (p. 258)

Utilizing Latour's (2005) theories in the parallaxic praxis, the teams espouse looking back through time and past understandings to better map out how specific collections are assembled and traced, and troubling the procedures and network tracings. In this model, using new materiality approaches, the team disrupts common understandings with artefact making, specifically through the creation of poems, artworks, and so forth.

When imagination is the method by which our research is conducted we come to the realization that we are not just constructing research projects in which methods are applied and results generated in some discreet academic context. Research is the generation of life worlds that are nothing less than our contemporary and future society. The researcher, the research participants, documents, and artifacts, come together to form a system or network of social relationships, that are not unlike any other kind of system or network of social relationships we might imagine or experience, such as a community, or a social movement. The social relationships constituted through research activities become one more element in the aggregate we call society. Imagination allows researchers to construct narratives, stories, and mythologies of the kind of world we wish to occupy.

As post-structuralist theorists have forwarded, the reproduction of education, culture, and society is an automatic process, and "*dominator culture*" (hooks, 2003, p. 197) encourages sameness and safety. Camus (1942) describes the philosophy of the absurd as man's search for meaning and clarity within a world that cannot be reduced to the rational and reasonable—accidents happen and events can deviate from the plan. Camus suggests that perpetual revolt or confrontation is the only way to live within the contradiction. He explains that metaphysical rebellion—what we refer to as outward moving political action (making)—is an act to refuse approval of the situation, that is to say, that to be political is to be awake to the notion that the foundation is always at once unstable and unsure. Camus (1956) concludes that the action, in our case "*making,*" is a call for "*clarity and unity*" and thus the making "*paradoxically, expresses an aspiration to order*" (p. 23). Political action, then, is fundamentally exercised through acts of creation that turn away from the externally imposed dominant ordering and give voice to the social and psychic threads of meaning.

Education, culture, and society are reproduced in systematic processes (Levinson, 2000) where safety and herd behaviours are perpetuated. Camus (1956) suggests that one must focus on the details of living and engage with the present as it is, not as hoped for. He offers that "*engagement with the world within a situated perspective is key*" (p. 58). Correspondingly, Pinar (1988) writes, "*Autobiography takes this task [of deconstruction] seriously, as it is the task of self formation, deformation, learning, and unlearning*" (p. 27).

Located in the theoretically innovative post-qualitative, this model affirms the possibilities of imagination as a method (Hayes, Sameshima & Watson, 2015; Sameshima, Wiebe & Hayes, in press). In the creative moment(s) of making there is a positive entanglement of the researchers' relational constructions of knowing, knowledge, the self, and the world. Because the content of what is imagined is both within and beyond shared perceptions, imagination as method can be detailed and precise; it can be coherent, informative, convincing, even compelling action, but it is, always, imaginative—and this is its promise for post-qualitative research.

A Pedagogy of Parallax

A pedagogy of parallax is made manifest through engagement with artful representations that creates a liminal space for deconstructing narratives. The encounters acknowledge common experiences but also breaks down conceptual dualism and honors difference.

Representations are dialogic when placed alongside other interpretations to form "*systems of analysis and interactions in the hybrid nexus spaces*" (Sameshima et al., 2009, p. 10). It is only through "*multiple perspectives and a varied system of representation,*" that fuller understanding and rich meaning making be gained (p. 8). Artful representation forms a multilayered, rhizomatic interpretation embracing diversity but also allowing for what is unsettled and in a dynamic "*place of agitation*" (Sameshima & Irwin, 2008, p. 6). The resulting aesthetic yield then becomes a medium to share, engage, and provoke further learning through dialogue. The model encourages the artist/teacher/ researcher to engage with the content in a personal, artful, conceptual, or metaphorical way. As well, when representative interpretations are presented alongside the other interpretations, systems of analysis and interactions in the liminal spaces can be considered.

Rendering content through new lenses affords the participant learners to reflect more critically and deeply about the content from a personal meaning-making perspective. Parallaxic pedagogy, as a method of understanding and reflection generation, produces artefacts, which can then spur further learning in others. The punctum of aesthetic representation can arrest single moments, so others are able to behold anew what was habitual, common, and unquestioned (Barthes, 1980; Ortega, 2008). Aesthetic inquiry is a narrative, ontological, and embodied invitation to react with body, mind, and heart. Subsequently, this reaction generates the ongoing conversation, critical reflection, and the shift in frame of reference that is needed for transformational learning (Butterwick & Lawrence, 2009).

Materiality & 'Ma'

The something (material) and nothing ('ma') is a key concept in understanding creative processes. The nothing is always an already conceived something.

The materiality of things plays an important role as a site for epistemological understandings. Making or materializing thinking is significant in parallaxic praxis because it offers concrete artefacts for empirical examination, reference points for symbolic interpretation, and a lens for de/reconstruction (Sameshima, 2019).

In the yin and yang of something and nothing, the nothing is also important in this model. Julia Kristeva (1980) has used the term prosody to refer to the space between musical notes and the space between words. Specifically, it is this space that determines the song, or meaning. The Analyses Phase of the Parallaxic praxis model is a space of play. In other works, Sameshima and Wiebe have attempted to describe this generative space as the liminal studio (see reprint in this issue, Wiebe & Sameshima, 2018) and as *ma* (Sameshima, 2019; Wiebe, 2019):

> *The Japanese concept of ma refers to the interval between two markers. Ma is somatically constructed by a deliberate, attentive consciousness to what simultaneously is expressed, repressed, or suppressed between two structures. . . It is a way of inquisitiveness, desire, imagining, learning, positioning, being, becoming.* (Sameshima, 2019)

The space of ma is the embryotic space where creative expression and knowledge generation can be birthed. Pilgrim (1986) expresses the ma space as a "*pregnant nothing*" (p. 259). In parallaxic praxis, artefacts can operate as pedagogic tools to metaphorically traverse points of understanding. Using the definition of ma as the interval between two markers, consider one marker as the self-starting point and the other as the point of understanding. With the belief that the body is the site of knowledge (Gallop, 1988; Sameshima, 2008), then the artefacts created are extensions of the self and thereby become the stepping stones across the void toward the other marker of knowing. The material artefact is thus a pedagogic tool, a convenor, a mediator of the unknown.

Reparative Residual Research

Community Engaged Methodology

Reparative residual research (see Sameshima & Slingerland, 2015; Sameshima, Wiebe & Becker, submitted) is an approach to pedagogic knowledge mobilization that seeks to functionally mediate social and intellectual action for and with broad audience communities.

Parallaxic praxis contributes to ongoing research on creative methodologies that develop new ways of interpreting data and designing methods for creating residual impact in the community. With this method, community members and research audiences are valued as social and economic innovators, a timely and necessary re-imagining of the agency of the public. The model supports: (1) how creative research pedagogies can develop through the multiple interconnections among imagination, making, and dialogue; (2) how research can have residual impact even after funding and research projects end; and (3) how research can have significant ongoing impact in communities. By engaging with material objects, exhibitions, and dialogue, we express "*the ways in which persons, memories and objects are interconnected and mutually constitutive*" (Nardi, 2014, p. 461).

Reparative pedagogies, while associated with service learning and civic responsibility, seek rather, to engage, contribute to, inspire, and renew community. Reparative residual research considers how artefacts can be used as catalysts to position research with ongoing effect/affect, as reparative and generative social action. For example, a permanent research exhibition installed within a community space works in a manner not unlike a residual income model, wherein there is a generated return even after the research project has been completed. Where possible, constructed artefacts are gifted back to the participants or to the community from which the study originates.

Artwork created by or for the community that it is exhibited in can inform and provoke viewers—offer pedagogic lessons; renew and remind the community of their contribution in the creation of institutional memory; or inspire—generating awareness that leads to action. Methodologically layered and exhibited in community, the quotidian familiar in tandem with form, attempts to pedagogically press the viewer/reader to imagine an expanded lens of interpreting the world.

Model Design

Elegant research design often returns us to functional design and patterns. We promote research design and methods that echo or sync with the inquiry itself (see Figure 4.1). For example, since one of the aims of Sameshima's work on a cervical cancer screening project was for women to become more aware of their health, PAR or Participatory Action Research was a good fit because the women were involved in narrating and creating their own health biographies (Sameshima et al., 2016). Figure 4.1 is a graphic that represents this idea of replication and patterning that creates project unity. This figure is a cellular automaton that follows encoded Wolfram Rule 90. The fractal created by this rule is a Sierpiński triangle. Attempts to pattern the internal research design with the project as a whole will create alignment and authenticity.

Figure 4.1. Cellular Automaton Wolfram Rule 90. Created by C. Sameshima, 2018.

The development of the perspectives used in each phase of the model follows concepts delineated by numerous scholars who cannot all be named. The following lists point to some of the early foundational building blocks of this model; however, over time, and with a decade of use, it is clear that the model is always dynamically constructed by the perspectives of the teams. Parallaxic praxis does not align with specific ontological or epistemological views. When working across disciplines, the researchers must accept the nature of training and that the possible views by each researcher are always limited and incomplete. Of particular import is that the notion of wholeness or unity is not through addition or combination, but that what is, is already full, but only materialized by the other's gaze:

> *Any subject requires another subject, located in a relation of outsideness (vnenakhodimost), in order to acquire what Bakhtin [1993] calls 'wholeness' or 'unity': the subject, person, individuality only becomes what he or she is—in a towering paradox—under the gaze of another.* (Renfrew, 2015, p. 47)

This idea transferred to the model accepts the data as complete but researchers, through their gaze, actualize possibilities of what is there.

Numerous research perspectives have been networked to imagine the possibilities for developing parallaxic praxis. Some of the key frames for thinking about the DATA PHASE include Sameshima's (2007a) 'pedagogy of parallax' and Pinar and Grumet (1976) 'currere.' The ANALYSES PHASE is supported by the works of Eisner (1991) 'self as instrument'; Ranciére (1991) 'authority of self'; Gadamer (1975/2004) 'fusion of horizons'; Bakhtin (1981) 'heteroglossia, polyglossia, intertexuality, chronotope, carnival, primacy of context over text, polyphony'; Hasebe-Ludt, Chambers, and Leggo (2009) 'Métissage'; Kristeva (1980) 'prosody'; Derrida(1982) 'Difference'; deLanda (2006) 'new materialism'; Deleuze and Guattari (1987) 'rhizome'; Sawyer and Norris (2013) 'duoethnography'; and Daignault (1992, 1993) 'liminal articulation as curriculum construction'. The RENDERINGS PHASE developed from considerations by Bakhtin (1993) 'architectonic model: I-for-the other'; Makiguchi (2002) 'value education—creation for community'; Sedgewick (1997) 'reparative position'; and Bourriaud (2002) 'relational aesthetics.'

Variations on the Model Design

An important aspect of the research design is that the model must be modified for each research project according to the team, participants, and the research goals. The types of process questions one can ask will also vary with the adaptions made to the model itself. The strength of the model rests in the expertise of the individual collaborators as well as connections between the artefacts and the audiences they are used with (see Renderings Section of this book). Following are three examples of project personalizations of the model.

Maarhuis Example

Maarhuis (2016) expanded on the earlier parallaxic praxis model (Sameshima & Vandermause, 2008) to create a research project that crosses multiple participant groups, phases of ekphrastic dialogue, time points of data collection, and locations of artful transactive expression. See chapter 7.1 for an expanded discussion on this project.

In the Replies to Wounds project (Maarhuis, 2016) the parallaxic praxis model (Sameshima & Vandermause, 2008) is utilized in the research methods and the pedagogy of parallax (Sameshima, 2007a) is utilized to understand implications for education in the results analysis. Artful representations are utilized as a means to render deeper understanding by creating thematic and interpretative artefacts that animate ongoing reflection and learning in others. Mediums such as poetry, collage, interpretive narratives, sculpture, and photography are applied in the analysis and meaning-making process. The ekphrastic representations are dialogic when placed alongside one another.

Parallaxic praxis is especially effective when studying contentious and complex societal phenomenon, such as the experience of violence, by addressing deep suffering and creating dissonance about experiences that are often hidden or cloaked. (Maarhuis, 2013; Maarhuis & Sameshima, 2012, 2013a, 2013b, 2015). Parallaxic praxis and arts-informed interpretive methods (Knowles & Cole, 2008; Knowles, Promislow, & Cole, 2008) are able to explore experiences and issues that, often, cannot be addressed fully by positivist methods, which may be singularly bound to academic vernacular, text, and routes of dissemination.

The *Replies to Wounds* project utilized arts-informed research and parallaxic praxis methodologies in a four-phased design with three points of data collection. The multi-layered data, made up of ekphrastic narratives and artful interpretations, was assembled to form an interactive collection of dialogic replies about the experience of interpersonal violence. Notably, these imbricated layers worked to shape the broad, artful, and transactive qualities of the data and subsequent analyses and interpretations (see Figure 4.2).

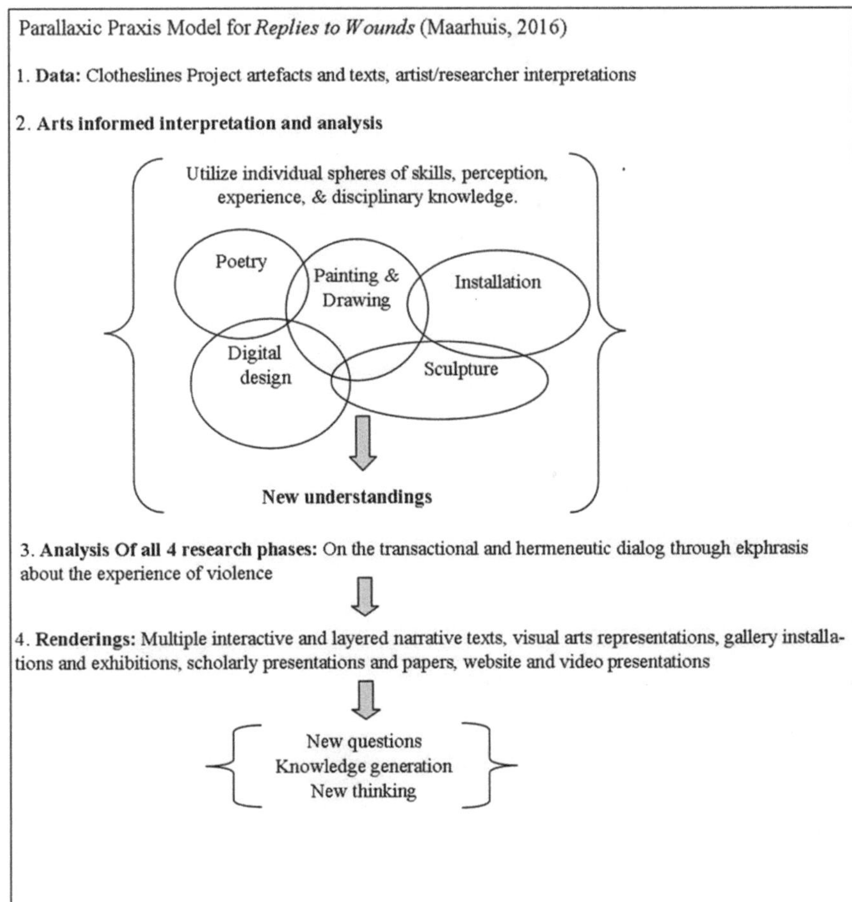

Note. Steps in the arts-informed data collection, analysis, and interpretive results process. The *Data Section*

Figure 4.2. Parallaxic Praxis Model. P. Maarhuis, 2016.

Saunders Example

In an earlier explanation of the model (Sameshima et al., 2009), the three phases of the model are described in a horizontal linear model (seen in the top right of Saunders' graphic). Saunders has recreated the model to embody a spiralling process of inquiry (see embedded graphic in lower left of Figure 4.3). Figure 4.3 is used with permission from:

- Saunders, V. (2014, October). *If you knew the end of a story would you still want to hear it?* PhD Pre-Completion Seminar, Cairns Institute, JCU, Cairns.

- Saunders, V. (2015). *"...": Using a non-bracketed narrative to story recovery in Aboriginal mental health care.* Unpublished thesis. Townsville, Australia: Nursing, Midwifery & Nutrition, College of Healthcare Sciences, Division of Tropical Health and Medicine, James Cook University.

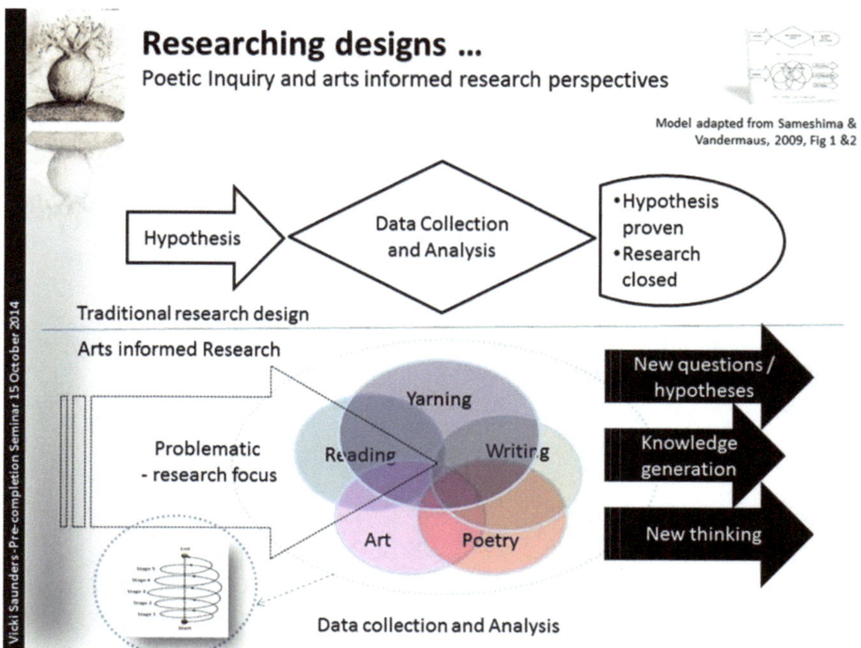

Figure 4.3. Research Design. V. Saunders, 2014.

Ingalls Vanada Example

Ingalls Vanada, D. (2017). Teaching for the ambiguous, creative, and practical: Daring to be A/R/Tography. *Art/Research International: A Transdisciplinary Journal, 2*(10), 110-135.

Used with permission.

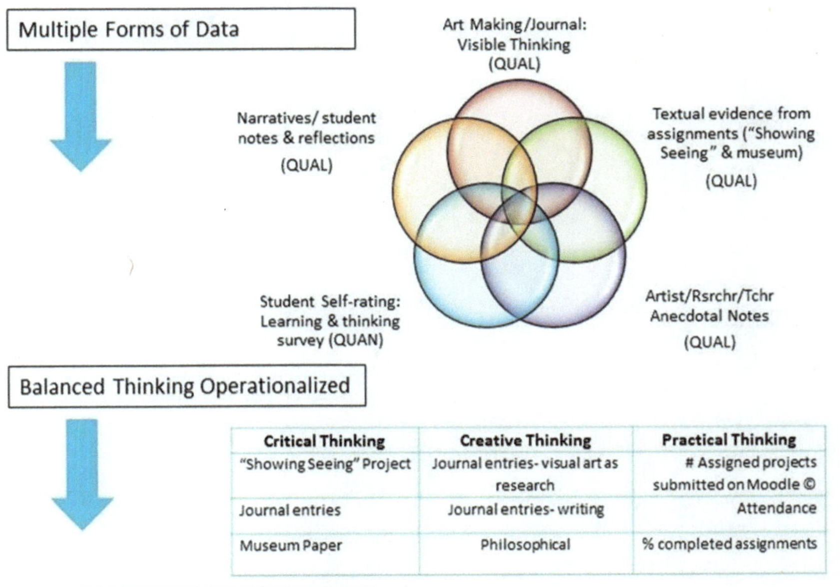

Critical Thinking	Creative Thinking	Practical Thinking
"Showing Seeing" Project	Journal entries- visual art as research	# Assigned projects submitted on Moodle ©
Journal entries	Journal entries- writing	Attendance
Museum Paper	Philosophical	% completed assignments

Figure 4.4. Mixed Parallaxic Design. Ingalls Vanada, 2017, p. 21.

Chapter 5

Cross-Domain Discourses

Multiliteracies Theories

The object of creating environments for the juxtaposition of artefacts and dialogue to rub up against one another is to instigate the *déclencheur*—a French word with no direct English translation, refers to ideas such as "to release a mechanism, activate, set off, trigger off an alarm, press a button; to launch, start, trigger off a debate" (Coffey, 2006, n.p.). Theories on performing research across modalities and across platforms of discourse require conceptualizations by the team members for the mechanics of relation. In thinking about the French to English translation, what are the mechanics of traversing thought and conception without direct pathways across platforms? From experience, interdisciplinary teams can be challenged not only by communication barriers due to differing ontologies and epistemologies, but also in understanding HOW platforms can be traversed. To understand the issue, we share a question posed by a colleague—a curious, supportive, and brilliant mathematician—'How do I read this poem?' From another angle, the poet might ask 'How do I read this semi-logarithmic graph?' The poem and the graph are both narratives, yet they are constructed of completely different building blocks.

Here we offer two views of how communications across discourse can occur. The first avenue is included in this volume as a reprint of an article written by Wiebe and an English language arts teacher, Clair Caseley Smith. Their study (Wiebe & Caseley Smith, 2016) examines the application of multiliteracies theory, thinking across literacy domains, and assessing literacies holistically. This study is important in thinking about parallaxic praxis because it offers a language for researchers who may have less experience working with arts integrated methodologies. While the discussion below on ekphrasis provides an avenue to understanding cross-domain thinking from a discourse of art, Wiebe and Caseley Smith's paper describes platform navigation through a discourse of multiliteracies. Of particular import is the development of the Threshold Concepts which conceptually mark constructions of intangible borders. This article confirms that in the act of making, the creator is in an analytical mode of thinking. As with the tenets of parallaxic praxis by way of ekphrastic interpretation, their research confirms that effective pedagogical strategies include linking analysis and creativity, and using metaphor and story. They conclude with a critical finding that multigenre instructional design increases motivation to revise. In the context of parallaxic praxis, this finding is interpreted as the adoption and acceptance of the notion of incompleteness and openness, giving rise to learning that continually seeks alternate possibilities.

Ekphrasis

With the parallaxic praxis model, we use polysemy (culturally constructed signs with many contextual meanings) performed through ekphrastic interpretations (translations of data across modalities) and collaborative dialogic practices to create multi-modal 'lines of sight.' Our aim is to 'broaden the semantic field: to develop a deep and wide space of thinking that goes beyond stereotypical thinking and canonical ideas (Sameshima & Maarhuis, 2013). Knowledge is generated from the dynamic relational interactions between people, place, and experience. This framework is compatible with theoretical approaches which acknowledge that transactional and comparative analysis, as well as meaning making, is inherently affected by perspective and context: time, space, movement, relationship, and position (Daiute, 2014; Dewey, 1934/2005; Mouffe 2007, 2008; Vessey, 2006).

Ekphrasis is a rhetorical device where one medium attempts to recreate an object's essence and form in another medium with the express intent of relating more directly with the audience. Prendergast (2004) has described the possibilities of ekphrastic inquiry—how educational researchers represent their interpretive work in poetic, visual, or other art forms. Ekphrasis is translation—an interpretive and often metaphorical play of the data. Etymologically, the Greek word means "*out*" or "*speak*" or to "*call an inanimate object by name*" (Wikipedia, 2018). The word is a historically contested term and has been traditionally defined as the use of verbal representation (poetry) of a visual representation (painting or sculpture) (Mitchell, 1994). We adopt a broader definition of ekphrasis referring to translation or representation between mediums (narrative text, poetry, music, painting, sculpture, etc.). We suggest that within the gap across discourse, language, discipline, and perspective, new thinkings can emerge. We follow Daignault's (1983) suggestion, that instead of trying to bridge the gap we instead find a new language. The gap is the curriculum and "*thinking is the incarnation of curriculum as composition*" (quoted in Hwu, 1993, p. 172). Thinking and making, are thus compositions of understanding and learning (See Sameshima & Irwin, 2008).

The use of ekphrasis within parallaxic praxis can generate novel ideas through the systematic interaction of multiple sight lines, multi-modal representation, and comparative analysis. The ekphrastic process is a process of storytelling—a narrative text that describes an interpretation of experience. For example, in the Women and Meth study, the stories of women are (re)interpreted into multiple representations through sculpture, poetry, collage, and photography to engage in "*active transformations*" of meaning, which advance "*polysemic values*" by having many connotative meanings or cultural significations (Hall, 2007, p. 483). The focal point of ekphrastic practice is a carrying through of 'essence' from one medium to another medium.

We use the word essence to refer to properties that make the entity itself, its identity (Jones, 2016). Essence is that which creates the identity of the thing. Various theorists have disagreed on whether existence precedes essence or essence precedes existence. We align with existentialist Jean-Paul Sartre (1946) and Martin Heidegger (1996) who suggest that existence precedes essence, that the identity of the thing becomes itself, through materialist existence. We take on this notion, that what is unthought or not yet generated has no identity until it takes form first, and through the material form, and through the gaze of the other, the relational essence (see Gadamer, 1980) of identity becomes fashioned. This is an underpinning notion of parallaxic praxis, that in the making we materialize new forms, which hold narratives and identities for meaning making.

Polysemy refers to phrases and words having multiple meanings while pluralism denotes multiple interpretive views. Polysemy etymologically stems from "*poly*" (many) and "*sêma*" (sign) – a sign with many meanings (Collins English Dictionary, 2012). A closer look at the word polysemy creates new ways of critically framing interpretive art creation research through a linguistic lens. The word polysemy refers to a term that has a large semantic field. Briton (2000) says a semantic field "denotes a segment of reality symbolized by a set of related words" (p. 112). For example, the following two sets of words are from the semantic field of 'color': Set 1: blue, red, yellow, green, black, purple. Set 2: indigo, saffron, royal blue, aquamarine, bisque. Set 1 words are called less marked and Set 2 words are marked. Marked words are less common, sometimes metaphorical, and themselves open new semantic fields. For example, saffron opens the semantic field of not just color, but spice (see Finegan, 2012, p. 196). Pressing dialogue forward through the opening of new semantic fields generated by the artistic interpretive translations is one of the critical aims of the parallaxic praxis.

Most helpful to this model is Eva Kittay's (1990) work on the semantic field theory of metaphor. As we know, words in a semantic field are specifically related to other items in the same field. A metaphor works by "*re-ordering the relations of a field by mapping them on to the existing relations of another field*" (Stern, 2000, p. 242). Stern explains that a metaphor "*typically conveys more information than its interpretation*" (p. 2). To reiterate, in parallaxic praxis, we use polysemy (constructed signs with many meanings) performed through ekphrastic interpretations (translating transcripts into art forms). Our intention is to critically reflect upon our ekphrastic metaphors to examine their semantic fields and thus better understand researcher assumptions and researcher interpretations within interdisciplinary research. Engaging in polysemy through ekphrastic research shifts the metaphoric work of art from a static object of representation to an 'ec-static' interpretive event, which fully embraces an affected, vitalistic and ontological becoming (Collins English Dictionary, 2018; Lash & Lury, 2007).

Stuart Hall's (2007/1973) work opens spaces for rethinking assumptions on producing, circulating, distributing/consuming, and reproducing messages. His work is particularly thought provoking since the research framework is concerned with the production of messages from interpretations of the same data sets. As discussed, Hall argues that polysemy and pluralism are not one and the same, challenging us to not only consider multi-modal and multiple interpretive views (pluralism), but to consider the multiple meanings connoted by words and phrases (polysemy) related to the interpretive artifacts created. Hall (2007/1973) suggests that similar repeated performative retellings of particular narratives create culturally specific interpretations which move these interpretations to 'common-sense' plausible truths, thus asking us as researchers if we are interpreting the data in similar ways (even in different modalities) because we are caught in established socialized normative narratives.

Dialogue and the Construction of Meaning

Parallaxic research draws upon three of the most influential of Bakhtin's ideas regarding dialogue and the construction of meaning through language: utterance, heteroglossia, and carnival (Morris, 1994; Stallybrass & White, 1986; Zappan, 2000). Essentially, meaning is dialogic, as it is established and sustained in the dialogue or "*double-voiced discourse*" (Zappan, 2000, p. 2), whether between various speakers or in reflexive work across contexts. Meaning does not belong to a single "speaker"; is modified through the interaction of the speakers; is never fixed or static, and comes about through the difference between the participants in any dialogue (Hall, 1997; Wiebe, 2012). In dialogic theories, meaning is socially constructed between interlocutors. The ability to see other sight lines through polyphonic play from a self-perspective can produce new kinds of interactions for provoking understanding (Wiebe, 2012). Bakhtinian ideas provide a theoretical basis for parallaxic praxis. Engaging a Bakhtian understanding of the construction of meaning holds that polysemy is ontologically brought about, and then continues to evolve through the interactive dialogue created by parallaxic ekphrastic interpretations. In this way, the researcher/artist moves discourse beyond pluralism into polysemy or stratification within interpretive modalities.

A very useful dialogic collaborative qualitative methodology employed during the analyses phase of this project was the method of Duoethnography (Norris, Sawyer & Lund, 2012; Sawyer & Norris, 2013); whereby, researchers examine personal artifacts, stories, memories, compositions, texts, and critical incidents within the gray zones between self and collaborative partner by way of writing together as a way to challenge socialized meanings. This method intentionally creates a transparency and articulation of perspectives, thoughts, and wonderings, purposefully creating self-reflexive reconstruction.

Signification

Stuart Hall (1997, 2007/1973) has explored how visual and textual representations or messages and communication are produced and disseminated, particularly in mediatized environments. The articulation of this practice employs the use of basic codes or signs which link a particular phenomenon or object to a particular representation. A sign is made up of the association of the signifier with the signified and refers to signification. A sign is a recognizable combination of a signifier (the material form) with a particular signified (the concept it represents) and connects to cultural concepts or meanings held by general beliefs, conceptual frameworks, or value systems of a society (Saussure in Hall, 1997). In his analysis of cultural communication Hall (2007/1973) pushes beyond language semiotics or the symbols to focus on the broader role of discursive formation or the effects and consequences of representations: the politics and power formations and how these discourses are deployed through representation. As this model relates to ekphrastic research, representations do not function merely to reflect or interpret meaning but act/perform to produce cultural meanings. The ekphrastic inquiry process is an explicit signifying practice, as it produces representations that are encoded cultural signs and, thus, is imbued with power relationships.

Hall (1997) addresses the cultural construction of meaning through representations in a four-stage theory of communication depicted as a complex structure of relations produced and sustained through a chain of distinctive stages: production, circulation, distribution/consumption, and reproduction. Each stage of communication forms a "*syntagmatic chain of discourse*" (2007/1973, p. 478). Discourse, in this instance, is specifically defined as "*a group of statements which provide a language for talking about – a way of representing the knowledge about – a particular topic at a particular historical moment. . . . Discourse is about the production of knowledge through language*" (Foucault, in Hall, 1997, p. 44). This chain of discourse is sustained through the presence of shared cultural codes or signs – signifiers and signified. The creation of representations or encoding of a message does, to a certain degree, control its reception or decoding; however, each stage has its own determining limits and possibilities and the stability and reception of a particular sign or message is never guaranteed. Hall (2007/1973) clarifies discourse as a system of representation.

> *It is in the discursive form that the circulation of the product takes place, as well as its distribution to different audiences. Once accomplished the discourse must then be translated . . . into social practices if the circuit is to be both completed and effective. If no 'meaning' is taken, there can be no 'consumption'. If the meaning is not articulated in practice, it has no effect.* (p. 478)

The purpose of representation is translation within the communication process: encode and transform as well as to decode, to render comprehensible that which is initially unfamiliar, to establish a preferred reading of an event or object (Lidchi, 1997). This preferred reading involves the dual processes of encoding and decoding which guide interpretation and delineates meaning making.

More specifically applied to parallaxic ekphrastic interpretations, Louise Rosenblatt (1978) describes the event that occurs between a reader and a text as a transaction, a give and take from both sides (see Figure 5.1). Readers bring to the text a unique set of experiences and the reader's background plays a major role in how he or she might interpret a piece of literature. This is integrally related to parallax—seeing something different based on the angle from which it is viewed.

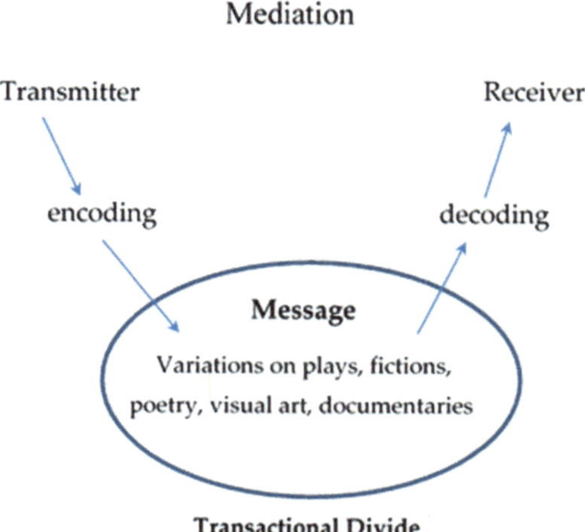

Figure 5.1. The Transactional Divide. Adapted from Rosenblatt (1978). *The Reader, the Text, and the Poem.*

The goal of the framework, and in particular, the utilization of the ekphrastic interpretations and collaborative dialogic method, is to intentionally play with the encoded message in the hopes that when the message is decoded from the transactional divide, the possibilities of new understandings become apparent.

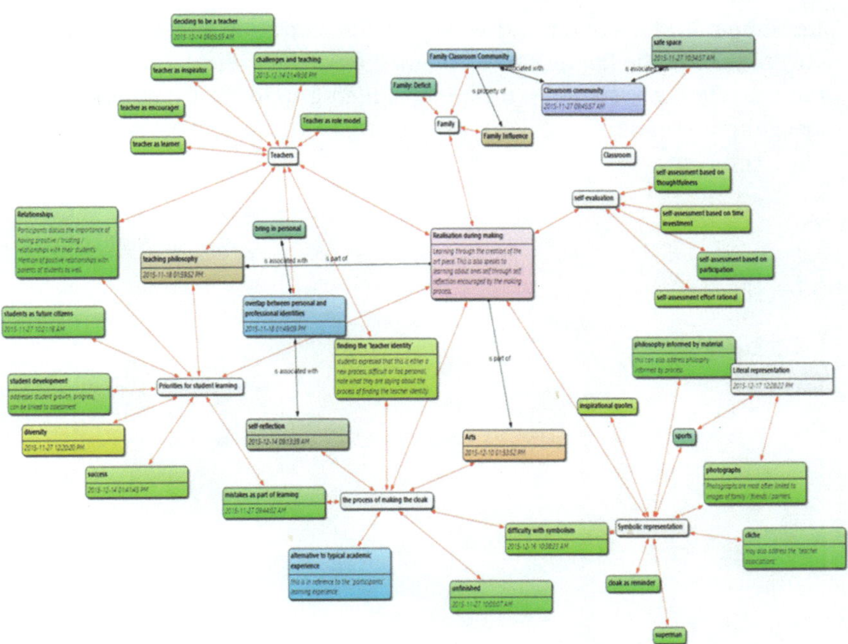

Figure 5.2. Example of ATLAS.ti Family Codes.

ATLAS.ti

ATLAS.ti as a qualitative data analysis computer program Sameshima's teams have found useful for analyzing relationships across large data sets. When working with large data sets with multiple forms of data, a program such as this could be used as a way to consolidate ideas before artful creation begins or both could be done simultaneously. The graphics generated by the program can themselves be considered renderings of the data. ATLAS.ti allows the researchers to annotate and tag across unstructured (i.e., audio, video, text) data sets offering consolidative features that support multi-site, multi-modal, and multi-user data. For example, in Sameshima's pre-service teacher identity project (see Chapter 7.5), where the participants created cloaks representing their conceptions of their teacher identity, the research team was able to tag various symbolic objects within multiple photos of each of 90 material cloaks the pre-service teacher had created. These same codes were used in tagging the pre-service teachers' writing reflections. Simply, if a cloak has an apple motif, they tagged that cloak and connected it to other cloaks that had apples. In the narrative reflections, they were then able to search the word 'apple' and annotate and create a network of how the apple was symbolic to pre-service teachers (see reprint in this volume by Stock, Sameshima & Slingerland, 2016). Figure 5.2 shows an example of a large network view of the family codes obtained from the same data. The ATLAS.ti program offers a systematic means of building markers to understand the most grounded codes.

Chapter 6

Ethics of Art & Simultaneity

Ethics in Arts Integrated Research

A catechizing process of using questions to press knowledge forward is the frame for the following discussion. As with all research involving participants, research protocols must be followed and ethics approvals obtained before research can begin. This is a potential pull-out section that could be used with the research team to discuss the ethics of using the arts in research design. The parallaxic praxis model has the capacity to evoke change because the arts are emotive and can powerfully re/injure or re/produce memories. Deep ethical care must be considered.

Since the 1980s, research that uses the arts integrally in the research process (data collection, analysis, and dissemination) has grown in educational research, health and social sciences, and other disciplinary fields (Barone & Eisner, 2012; Boydell et al., 2015). While examples of arts integrated studies and boundary-crossing research are growing comprehensively and archives of methodological perspectives and frameworks have developed, discussions on ethics are disparately minimal and urgently need to be addressed (Akesson, et al., 2014; Boydell et al., 2015; Cox et al. 2015).

A consortium of international delegates met in 2011 to discuss ethics in arts-based research. Key ethical concerns raised in the initial foray were framed as follows: authorship/ownership of the work; 'truth', interpretation and representation; informed consent/anonymity/ confidentiality; dangerous emotional terrain; and issues of aesthetics (Boydell et al., 2012). This framing has been updated to address emerging challenges: informed consent to maintain confidentiality; design and conduct to minimize harm; managing fuzzy boundaries; addressing authorship and ownership of visual products; and representation and audiences (Waycott et al. 2015). Both groupings accurately umbrella key dilemmas and types of concerns. Instead, to frame this discussion we focus on the human aspect: Risk to the Audience; Risk to the Participant; and Risk to the Researcher. Understanding risks and benefits are always in relation to people in that what may be a risk in one study, may be a benefit in another. For example, blacking out the eyes on a photograph to protect the identity of the participant is highly ethical in one study but could be viewed in another study as the reproduction of non-identity of a vulnerable population. We present snapshots of personal examples Sameshima has experienced through dilemma vignettes, followed by a mini discussion and a group of conversation starters for teams to consider. This section could also be used with students planning to use arts integrated methodologies as many of these issues often are not anticipated. As the vignettes are based on Sameshima's personal experience, the select issues covered by no means represent all possibilities.

Ethical Standards

Researchers need to consider that fine line between intent and effect. Ethical standards including respect, trust, honesty, compassion, empathy, fair-mindedness, social justice, integrity, rigour, and more, are expected to be part of a researcher's commitment. Since research ventures intentionally seek to illuminate unfamiliar territories, all research will entail risk, whether negligible or severe. Risk is especially heightened in research through the arts because they engage emotion and identity on a deeply personal level.

In Canada, respect for human dignity is a key value of the Tri-Council Policy Statement 2nd Edition for Ethical Conduct for Research Involving Humans (TCPS2, 2014). TCPS2 is a Canadian document governing ethics for three federal research funding agencies. The Policy (2014) defines respect for human dignity as research that is "*conducted in a manner that is sensitive to the inherent worth of all human beings and the respect and consideration that they are due*" (p. 6). Core principles provide consideration for: Respect for persons (value, autonomy, consent, participation, commitment to accountability, and transparency); Concern for welfare (impact of the research on individuals, privacy, control of information, and treatment of materials; and Justice (fair treatment, consideration of vulnerability and power balance) (see p. 6-9).

Navigating the variable path between "*the two main goals of providing the necessary protection of participants and serving the legitimate requirements of the research*" (p. 17) is the terrain this discussion navigates.

Risk to the Audience

Dangerous Conference Presentations?

a celebrated keynote speaker jogs into the ballroom, arm waving high

applause smiles, praise for her scholarship, someone I've admired.

she presents research on inhumanity through photo slides

I am traumatized, wounded still now

I am not innocent, the more graphic the better

so I thought in my grade 9 social studies presentation

on the bombing of Hiroshima

Danger in the Hallway?

as a curator, I have offended by hanging juried art

a painting of a nude reclining woman
illustrating documented reactions to

medication for polycystic ovarian syndrome,
a master's thesis investigation

health and safety complaints, "a mixture of shock and repulsion"

a deleted heated facebook discussion, appeals for removal

Danger in Dissemination?

for a study on prenatal education access

a red foil armature of a uterus is part of a costume

specifically made for a juried runway exhibit on wearable art

hosted by the local chic contemporary art gallery in a bar

standing room only, music booming, photos going viral

can this artwork be shown in the participants' own cultural space?

Discussion and Considerations

Arts integrated investigations incorporate the arts to catalyze creative innovation, share research as a pedagogical strategy to broad audiences, and promote the capacity of interdisciplinary multimodal inquiry. The arts press us into states of reflection on how we make meaning of the world, how we position ourselves in relation, and how we acculturate ourselves in the larger cultural community.

What provokes some and not others? Barthes (1980) uses the term the stadium as the most obvious symbolic meaning of a photograph—for example, a random picture of baby—and the punctum which connects or 'pierces the viewer'. The punctum is personal and unique to each viewer. When a mother looks at her baby in a photograph, the punctum leaps out and touches her. The punctum in the artwork is what generates a connection to feel, to transform, to learn, to generate new ways for seeing. The word punctum means to wound; its Latin root makes reference to trauma. Appropriately, Barthes wrote, "*the punctum shows no preference for morality or good taste: the punctum can be ill-bred.*" (p. 43). Can one be 'wounded' but not take offence? This idea puts the responsibility on the viewer to be able to navigate uncomfortable feelings without taking offence. Is being on the offensive an attitude to avoid engagement?

And to what extent is provocation acceptable? Tavin and Kallio-Tavin (2014) present a pedagogy of provocation in their discussion of including violent contemporary artwork in art education. They muse that "*perhaps the [violent] artwork's otherness is so stunning that it pushes toward denying the artwork's alterity. The artwork represents the absolute Other, and forces viewers to question their abilities to confront the alterity of Other*" (p. 67). The authors use Levinas' (2008) explanation of the totalized world, where the Other is conceived through our own sameness limiting our views of the Other's possible worlds. The authors contend that to experience art works that intentionally shock us from our normative framings makes 'the act of violence less violating and, therefore, paradoxically more moral' (p. 68). In regards to the art genre called exploitive reality, art critic Arthur Danto says 'Morality trumps ethics' and Tom Eccles, an art director at Bard College suggests, "*it's not about what the public should or shouldn't be exposed to; it is what you should or shouldn't be complicit in*" (Hoban 2008, p. 1).

Questions to Discuss:

- If provocative research aims to stimulate learning, what is too much provocation?
- How might we consider audience consent in research dissemination?
- What responsibilities do curators have for artwork in open public spaces?
- What do you think of the artist, Acconci's words: *"Sometimes you need to disturb in order to make the space for somebody to think"* (Hoban 2008, p. 1)?
- Can artworks based on participant data offend the participants and their cultural ethical boundaries?

Risk to the Participant

Dangerous Researcher Intention?

a PhD applicant wants to shame her abuser

and call it arts based research

Danger in Research Design?

a playlist created by a music researcher

of key songs instrumental in recovery for a

methamphetamine addict elicits distress and triggers use

Dangerous Class Assignment?

a scholar shares a high school art student assignment

students emulating a particular artist's style
explore the theme of identity

self-created staged photographs
dressed up in provocative and sexualized

scenes accompanied with names and unedited artist statements

not the kind of pictures you would show your parents

Discussion and Considerations

There is growing debate on using identifiable images versus obscuring the data in arts integrated studies. Clark, Prosser, and Wiles (2010) propose that ethics in image-based research is different from word-based research and situated approaches must be negotiated. In the art assignment example, spelling or grammatical errors in the young people's artist statements and their accompanying named photographs can create unfair audience bias. Pixelating or obscuring of faces raises issues of 'othering' young children in research (Nutbrown, 2010), or rendering data meaningless (Wiles et al., 2008). Boydell et al. (2012) point to the criminalizing effect of the black bar across the eyes when used to anonymize facial data.

Boxall and Ralph (2009) suggest that while 'tighter ethical regulation of social research, combined with the multitude of ethical issues raised by the use of image-based approaches may be discouraging the use of creative visual approaches in intellectual disability research' (p. 45), the inclusion of underrepresented populations is a major concern. Along similar lines, Ritchie's (2013) work found conflicting views in response to photo essay work on aging bodies, revealing both supporters of ageism with the desire to protect, while challenged by others who promoted "*acceptance of older people as competent, autonomous beings*" (p. 101). Vanderwees (2015) submits that 'exploitive or voyeuristic' photos (as used in Jonathan Safran Foer's novel) can be used to "*consider ethical relationships between [readers] and others*" (p. 177). Further, the multiple benefits of ethnographic video methods present exceedingly complex ethical challenges when working with vulnerable populations or minors, as well as when filming within community-oriented environments (Puurveen et al. 2015).

Questions to Discuss:

- Where is the line between preserving anonymity and reducing stigma, particularly with vulnerable research populations or minors?
- What are the researcher's responsibilities to participants taking on roles in performance or embodied inquiry processes?
- How is researcher integrity 'policed'?
- How might ethics change between modalities: For example, between the visual and the acoustic?
- What are the responsibilities of the mentor or primary investigator as ethical advisor?
- How might supporting characters in autobiographical and life-writing work be protected?

Risk to the Researcher

Dangers for Participants as Co-Researchers?

graduate students explore gender roles and violence against women

through the reading of a play. 'Carmen' "felt really, really vulnerable"

'Ruby' was surprised at "how much more emotionally involved you get

with the characters when they are actually people
and not just words on a page"

most participants disclose feelings of unpreparedness for the

emotional impact and intensity of participating in the study

Dangerous Uncontrolled Research?

as a non-Indigenous co-researcher, I reflect on my role

with a large interdisciplinary research team doing research

in Indigenous communities, slow and patient I weave

myself in the piercing motion of a needle felting practice

introducing each fibre into a background already formed

my interwoven learnings intertwined and meshed

supported in entanglement but always without roots

Discussion and Considerations

Is it enough to offer de-identification, withdrawal at any time in the study, or direction to appropriate health and counselling services in participant consent letters? Boydell et al. (2012) note that "actors and other artists and their experiences of depicting suffering and violence, for example, remain relatively unexplored" (p. 11). Sensitive research has social or psychological costs potentially including guilt, shame, stigma, judgement, or embarrassment (2012).

The TCPS2 (2014) echoes Sameshima's needle felting acknowledging that "*building reciprocal, trusting relationships will take time*" (p. 109). Nilan (2002) uses the term "*dangerous fieldwork*' (p. 383) to describe a researcher's anxiety over a perceived lack of control of research. In her examination of fieldwork, Nilan (2002) challenges the ethnographer's "*desire for mastery*" (p. 383) explaining that "*the very analytic texts we produce are themselves constitutive effects of discourse . . . because of the necessity to write within the acceptable discourses of academic prose and disciplinary genre*" (p. 383).

Aside from the unexpected risks, art-making can reveal to the researcher, the ongoing engagement with intense, painful data sets involving emotional interviews or traumatic data can be significantly impactful on the welfare of the researcher's life. Especially in interpretive ekphrastic practises (translating textual data into artworks), intensive indwelling in the data over extended periods of time can be draining on the researchers.

Questions to Discuss:

- How many interpretations of data can there be?
- Who owns artefacts co-created by artist-researchers in participatory research?
- Whose interpretation or analyses of data is privileged?
- How might researchers working with emotional data sets be supported?
- What are researchers' responsibilities in responding to traumatic responses experienced by participants as co-researchers (beyond a helpline provided in the consent form)?

Although ethical norms are often regarded as common sense, respect for human dignity involves addressing ethical dilemmas and the arts themselves can be used to creatively bridge divides. Cox et al. (2015) editors of a special issue on ethics and arts-based research, draw attention to the key recommendation across the full collection, of the importance of explicit and self-reflexive accounting of the ethical and methodological arisings during the research process. Ethics conversations must become integral to arts integrated methodology courses, research team meetings, and ongoing mentorship practice with doctoral students. Leggo's (2011) narrative example that the artist's practise is the work of opening fractious and undisciplined possibilities is resilient advice:

> *As I write and critically reflect on my writing, I am constantly challenged by the ways that writing opens up possibilities for hope, even at the same time that I grow more aware of the dangers of writing, the ways that writing seductively weaves hopeful possibilities while always remaining wild and uncontrollable.* (p. 116)

Navigating Trauma and Suffering[1]

Questions Explored:

- What am I (as a researcher and artist) doing and creating? What is it called?
- How is the concern of re-inscribing dominant discourse addressed?
- Where and where within the interpretive works is the narrative authority of the researcher located?
- What is a 'defensible' or 'ethical' interpretation?
- How can research methodology work to address the concern of reinscription?

In broad terms and specific events, many artists, theorists and philosophers have wrestled with narrative images and aesthetic depictions of suffering and violence (Adorno, 1962; Arendt, 1963/2006; Barthes, 1980; Benjamin, 1968/2007; Butler, 2007; Coetzee, 1999; Ensler, 2008; Higgins & Silver, 1991; Knowles, Luciani, Cole, & Neilsen, 2007; Levine, 2009; Marais, 2006; Matus, 1998; Morrison, 1970; Ortega, 2008; Pink, 2007; Sontag, 1977, 2003). The word trauma is understood as a direct or indirect experience of interpersonal violence that produces iterative pain and suffering for individuals and communities. Further, it "*fragments experience and prevents any totalization into a whole. In so doing, it robs suffering of its meaning. Trauma doesn't mean anything, it just is*" (Levine, 2009, p. 16). Given this perspective, how do we approach researching, interpreting, and learning about trauma in an ethical and respectful way, especially in regard to an arts-informed phenomenological study – by definition a project of meaning making? How can we represent trauma without giving it a meaning that would harmonize or frame it into an orderly and essentialized whole, ridding it of its chaotic and brutal character?

---

[1] This work was excerpted from a presentation by Maarhuis and Sameshima in 2013 and an independent research course Maarhuis took with Sameshima at Washington State University at the time. Maarhuis, P., & Sameshima, P. (2013, March). Place of agitation, place of learning: The narrative canvasses of a Clothesline Project. Paper presentation. *National Art Educators Association (NAEA) Conference.* Fort Worth, TX.

Understanding and navigation may come about through imaginative poiesis or to actively re-image and reveal trauma through the incorporation of the fragmented, chaotic, and meaningless character of violent experience. As applied to examining the experience of violence, it is the combination of praxis in research and pedagogy, as well as poiesis of arts informed analysis and interpretation, that allows for productive-imaginative comportment and ontological Being (Heidegger, 1933-34/2010; Sinclair, 2006). To achieve this, one must step away from the notion that mere retrospective 'thinking' can give one the means to develop an empathetic understanding of the totality of traumatic experience. There is no deliverance to understanding through blunt cognition and systematic knowledge. Poiesis must "*consist of a series of inquiries linked by an underlying concern, inquires that proceed circuitously along different pathways but nevertheless attempt to arrive at the same destination*" (Levine, 2009, p. 20). Artful renderings and "*poetic knowledge*" make present and reveal truths about the experience of violence (p.159). As well, the idea that art and artful presentation provides meaning in and validation of extreme pain and suffering is rejected. Such ascription can render traumatic suffering into what is prurient and superficial. It turns the act of bearing witness into a remote and delusive venue for hopeful feelings of well-being. Rather, imaginative poiesis opens one's capacity to be present with, to be changed by, and to respond to suffering.

The combination of arts-informed phenomenological research, parallaxic and transformative pedagogies, opportunities for imaginative response, and ethical knowledge dissemination is of particular importance in addressing and understanding the multi-determined etiology, pervasive perpetration, and negative consequences of interpersonal violence. But why? Why is this combination multi-modal and imaginative practices deemed important and effective? First, it is work with disturbing narratives and renderings that demonstrate the value of opening to the expressiveness of images and richly textured qualitative research and "*embodied relational understanding*" *by sensitizing practitioners and cultural practices*" (Todres, 2008, p.1566). Second, aesthetic study, interpretation, and pedagogies expose and threaten the existing social order that tolerates interpersonal violence. Third, imaginative and artful poiesis gives rise to ethical interruptions and then invites one to sit in the dissonance and reflection (Spivak, 2012). And fourth, at its core, a process of imaginative poiesis and mimetic re-presentation can provide the means to "reply to one's wounds" (Levine, 2009). Trauma, imagination, memory, and re-presentation are coalesced within our way of being through acts of poiesis. This focuses research, pedagogy, and dissemination efforts away from an objectifying duality of the traumatized/non-traumatized and refocuses everyone – the researcher, participants, and viewer – on creative capacities:

> *I think the dominant conception of trauma is based upon a vision of the human in which suffering is purely extrinsic, a phenomenon that is merely factual and that overlies the existence of a non-traumatized being. I would rather say that existence itself is a trauma.* (Levine, 2009, p. 178)

The educational importance of doing difficult research through parallaxic praxis must be considered. First, exercising multiple theoretical and pedagogical perspectives, combined with artful interpretations, leads to deep and rich understandings as well as methodological discovery. Second, as with many studies, despite activism, growing awareness, and decades of research, certain challenges continue to plague families, communities and schools/universities. Aesthetic education and arts-informed research results stimulate fresh thinking and alternative perspectives, which can lead to new learning, new becomings, and the generation of unattended questions regarding the experiences at hand. Third, the use of transformative learning theory and a pedagogy of parallax allows the facilitator/teacher/researcher to present materials and information in a liminal space and a supportive manner, which allows for tempered and mindful exposure to disturbing materials as well as the needed reflection and interpersonal processing. These research and pedagogical approaches address ethical concerns regarding issues of harm and one's duty to care for participants/students/viewers/ researchers who may be adversely affected by the often frank and brutal content of some of these traumatic research projects.

The Ethics of Simultaneity

In the section of the book called Model Design, a number of researchers and their ideas are listed as building blocks in the development of this research design. The naming of the researchers and their ideas, along with the choice of unnaming those who have been influential creates pause. To name is to take a stance, to select, to close another. The issues of working across disciplines and across modalities within multiplicity demand a conscious holding in reserve, a knowing that decisions are made, always, from an array of incompleteness. Wiebe and Sameshima, in a paper drawing from the novel, *The Sympathizer* (Nguyen, 2015) suggest that the liminal studio, the play space of these relational tensions, is where the something of nothingness can be "*a language of resistance for a reimagined politics of creativity and generation*" (p. 25). In each parallaxic praxis the drawing out of a network of theorists and theories become the basis of a collective team ethic. We explain:

> *In the Western history of knowledge, the human energy empowering the canonic drive has been a synoptic one (Schubert, 2010). In synopsis is*

> *the desire for clarity, refinement, prioritization. It is the pursuit to define so that concepts can be distinguished and recognized, enough so that they can be passed on to the next generation, a process called education (Aoki, 2000). Despite this, Einstein urges us that while knowledge can be made as simple as possible, it should be no simpler (Yale book of quotations, 2006, p. 231). In other words, synoptic processes need a complement of expansive ones. Knowledge assemblage processes need to be both synoptic and expansive. With every rule there is an exception. With every and, there is a but. In early Hebraic language, the sign wav, could signify either and or but. As a coordinating conjunction the sign wav had multiple, even oppositional meanings, and it was up to the reader to understand meaning through context and tradition. And, in the way that paradox often operates as a poetic trope, there is always the possibility that oppositional meanings were meant to both be true at the same time.* (Wiebe & Sameshima, 2018, p. 26, See Chapter 7.7)

Tracing the Development of Ethical Frameworks

In a parallaxic praxis, the questions and choices within the development of a research project call for complex thinking and, at times, complicated decision-making processes. To illustrate, the following section shares excerpts from Maarhuis' dissertation. Integrated with ideas developed through this book, this tracing of the development of a framework from Maarhuis' voice, of the Clothesline Project, demonstrates the navigation of conceptualizing an ethically aligned framework using parallaxic praxis. For a fuller explanation of Maarhuis' dissertation project, please see Chapter 7 of this book.

The purpose of the *Replies to Wounds* study (Maarhuis, 2016) was to describe hermeneutic phenomenological research on the Washington State University Clothesline Project (1993–2012) and ekphrasic artefacts about the experience of interpersonal violence utilizing a Deweyan (1934/2005) theoretical framework with reference to Bakhtinian notions (Holquist & Liapunov, 1990); parallaxic praxis (Sameshima & Vandermause, 2008); agonist activism (Mouffe, 2007), and transformative teaching and learning strategies (Mezirow, 2012).

Theoretical Framework

The writings of Dewey (1934/2005;1958) that focus on artful transactional experience serve as the primary theoretical framework for analysis and understanding the Clothesline Project event, participant narratives, and ekphrasic critique. To dig deep into the analysis of the structure, discourse, as well as narrative content, I also consider ways in which the philosophies of Dewey and the linguistic and literary insights of Bakhtin (Holquist, 2004; Morris,

1994; Stallybrass & White, 1986) are complementary, contrasting, and interactive. Notably, Bakhtin's ideas are applied due to a lack of specific discussion in Dewey's work about the ways in which literary texts and narrative language function as a dialogic focal point within disruptive communal events (Dressman, 2004). The concepts of Chantal Mouffe (1999, 2005, 2007, 2008, & 2013) about conflictual consensus/dissensus, agonism, and the use of critical art are added to the theoretical framework due to a lack of specific discussion in Dewey's work about means to address deeply embedded societal problems, such as interpersonal violence, within democratic deliberation and education. A combined Deweyan, Bakhtinian, and Mouffian lens allows for an intensive, complex, and distinctly positioned analyses of aesthetic phenomena and ekphrastic works that are simultaneously chaotic and ordered, beautiful and brutal, violent and harmonious, disturbing and transformative.

Deweyan Concepts

Knowledge and meaning making in a hermeneutic phenomenological research project are understood as ongoing, ontological, incomplete and generated from an interaction between people, their experiences, ideas, and contexts (Dewey, 1934/2005, 1958). Though a prominent scholar, author, and social activist of his day (1859–1952), questions arise as to present day relevance and applicability of Deweyan ideas (Rud, Garrison, & Stone, 2009). How does one apply Deweyan theories—almost 100 years after their penning—to contemporary societal problems such as violence, shifting aesthetic experiences, radically different technologies, and modes of communication?

Throughout Dewey's work the elements of experience are a major theme, as is my analytical focus here; however, given the limits of this dissertation excerpt, only a few of his philosophical notions will be discussed here. In *Art as Experience,* Dewey (1934/2005) systematically considered aesthetic experience, as generated by works of art and emergent from the prosaic rudiments of everyday experience (Mandoki, 2007).

Experience. The ordinary interactions of beings, things, and environs or experience are understood as being situated in a particular context. It is transactional and relational (Dewey, 1934/2005; 1958; Jackson, 1998). Thus, given the large number of those directly and indirectly affected by interpersonal violence, the experience of violence can be called an everyday, even an ordinary experience.

Experience is determined by the interaction, context, and conditions of existence (Dewey, 1934/2005). In this, human beings are not separate from objects, events, or other beings. Additionally, the temporality of experience is a result and a consequence of the ongoing and cumulative interaction of the self in the world.

The Clothesline Project event displays the traits of an experience, including completeness or a sense of fulfillment, uniqueness, or unity of a single quality, and unifying emotion or coherence (Jackson, 1998). The experience of violence and participation in the Clothesline Project is generative in that many undergo a transformation of the self, perspective, attitude, and/or knowledge. For example, Clothesline Project participants move beyond their individual expression into a collective that translates the meaning of the everyday experience and interpersonal violence.

Order and harmony. Deweyan thought can provide a foundational framework to understand the experience of the Clothesline Project; however, the application, felt unfinished and even avoidant. Still, I wrestled to reconcile Dewey's consistent reference to order, harmony, experience, and artwork (1934/2005, 1958).

Considering Deweyan thought:

- What do I do with works that do not depict what is harmonious, such as the Clothesline Project?
- What about aesthetic forms and medium that are not positive or beautiful?
- How do notions of transformation regarding difficult topics figure into Dewey's thinking?
- Is Deweyan philosophy too dated and superficial to use as a framework for defiant and contentious works of art?

First, these questions are difficult to answer when ideas about art tend to be object-centric, primarily focused on static form. While form (or aesthetic and materialized existence of the artwork) visibly precedes the essence or relational identity of the artwork, this form could conceivably communicate various relational identities. With deeper analysis into Deweyan thought and a re-focus on the creative and transactional process of the artists and audience, the necessary use of order and harmony became clearer. Here is a lengthy but important quotation from Dewey (1934/2005):

> *The rhythm of loss of integration with environment and recovery of union not only persist in man but becomes conscious with him; its conditions are material out of which he forms purposes. Emotion is the conscious sign of a break, actual or impending. The discord is the occasion that induces reflection. Desire for restoration of the union converts mere emotion into interest in objects as conditions of*

> *realization of harmony. With the realization, material of reflection is incorporated into objects as their meaning. Since the artist cares in a peculiar way for the phase of experience in which union is achieved, he does not shun moments of resistance and tension. He rather cultivates them, not for their own sake, but because of their potentialities, bringing to living consciousness an experience that is unified and total.* (p. 14)

It is the actual process of creation and the specific form of the work of art that is purposeful and ordered, even though the experience depicted in the artwork may be brutal and the works of art may produce feelings of dissonance and discord. Dewey (1934/2005) focuses on the work of creativity or ideas behind the work of art that needs to be harmonious and orderly, not the artwork itself. The artist (in this case, the Clothesline Project participants) used chaos, pain, tension, and discord. They converted it into an art form—through the use of a particular medium—so interest, reflection, and transformation can take place. It is essential to remain focused on the artist's purposeful creation of the artwork and the resulting communication or transactional experience through medium. Fundamentally, without the materialization of some order and harmony within the process of creativity and production of a communicative form, the artist and the audience cannot have a fully transactional and dialogic experience.

Second, and more broadly applied, Dewey (1934/2005) describes an embodied reconstruction when discussing a shift in perspective, understanding, and actions after an experience, such as the Clothesline Project event. He states:

> *For "taking in" in any vital experience is something more than placing something on the top of consciousness over what was previously known. It involves reconstruction which may be painful. Whether the necessary undergoing phase is by itself pleasurable or painful is a matter of particular conditions.* (p. 42)

Reconstruction, no matter where on a continuum of painful or pleasant experiences, can open the capacities of the participant, event organizer, researcher, educator, and the audience to be present with, to be changed by, and to compassionately respond to the difficult experiences of another. Coming to a different perspective is about harmonizing or adjusting one's previous understanding to take into consideration new information, thinking, and experiences. Thus, while Dewey did see working toward democratic consensus and education as a vital means to address relational wellbeing and social ills (Hickman, 1992), Deweyan notions of order and harmony in transactional aesthetic expressions are more about ongoing alignment or adjustment to new experience and information (Fesmire, 2003; Jackson, 1998; McClelland, 2005), than about maintaining undisturbed societal agreement.

Thus, Deweyan pragmatism is relevant to contemporary inquiry through a broad and overlapping emphasis on the transformative experiences of agency, activism, art, reflection, and cultural and civic identity. Artful works and events, such as the Clothesline Project, have a distinct function and act as a form of language and tool in communication, which, in turn, allows for communal deliberation, dialogue, and disruption of dominant discourse (Droogsma, 2006; Hipple, 1998). Aesthetic experience and the arts have a distinct purpose in identifying common problems, the formation of dialogic spaces, and the dissemination of knowledge (Jackson, 1998; Mattern, 1999; Waks, 2009). Specific concerns about the application of Deweyan thought to painful and difficult experiences and the responsive creative expressions can be addressed through the two notions described above (a) materialization of order within the process of creativity and art form to enhance transaction and (b) embodied reconsideration and reconstruction through aesthetic experience and dialogue.

However, while the central premise of this project is that Deweyan theories do still apply within my theoretical framework, there are ongoing contested critiques and debates about Dewey's writings on conflict, authority, power, and violence (Diggins, 1994; Hickman, 1992; Johnston, 2001; Saito, 2009; Westbrook, 1991). As well, there is a lack of detailed analysis of privilege, power structures, and the experience of interpersonal violence in Dewey's own work (1916, 1916/2011, 1922, 1927/1988, 1930, 1939, 1958). Given this, I need to include the complementary theoretical ideas of Bakhtin (Bakhtin, 1919/1990, 1984, 1993; Holquist, 2004; Morris, 1994; Stallybrass & White, 1986).

Bakhtinian Concepts

The addition of Bakhtin theoretical notions provides a way to address the meaning of acts of violence, the use of embodied speech within the narratives, and the power of attenuated and then re-enacted socio-cultural discourse and power structures. While the dissertation draws upon many of the most influential Bakhtinian ideas, given the limits of this dissertation excerpt, only a few of his philosophical notions will be discussed here.

Dialogue. Within Bakhtinian thought, dialogue is made of three basic elements: an utterance, a reply, and, most importantly, a relation between the two that allows for meaning making (Holquist, 2004). Dialogism is made up of an ongoing simultaneity in that "*speakers are different from each other and the utterance each makes is always different from the other's; and yet all these differences are held together in the relation of dialogue*" (Holquist, 2004, p. 40). An example of differential relation within dialogism can be found in a "double-voiced" discourse or "the presence of two differently oriented speech acts inhabiting the same words" (Morris, 1994, p. 13) that contains utterances and specialized speech genres (Morris, 1994; Holquist, 2004). Utterance is an active unit of speech, always placed within the relational context of dialogue together with other utterances, which take meaning and shape within a particular historical moment in a socially specific environment. The nature of "*embodied*" and "*intoned*" utterance is never singular and is part of a whole chain of utterances (Morson & Emerson, 1990, p. 133). Authorship of an utterance, in communion with the whole of being, becomes a dialogic event. While an utterance is specifically defined, or bounded, within a sphere of communication, it is also inherently interactive and relational between speaker(s) and audience (Zappan, 2000). It is a linguistic concept as much as it is a form of dialogic being—always in response and always expecting a reply (Morris, 1994).

As well, speech genres are a type of collective dialogue or a grouping of utterances that are developed and performed within a textual space where a particular discourse coalesces into a recognizable form. Given this, the Clothesline Project can be understood as a dialogue—a group of utterances—that utilizes a particular form of speech genre, in that it is identified with a particular sphere of communication (i.e., the annual Clothesline Project event); it has developed into stable thematic content (i.e., experience of violence); and it has developed a style and compositional structure (i.e., short narrative on colorful t-shirts, publicly displayed).

Answerability. Bakhtin (1919/1990) specifically positions art, being, responsibility, and relationship within aesthetic dialogue in his short essay Art and Answerability by noting that "*art and life are not one, but they must become united in myself—in the unity of my answerability*" (p. 2). Answerability is rooted in the Bakhtinian notion of transactional being (I/you) that is constructed through aesthetic dialogue and expresses the ethical responsibility of engagement of self and Other within context and over time (Holquist, 2004). This is not about identity but about the production or enactment of meaning through artful text. In other words, for Bakhtin (1919/1990), to be in dialogue is to be answerable to self as well as to respond ethically to the shared context of relationship and being with others. From this perspective, Bakhtinian dialogic ethics and responsibility are not a unified or essentialized set of community values, but are ongoing constructed understandings and responsive acts found within and through aesthetic dialogue. Using this lens, the Clothesline Project is a venue for answerability and ethical aesthetic response to acts of violence. Further, Bakhtinian ideas of art and answerability do not demand consensus or a harmonized response, and consequently, link with Mouffian ideas of agonist and critical art (2007, 2008) and Deweyan ideas of *Art as Experience* (1934/2005).

Carnival. One way that the act, dialogue, utterance, and heteroglossia are made manifest is in the enactment of carnival, a chronotopic and intersectional concept that describes spatial and temporal elements of an individual and communal generative event. For Bakhtin, the notion of carnival is derived from the way folk culture attenuates official hegemony, or dominant culture, through festivals, celebrations, seasonal rituals, pageants, public speech and performance, and market-place spectacles (Stallybrass & White, 1986). Carnivalesque acts are distinct from sanctioned community events, suspend official hierarchical power and rank, and are a means to undermine hegemony (see Morris, 1994, p. 20).

The phenomena of carnival, in effect, embody secular-social relations and draw attention to the fragile cultural construction of place, power, and social roles. Carnivalesque performance and language are intermittent expressions of freedom from official social norms (see Zappan, 2000, p. 7). Surging communal expression, through costume and color, brings about the productive process of re-generation or re-presentation, which frees human consciousness from dominant and hierarchical perceptions of the world and opens up the possibility for new awareness, understanding, and change (Morris, 1994). Yet, participants in carnival live within a performed duality: freedom from social norms and dominant culture, yes, but a freedom strictly contained within specified time and space (Stallybrass & White, 1986).

Carnival, violence, and the individual. The complexity of interpersonal violence demands that my Bakhtinian analysis goes beyond notions of the act, dialogue, and utterance. Thus, while collective carnival may be acting out transgressively against dominant or official discourses, there is also re-enactment of "*licensed complicity*" and the "*displaced abjection*" of weaker social groups within the chaos (see Stallybrass & White, 1986, p. 19). This process of "assertion violence," takes place when an individual or group attempts to affirm his or her position and power in the community through performative, aesthetic, and harmful acts (Kupfer, 1983, p. 45). Self-affirming violence, however, is evidence of a lack of true agency. It is oft enacted to maintain an internal and secure sense of power and position within one's community, which is, in turn, a re-enactment of the violence of dominant discourse and power structures.

Dialogic community and bacchanalian acts. Additionally, Bakhtin hyper-emphasizes the plurality of the dialogic community as a whole and infinite regenerative revelry; thus, there is an almost complete neglect of the experience of the individual within the violence and degradation of carnival (Emerson, 1993; Hollis, 2001; Ryklin, 1993). Curiously, in his writings about carnival, Bakhtin (1984) theoretically retains the transactional notions of the act, being, and transactional dialogue (Morris, 1994; Zappan, 2000), but does not integrate in his ideas of answerability, art, and responsive ethics (Bakhtin, 1919/1990). In Bakhtinian writings about carnival there is a propensity toward the abstract, as he works to use bacchanalian acts to emphasize the sweeping away of institutions, social norms, and doctrine for the supposed renewal and betterment of community (Morson & Emerson, 1990).

While Bakhtinian theory and text about the chaos and dialogic regeneration in a community may not be harmful, the Clothesline Project narratives affirm the trouble, trauma, and despair that can occur when acts of carnival become involved in real violence. The aesthetic and critical display of the Clothesline Project provides both vision and voice to the experiences of harm, trauma, and death of individual bodies during episodes of violence embedded societal practices of reoccurring hegemony. So, ideas of responsible answerability (Bakhtin, 1919/1990) do provide some grounding for artful critique in my theoretical analysis, but it is disingenuous to singularly apply utterance, heteroglossia, polyphony, or the nostalgic Bakhtinian notions of carnival to a contemporary discourse on violence (Hollis, 2001; Ryklin, 1993). How do I sharpen the focus of my theoretical lens?

Mouffian Concepts

Initially, one of the challenges at the beginning of this study was how to apply Deweyan and Bakhtinian theories to present day understanding about experiences of violence and participation in activist events such as the Clothesline Project. Dewey (1916/2011, 1934/2005, 1939) emphasized artful practices as a medium for political deliberation, education, and unified community-based problem solving; however, he did not develop these ideas for pragmatic application to specifically address contentious problems and confrontational political action (Mattern, 1999). Additionally, as I proceeded in the research project, there were other challenging questions in regard to relating the theoretical framework and applied notions of time, dialogue, display, and platform in the process and methods of research and analysis.

Questions:

- The Clothesline Project has been in existence for approximately 25 years. How do researchers and educators analyze and understand the Project as an ever-evolving aesthetic and dialogic platform in our communities today?
- What research methods are best suited to promote ongoing dialogue, education, and democratic practice as part of the analysis and dissemination process?
- What methods of research are best suited to answer questions about qualitative phenomena that are aesthetic, activist, and artful in form and expression?

There are strong calls for a feminist critique (Seigfried, 2002a, 2002b) of Dewey for a more concentrated analysis of power relations as opposed to prescribed approaches to ongoing community problems and concerns (Hickman et al., 2009). The inclusion of feminist critique as well as concepts of antagonism, agonism, and pluralism (Laclau & Mouffe, 2014; Mouffe, 1999) can advance pragmatist social thought and combat hegemony and dominant discourse (Hickman, et al., 2009). Likewise, Saito (2009) points to the need for a significant reconstruction of Deweyan pragmatism by shifting away from equilibrium and problem solving by moving "*toward dissolving and dissolution . . . to sustain a sense of the unsolved tension*" (p. 93) when addressing personal relations, citizenship education, and creative democracy in present-day society.

As I move deeper into the development of a theoretical framework, these questions and concerns call for the inclusion of yet another theorist.

Agonist pluralism. To address this dilemma within my theoretical framework, I return to expand on the ideas of transaction and dialogue. Mouffe (2007, 2008, 2013) asks: How can artistic practices contribute to the questioning of dominant hegemony within democratic society? For my purposes, this question applies to the research of the experience and communal response to interpersonal violence, as expressed in the Clothesline Project event. Like Dewey (1916/201, 1934/2005, 1939), Mouffe (2007, 2008, 2013) methodically and pragmatically builds a unified analysis of communication, art, education, and democratic practice in public spaces. And, like Bakhtin (1984, 1919/1990), she acknowledges the ongoing existence of and need for agonism and responsible answerability in human relations and communal living.

In challenging democratic theory and practice Chantal Mouffe (1999, 2005, 2013) rejects a deliberative democratic model and espouses the development of agonistic pluralism, through the need to acknowledge the limits of rational consensus. Agonism, "*a struggle between adversaries*" (Mouffe, 2013, p. 7), requires the provision of a means through which all members of the community have ways to ardently express themselves. The prime task of agonistic pluralism is not to exclude passionate and discordant voices from public spheres in the name of rational consensus, but to mobilize those energies toward democratic aims through conflictual consensus (Mouffe, 1999, 2005, 2013). Essentially, agonism addresses the inherent societal configurations of power and political relations that cannot be eliminated and cannot be reconciled through technical and rational dialogue alone. Mouffe (2008) rejects political naiveté and the reduction of politics to technical maneuvers and non-adversarial procedures:

> *Society is always politically instituted and never forgets that the terrain in which hegemonic interventions takes place is always the outcome of previous hegemonic practices and that it is never a neutral one.* (p. 9)

Critical art. Later, Mouffe (2007, 2008, 2013) applies these ideas to art as an agonist intervention in public space—beyond the modernist idea of the avant-garde and the remote privileged artist—to movement, displacement, and negotiation practices that widen the field of artistic intervention by directly intervening in a multiplicity of public and social spaces, in order to oppose ongoing and overlapping dominant and hegemonic practices. Art, democratic practice, and politics or power relations are constituted on one non-violent and discursive field toward the possible formation of critical art or artful practices that foment "*dissensus that makes visible what the dominant consensus tends to obscure and obliterate*" (2007, p. 4), giving a platform and voice to those muted by dominant discourse.

Current challenges for the Clothesline Project include access to a multiplicity of public and social spaces that go beyond institutional confines as well as questions about how to develop ongoing displays and dialogue. Using Deweyan, Bakhtinian, and Mouffian ideas as a theoretical framework for future research methods and dissemination of the Clothesline Project serves to address these challenges. Notably, the Mouffian notion of agonistic art is a practice of critique that is suited to the highly mobile and technological nature of current daily life and embraces the use of variety of ever-evolving media and platforms to remain part of democratic dialogue. Agonistic pluralism and critical art include multiple art forms, media, and technology by activists, artists, educators, and researchers, which allow for the inclusion of a new generation of young community members, who are accustomed to multiple spaces for dialogue. From this perspective, activists and participants in the Clothesline Project can continue to be flexible and move in response to the dominant and hegemonic discourses they oppose (Droogsma, 2009; Gregory, et al., 2002; Harrison & Barthel, 2009; Hipple, 2000; Jones, 2009), through purposeful and pragmatic artistic acts that work to construct new subjectivities.

Making as Ethical Constructions of Our Futures

Maarhuis: When fully embracing the aporia of difficult topics like interpersonal violence the researcher, viewer, and participant must sit in the dissonance of simultaneous and seemingly contradictory life circumstances, that don't fit into familiar cultural narratives and truths (Fesmire, 2003; Spivak, 2012). In this way dissonance, imagination, memory, and interpretation are coalesced within our way of being through acts of poiesis and ethical representation, as "*a reshaping of the world as it is given to us, with all the wounds and suffering we have experienced, and 'making them new'*" without denying, justifying, lessening, or accepting the harm and its damaging effects (McNiff in Levine, 2009, p. 10). Research findings (Maarhuis, 2016, See chapter 7.1) suggest that a process of imaginative poiesis, ekphrastic re-presentation and transactive dialogue can provide effective means to reply to wounds. Levine (2009) reflects on the role of poiesis:

> *[It] takes us outside of being 'the ones who are done to.' How can we make something out of what's been made of us? This is the basic question and one that leads us to the fundamental human capacity to respond to history through the creative act.* (p. 178)

As a compassionate reply to difficult experiences, artful methods of inquiry and parallaxic praxis can open up the possibility of transformative teaching and learning, agonist activism, and new ways to engage in the promotion of human understanding and knowledge generation. My process of in depth deliberation and the intersection of Deweyan, Bakhtinian, and Mouffian theories provide a flexible foundation for understanding the transactional dialogue of the Clothesline Project and a pragmatic mode of dissemination for how to bear witness and reply to the wounds of violence and suffering. Artful methods of activism, protest, and inquiry open up the possibility of fresh perspectives, agonist transactions, and new ways to engage in reflection for the promotion of human understanding and knowledge generation thus, ekphrasic transactional dialogue considers art as experience and enacts art as critique.

Sameshima and Wiebe. Nguyen (2015), in his Pulitzer prize-winning book, *The Sympathizer*, asks,

> What is more important than independence and freedom?" "What do those who struggle against power do when they seize power? What does the revolutionary do when the revolution triumphs? Why do those who call for independence and freedom take away the independence and freedom of others? (p. 178).

Using a parallaxic praxis, we, too, wrestle with answerability. The question of ethics can never be bandaged with pat answers and the work of dialogic wrestling integral to researching with integrity. We draw on Bruner's (2002) idea of canon and breach and Schubert's description of curriculum as synoptic and expansive text to suggest that as creatives, we breach the social canon of knowledge through making—through the materialization of forms not yet in existence and through the form, new essences of identities are born (See Chapter 7.7).

We share the following from a publication in press, locating imagination as a cornerstone to parallaxic praxis. The critical point being that a politics of the imagination turns *away from* a source of contention or a system that is struggling to generate new networks and systems of social relationships: it is not a rebellion or resistance but a making[2].

Imagination is the creative energy of society (Castoriadis, 1975). As we think and imagine, we construct a new social. The creative moments of making are not only a positive entanglement of our relational constructions of knowing, knowledge, the self, and the world; but also recognition of our moral and political obligations as researchers.

Imagination is the engine of society and its production acquires a distinct political form (Castoriadis, 2002). Political here takes on a connotation that is more about intentional creation and generation rather than participation in political institutions. As Shukaitis (2009) argues, the radical imagination allows for a collective liberty or self-determination to emerge. He argues for imagination *"as a composite of our capacities to affect and be affected by the world, to develop movements toward new forms of autonomous sociality and self-determination"* (p. 10).

Through imagination the political acquires an aesthetic dimension that embraces openness and refuses closure. This is achieved through the multiplicity of psychic, social and aesthetic openings: a flow of constant movement and transformation (Kristeva, 2003). Here imagination is a quotidian politics; the everyday revolution that is lived in the moment. In our everyday lived experience the familiar language of resistance, revolt or revolution should be reimagined for a politics of creativity and generation. We are cognizant of how language shapes our conceptions. These words are usually used with the word against,' so energies are in opposition. A politics of the imagination *turns away* from the source of agitation, using that energy to generate new networks and systems of social relationships: it is not a rebellion or resistance but a making. As a political imagination, research in this way is a generative poiesis that emerges through and within specific acts of creation.

---

[2] Sameshima, P., Wiebe, S., & Hayes, M. (in press). Imagination: The generation of possibility. In B. Andrews (Ed.), *Perspectives on arts education research in Canada. Vol. 1: Surveying the landscape.* Rotterdam, The Netherlands: Brill.

Chapter 7

Examples

Example 7.1: Replies to Wounds

Meaning Across Multiple Ekphrasic Interpretations of Interpersonal Violence and the Clothesline Project[1]

Patricia Maarhuis

Overview

The purpose of this study was to describe hermeneutic phenomenological research on the Washington State University Clothesline Project (1993–2012) and ekphrastic artefacts about the experience of interpersonal violence, utilizing arts-informed research methodology (Cole & Knowles, 2008) in a Deweyan (1934/2005) theoretical framework with reference to Bakhtinian (Holquist & Liapunov, 1990) and Mouffian ideas (2008). The project examined emergent themes, meaning making, and forms of artful expression across 4 phases and 3 points of data collection. The research methods map a linked process that combined arts-informed research (Cole & Knowles, 2008), parallaxic praxis (Sameshima & Vandermause, 2008), agonist activism (Mouffe, 2007), and transformative teaching and learning strategies (Mezirow, 2012). Emergent themes and expressed meaning across the four phases of transactive and ekphrastic interpretations were highly complex and re-presented the contextual experience of violence as intersected with time, emotion, cognitive reappraisal, memory, the body, culture, relationships, and other variables. Findings provided evidence for a generative process made up of deliberative reflection, artful interpretation, transactional dialogue, and transformative learning. The physical, spatial, and relational materialization of one's thoughts, feeling, and ideas through various art forms was a way for participants to construct meaning and to learn about the experience of

[1] Excerpted from: Maarhuis, P. (2016). *Replies to wounds: Meaning across multiple ekphrastic interpretations of interpersonal violence and the Clothesline Project* (Doctoral dissertation). Washington State University, ProQuest Dissertations (#10163970).

violence. Findings link the process of ekphrastic interpretation to pragmatic educational strategies. Effective use of transformative teaching strategies and demonstration of transformative learning affirmed the potential for parallaxic praxis and transactional ekphrastic responses to be efficacious and ethical pedagogic tools for the difficult issue of interpersonal violence. Also, analysis indicated that the research phases were events of agonistic activism that engaged critical art (Mouffe, 2007). This finding suggests that the research methods and educational strategies utilized in this project may be a means to expand individual and community activist engagement.

The Project

"I was particularly interested in the type of conversations that are generated and amongst groups of young people. I wanted to explore their inter-connected micro-communities, and that boundary between the public and the private" said British artist, Sonia Boyce (Boyce in Peckham Space, 2011, p. 1), about her film and gallery installation, *Network*. Featuring young people in Southwark Children's Services, the film follows the journeys of four young women from their homes to their weekly visual and performing arts group meeting through the different street systems of South East London. Once there, the young women draw out and map their networks, social experiences, and friendship groups on writing boards on the walls and pillars within the gallery. Boyce's (2010) work is an example of cross-discipline practice that challenges the definition and understanding of creation, research, and display of artwork across diversified sites, artists, audiences, situations, time, and conditions (Bourriaud, 2002; Kwon, 1997; Meyer, 1996; Mouffe, 2007, 2008; Simon, 2014).

Over recent decades and with growing momentum artistic practice has tested and interrogated foundational notions and acceptance of aesthetic works by asking relational questions of what, when, where, by whom, for whom, how, and why (Bourriaud, 2002; Meyer, 1996; Simon, 2014). In her essay on current tensions within site-specific and relational artistic practices, the art historian Miwon Kwon (1997) observes that art's relationship to actual location as site and the social conditions as site are:

> *subordinate to a discursively determined site that is delineated as a field of knowledge, intellectual exchange, or cultural debate. . . this site is not defined as a precondition. Rather, it is generated by the work (often as "content"), and then by its convergence with an existing discursive formation.* (p. 92)

Further, the philosopher Mouffe (2007, 2008, 2013) views the work of art as a critical and an agonist intervention in public space—beyond the modernist idea of the avant-garde and the remote privileged artist—to movement, relationship, displacement, and negotiation practices that widen the field of artistic intervention by directly intervening in a multiplicity of public and social spaces, in order to oppose ongoing and overlapping dominant and hegemonic practices. In this way agonist pluralism and the use of critical art is a means to include discordant voices in public discourse through conflictual consensus and dissensus.

In this same spirit, I proposed a project that takes on the relational task of addressing adjacencies and distances—between multiple persons, places, things, and experience—within a linked and stepped transactional dialogue. The Replies to Wounds project (Maarhuis, 2016) is qualitative research centered on artful and imbricated interaction about the experience of interpersonal violence, in particular, the Clothesline Project narratives (National Network Website for the Clothesline Project, n.d.). Freed from the anchorage of singular site, event, and artist/author-specific works, I engage in parallaxic praxis (Sameshima & Vandermause, 2008) and arts-informed research (Sameshima & Knowles, 2008)—positioned afloat and attentive—in the analysis of experience, context, time, and interaction (Dewey, 1934/2005).

Like Boyce (2010) at the Peckham Space, I am interested in narrative expressions generated in and amongst groups, but with explicit attention toward educational research, meaning making, and educational strategies about interpersonal violence, difficult topics, activism, and social justice. The innovative use of multi-layered and interactive interpretations in research can open up linguistic and aesthetic expression to researchers and participants, thereby opening up the potential for transactional means to engage, bear witness, and reply to the wounds of interpersonal violence and assault.

Project:	Replies to Wounds
Type:	Qualitative research: Hermeneutic phenomenology
Theoretical Framework:	Dewey with reference to Bakhtin and Mouffe
Methodology:	Arts Informed Research, Parallaxic Praxis, Narrative Inquiry
Methods:	Four dialogue phases with 3 points of data collection on ekphrastic and narrative text
Data Analysis:	• Coding (emergent & conceptual themes) • Artefact form and media • Narrative text content • Expressed significance (referential & evaluative) • Time & situation

Table 7.1.1. Methodological Approach for *Replies to Wounds*.
Steps and Elements of the Research Project.

The purpose of this study was to describe hermeneutic phenomenological research on the Washington State University Clothesline Project (1993–2012) and ekphrastic artefacts about the experience of interpersonal violence, utilizing parallaxic praxis (Sameshima & Vandermause, 2008) and arts-informed research methodology (Cole & Knowles, 2008) in a Deweyan (1934/2005) theoretical framework with reference to Bakhtinian (Holquist & Liapunov, 1990) and Mouffian ideas (2008). The research methods map a linked process that combined arts-informed research (Cole & Knowles, 2008) and parallaxic praxis (Sameshima & Vandermause, 2008) with agonist activism (Mouffe, 2007), and transformative teaching and learning strategies (Mezirow, 2012). The emergent themes and expressed meaning across the four phases of transactive and ekphrastic interpretations were highly complex and re-presented the contextual experience of violence as intersected with time, emotion, cognitive reappraisal, memory, the body, culture, relationships, and other variables.

Phases in Research Design. The research project examined emergent themes, meaning making, and forms of artful expression across 4 phases and 3 points of data collection (see Figure 7.1.1). In particular, the research design relied on and tested the evaluative methodological process of *Evanagnostos,* the Greek word for something being easy to read and legible (Online Liddell-Scott-Jones Greek-English Lexicon, 2018). Within the ekphrastic process, interpretive artful works must be legible to audiences, which can then bring about transactional dialogue and understanding. The semantic labor (Kester & Strayer, 2005) in the meaning making process takes place over time and upon reflection by the artist and audience. If an interpretive work of art is highly readable and legible, then there is opportunity for the audience to look beyond the medium of the artwork toward broader meaning making. Readability and legibility of artful interpretations are directly linked to the research question and animates the research design, which is concerned with the transactional dialogue between the ekphrastic works. Comprehension and understanding gained by the audience through *Evanagnostos* can depend on the level of direct representation and the use of responsive images, graphics, and narrative text between the multiple interpretive works and during the linked ekphrastic dialogue (see Table 7.1.2).

The research design in *Replies to Wounds* relied heavily on the transactional readability or communicability of the ekphrastic works within each of the design phases, in particular, the Phase 2 or the artist-researcher works. The project results found a high level of *Evanagnostos* within and between Phases 1, 2, and 3. In other words, the participants and artist-researcher ekphrastic works clearly interacted with each other and, because of a high level of readability and legibility in the ekphrastic works, there was also a high level of transactive dialogue between the artful works.

Phase	Participants	Data Type	Space (S)/Time (T)
1	P1: Clothesline Project participant	128 ekphrastic artefacts or interpretations	S: Campus event on public mall T: Year round creation, annual display
2	P2: Artist-Researcher (A-R)	Ekphrastic interpretations of Clothesline Project artefacts	S: Display installation in open studio room T: Created from 2011 to 2015 in office and home studio
3	P3: Recruited participants at installation display & open studio	Participant's ekphrastic interpretations of A/R artefacts & installation display. Survey & Observation	S: Interactive open studio room on campus T: Single session of ~4 hours
4	All 3 participant groups: P1, P2, P3	All 3 data sets	Across all 3 data sets
The research design for the *Replies to Wounds* project over 4 stepped phases with 3 points of data collection. The Space/Time column indicates where and when the data or event are created and/or displayed.			

Table 7.1.2. Phases in the Research Design.

In Phase 1, the interpretive artefacts (the Clothesline Project t-shirts) were cataloged, coded, and analyzed, which included the creation of a digital video with music soundtrack of all the artefacts (https://www.youtube.com/user/InBricolage?feature=mhee; Inbricolgage.com: https://www.inbricolage.com/phase-1-clothesline-canvases.html). The Clothesline Project narratives and artefacts were found to be ekphrastic works of art that re-presented, re-interpreted, and re-framed the victim-survivor experiences of violence. The Clothesline Project was a *bricolage* of expression -figuratively and actually–as demonstrated in the various forms of narrative texts, artefacts, and in its public display. Also, the Clothesline Project artefacts, event, and these research results were constructions of parallaxic perspectives–figuratively and actually–where the researcher, participants, and audience members can dwell in a particular space, listen, reflect, and re-interpret experiences of violence.

Figures 7.1.1 – 7.1.2. Clothesline Project Event. 2012. P. Maarhuis. Glenn Terrell Mall, Pullman, Washington State University.

In Phase 2 the interpretive artefact (Clothesline Project t-shirts, see Figures 7.1.1 - 7.1.2) and the data analysis from Phase 1 were used to respond and create artist-researcher ekphrastic works of art and gallery installation (Inbricolage.com: https://www.in bricolage.com/phase-2-interperative-works.html). I created 4 artist-researcher interpretive works: *Reflective Transaction*, a collection of 10 mixed media works with layered digital photography and poetry; *Tell*, a mixed media and found object sculpture; *Alibi*, a mixed media and found object installation; and *Labyrinth*, a print collage collection of 4 works.

The Phase 2 work re-presented themes found in Phase 1 in condensed and intensified art forms. My works were relational and intersectional and, consequently, challenged binaries, cultural tropes, and easy conclusions about the experience of violence. Additionally, there was strong inter-artefact and inter-textual dialogue between the Clothesline Project and the artist-researcher interpretations, as seen through Clothesline Project narrative quotes and t-shirt artefacts that were layered within my artist-researcher work (see Figures 7.1.3 to 7.1.11).

Figure 7.1.3. Reflective Transaction [Digital print & poetry series of 10]. P. Maarhuis, 2015. Washington State University, Fine Arts Center. Gallery 3. Pullman, WA.

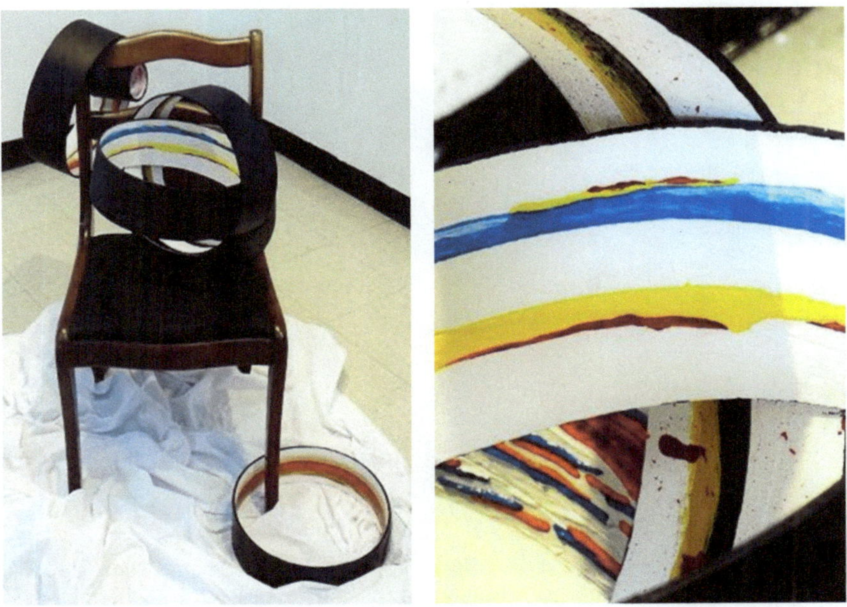

Figures 7.1.4 – 7.1.5. Tell [Mixed media sculpture installation]. From *Replies to Wounds: An aesthetic dialogue about experiences of violence* [Dissertation exhibition November, 2015.]. Washington State University, Fine Arts Center. Gallery 3. Pullman, WA. Photography by Becky Bitter.

Figure 7.1.6. Alibi [Mixed media sculpture installation]. *From Replies to Wounds: An aesthetic dialogue about experiences of violence* [Dissertation exhibition, November, 2015.]. Washington State University, Fine Arts Center. Gallery 3. Pullman, WA. Photography by Becky Bitter.

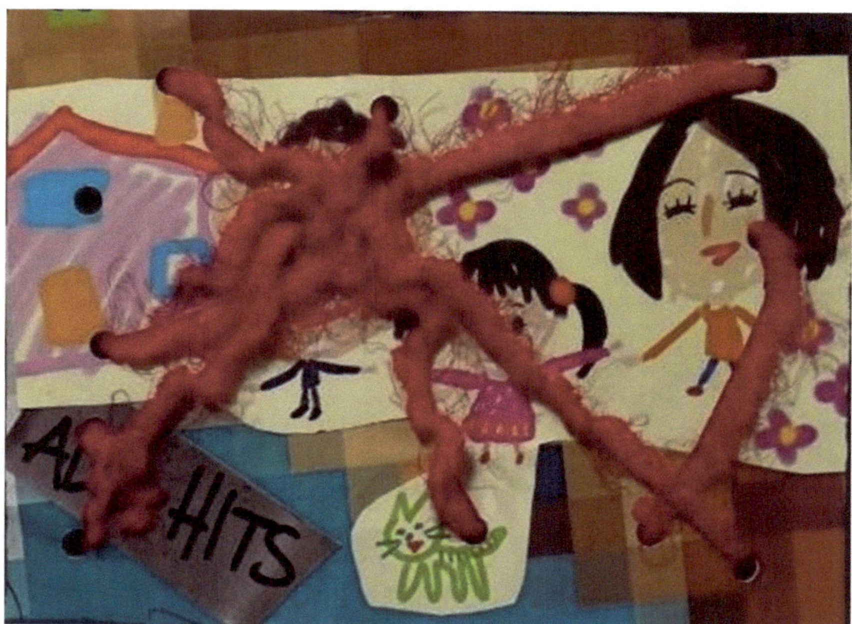

Figure 7.1.7. Labyrinth: All in the Family [Print and fabric collage, 6 x 8, Series: 1 of 4]. From *Replies to Wounds: An aesthetic dialogue about experiences of violence* [Dissertation exhibition, November, 2015.]. Washington State University, Fine Arts Center. Gallery 3. Pullman, WA.

Figure 7.1.8. Labyrinth: Untitled [Print and paint collage, 12 x 16, Series: 2 of 4]. From *Replies to Wounds: An aesthetic dialogue about experiences of violence* [Dissertation exhibition, November, 2015.]. Washington State University, Fine Arts Center. Gallery 3. Pullman, WA.

Figure 7.1.9. Labyrinth: Untitled [Print and paint collage, 12 x 16, Series: 3 of 4]. From *Replies to Wounds: An aesthetic dialogue about experiences of violence* [Dissertation exhibition, November, 2015.]. Washington State University, Fine Arts Center. Gallery 3. Pullman, WA.

Figure 7.1.10. Labyrinth: What You Say [Print and paint collage, 12 x 16, Series: 4 of 4]. From *Replies to Wounds: An aesthetic dialogue about experiences of violence* [Dissertation exhibition, November, 2015.]. Washington State University, Fine Arts Center. Gallery 3. Pullman, WA.

The results of Phase 2 shows how I purposefully engaged transactional dialogue in 4 ways: (a) through the creative design and choice of media; (b) through the aesthetically expressed and parallaxic themes in the narrative text and artful forms; (c) through parallaxic praxis in the spatial positioning of the A-R works in anticipation of relational dialogue with Phase 3 works of art; and (d) through attention to movement of the audience through the gallery during the exhibition.

For example, artist-researcher works were positioned purposefully by content themes and media type around the periphery of the gallery with open places left on the wall and floor. This was done so the Phase 3 participants would have a space to engage with media material; to do the work of art within the gallery space, and to position their own artful interpretations in relation to the artist-researcher works. Additionally, adequate space was left for a general audience to move through the gallery and view the transactive works. Thus, each of these purposeful actions toward parallaxic and transactional dialogue as well as spatial position influenced the engaged dialogue and reflection process of the Phase 3 participant's actions and experience, as is discussed in the P3 section.

Within Phase 2 there were three layers of transactional dialogue across multiple audiences, which were enacted by me, as the artist-researcher, through (a) ekphrastic replies to the Clothesline Project participants' expression about violent experiences, (b) artful communication with the Phase 3 participants, and (c) a gallery exhibition for a community general audience.

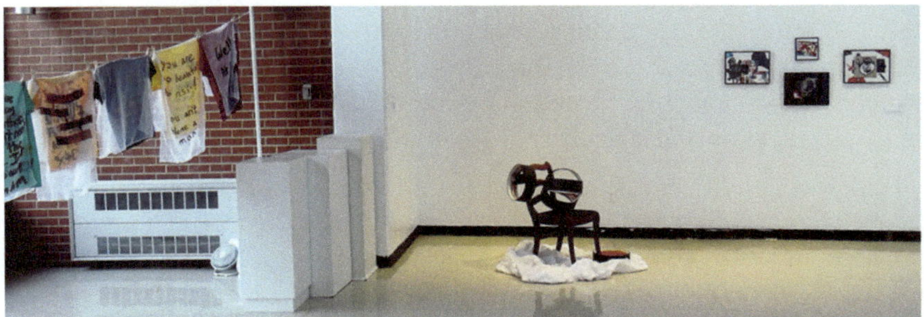

Figure 7.1.11. Exhibit. *Replies to Wounds: An aesthetic dialogue.* [Dissertation exhibition, November, 2015.]. Washington State University, Fine Arts Center. Gallery 3. Pullman, WA.

For Phase 3, within the gallery installation, a small group of 8 participants interacted with and created transactive and ekphrastic responses to the artist-researcher's interpretive works from Phase 2. (Inbricolage.com: https://www.inbricolage.com/phase-3-open-studio.html). All works were created in the gallery space and in reply to the Clothesline Project and artist-researcher works. As well, the Phase 3 participants positioned their own works within the intensified aesthetic environment of the gallery exhibition, as a means to engage transactional dialogue with my artist-researcher work.

Like Phase 2 artworks, the Phase 3 ekphrastic artefact forms and narrative were intensive, metaphoric, and transactional. The type of form, text, design, color, and media was chosen purposefully by the Phase 3 participants and maintained a consistent dialogue with the Clothesline Project artefacts as well as my artist researcher works. Notably, the Phase 3 interpretive artefacts continued to shift the artful dialogue, away from a collection of individual victim-survivor expressions and toward a deep examination of the systemic patterns in the perpetration of violence initiated within my artist-researcher works. For example, the Phase 3 participants moved the transactive dialogue to include consideration of specific cross-cultural contexts of interpersonal violence as well as offered future possibilities and hopeful solutions.

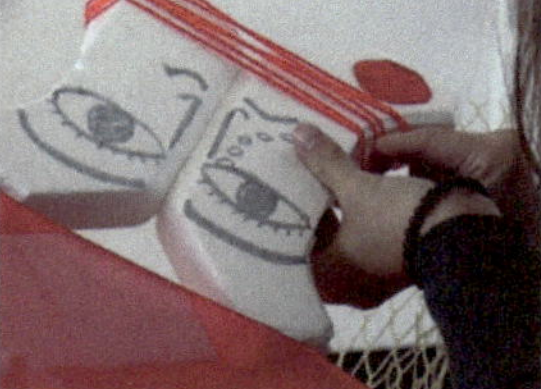

Figures 7.1.12 – 7.14. Making.

In all, through the use of specific artefact and narrative forms, the Phase 3 participant artworks advanced the transactional dialogue about interpersonal violence and maintained an intensive aesthetic environment, designed for ongoing reflection and layered interaction within the gallery exhibition.

Post open studio survey responses provided additional results and deeper explanation about Phase 3 participant experience in the research project, the creative process, and about the ideas and feelings expressed in their ekphrastic works.

In terms of interaction with the artist-researcher gallery exhibition and its influence on the participant thinking, feeling, and sensing experience about interpersonal violence, Phase 3 participants indicated a strong impact on their level of awareness and empathy as well as their ability to relate to the complex contexts of violence. Additionally, open studio participants reported engagement in a process of critical and creative reflection, action, and expression. This critical and creative process of interaction in the open studio influenced the participants' responsive art by sparking motivation to expressively respond. As well, the gallery exhibition modeled aesthetic options for expanded thinking and communication about interpersonal violence. Because of the quiet and non-judgmental atmosphere, participants were open to sitting in the dissonance of strong emotions and difficult reflections. In turn, Phase 3 participants were able to then directly reply to the topics, theme, and artful work found in the artist-researcher interpretations.

Making responsive artwork in an open studio had an impact on the participants' thinking, feeling, and sensing experience about interpersonal violence as an embodied and aesthetic process. The making of responsive artwork and the reflection process about interpersonal violence brought about strong feelings and emotions for participants. Together, this impacted how the participants' expressive interpretation was made, the choice of themes, and the choice of art materials. Further, the process of making art channeled sustained attention and energy (thoughts, ideas, and emotions) into a physically active dialogic project. This purposeful process of making responsive artwork was a means to move beyond linear thought, toward critical, embodied, and creative action and activism. As well, making responsive artwork was a means to portray the participant's own personal experiences and perspectives and to relate these personal experiences to the Phase 1 and Phase 2 ekphrastic dialogue about violence.

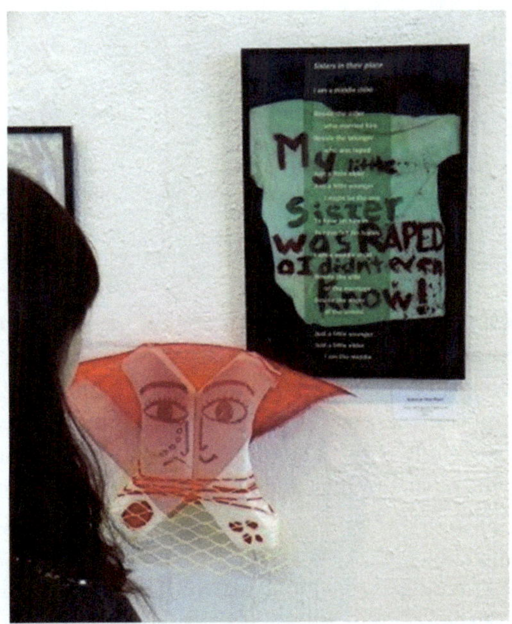

Figure 7.1.15. Exhibit. Participant *Snowy* and her interpretive sculpture. [Found object sculpture]. Washington State University, Fine Arts Center. Gallery 3. Pullman, WA. Photography by Becky Bitter.

Participants reported new learning through the open studio experience, which included the realization of having the capacity to create meaningful art and of being able to effectively use particular media or art forms. There was an expressed understanding that the characteristics of courage, empathy, consideration, sincerity, and passion were needed to creatively expressive one's thoughts and ideas when replying to the violent experiences of others.

When asked how the combination of gallery artwork and making responsive artwork influenced their thinking about interpersonal violence, open studio participants answered this question by describing varying depths in a process that included 6 elements or steps: (a) reflection, (b) dissonance, (c) empathy, (d) critical thinking, (e) engagement in expressive artwork, (f) sense of resolution or possibility found in new/different thinking and actions.

Figure 7.1.16. Exhibit B.

To better understand the relationship of spatial placement to transactional dialogue of ekphrastic works, participants were asked about the influence of space and placement of their work in the gallery exhibition. Results showed this was an important aspect of inter-artefact communication. Phase 3 participants purposefully chose a space to fit media and art form or vice versa and replied directly to one of my specific artist researcher works or expressed theme. Additionally, they chose a particular placement to reflect ideas expressed in the participant's artwork, and/or chose a particular placement to impact audience interaction with the artwork and in the gallery exhibition.

Interaction within the open studio was focused on aesthetic and artful dialogue and purposefully shifted away from verbal engagement between participants. When asked about how their open studio experienced was influenced by the presence of or interaction with other participants, the respondents noted that the interaction was minimal and that, overall, this generated a positive effect on the atmosphere and their ability to focus on creative artwork. As well, being part of a diverse group of participants with multiple identities was experienced as positive and enriching to the creative process. Even though participants did not engage verbally for any significant amount of time, they did engage in artful dialogue through their creative interpretations. This artful communication was described as interesting, positive, and as an enhancement to their own individual creative works.

Overall, open studio artful expressions, additions to the gallery exhibition, and survey responses continued to expand parallaxic perspectives and opportunities for transactional aesthetic dialogue about interpersonal violence. Moreover, participants expressed the desire to participate in similar creative events and activities in the future as well as the intention to take part in activism.

In Phase 4, the narrative and artful interpretations across Phases 1, 2, and 3 were analyzed as bundles of webbed and transactive dialogues. These imbricated layers worked to shape the artful and transactive qualities of the data as well as subsequent analyses and interpretations. Additionally, the patterns of relationship across Phases 1 through 3 were discussed across the categories of difference and change, similarity, conflict and contradiction, and consistency and coherence and in terms of how these occurred across narrative expression, time, event, and group (Daiute, 2014). Across the sets of data, tensions were noted that allowed contradictory meanings, complex stances, and interactive relational dynamics to become evident within the process of relating experiences of violence from varying perspectives across differing space, event, and time.

In sum, the research methods utilized in this project allowed me to look at three things: (a)what is being experienced; (b) how the experience is expressed across time, event, group and form; and (c) how the successive ekphrastic interpretations transact across narrative expression, time, event, and group.

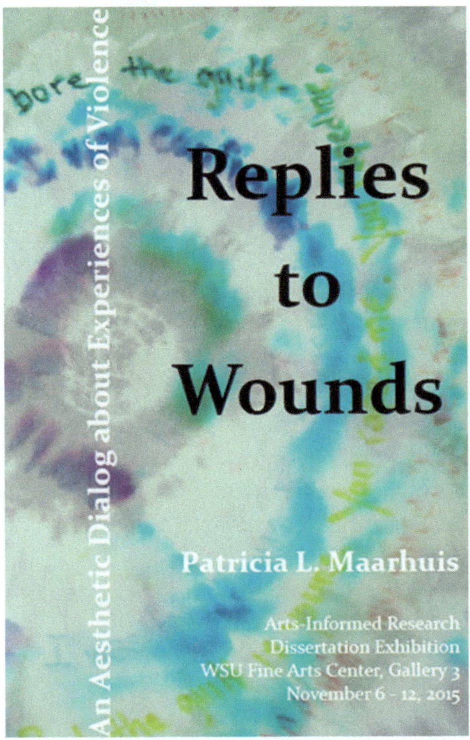

Exhibit 7.1.17. Dissertation Exhibition Poster [Digital print with Clothesline Project artefact image in background]. From *Replies to Wounds*: An aesthetic dialogue about experiences of violence [Dissertation exhibition, November, 2015.]. Washington State University, Fine Arts Center. Gallery 3. Pullman, WA.

While trying to understand the methods and practices within this research project, I explored contemporary writings about artwork, accumulation, and the archive. After an afternoon of reading, I felt a coming-home kind of recognition, a kinship when reviewing the artwork and writing of Renée Green (2002). Green's work wanders through alternative interpretations and layered representations of narration, subjectivity, history, memory, space, time, and documentation to depict complex negotiations of past events from a present and on-going dialogue (in Zapperi, 2013). Her writings include whole paragraphs that list question after question about who is narrating and how; what is represented; and why one thing is included or another excluded. Likewise, the research project I conducted put me at the brink of amassing layers of complex dialogic data and led me to ask similar questions.

I empathized as Renée Green (2002) described her feelings and thoughts about collection, archives, artwork, and reinterpretation:

> Collecting and the subsequent ordering of masses of material—including fictive attempts—led to a feeling not merely of wonder, but also of fatigue, attention deficit. Negation in abundance can be read as the cancelling out effect . . . which is mind numbing, more than one can bear. (p. 49)

Reading this induced me—with some trepidation—to reflexively inquire: Why this research project, this way? It could be strictly about matching methodology to the research question or about a researcher's positionality and identity; however, for me, it was really something more expansive and inevitable. Further along in Green's musings about documentation and the means for coping with life, one particular question, caught my eye: "*How can a relationship with the past exist in which memory functions as an active process, allowing continual reconsideration, rather than as a form of entombment, to which archives and museums are sometimes compared*" (2002, p. 54)? In search of an answer, Green is led to the writings of Agamben (1999), the *Remnants of Auschwitz*, and a critique of subjectivity. But I went in a different direction. The question grabbed a hold and, I thought, yes, that is what I want to explore in the narratives and artwork generated by *Replies to Wounds*: an active process allowing continual reconsideration that flows and reveals, rather than entombs. That is why I conducted this research project, this way.

Possible Post Analysis Questions

These were used with Artist-Researchers and Participant-Creation Projects

Interaction with artwork

- How did your interaction with the artworks influence your thinking, feeling, and sensing experience of the project?
- How did your interaction other's artwork(s) influence your process of making?
- How did your interaction with the data influence the type of media (paint, paper, metal, wood, etc.) and form (sculpture, poetry, painting, etc.) used in the making of your responsive artwork?
- How did your interaction with the artwork influence what you created?

Process of making your responsive artwork in the Open Studio

- How did the process of making your responsive artwork in the Open Studio influence your thinking, feeling, sensing experience of the Clothesline Project?
- How did the process of making your responsive artwork in the Open Studio influence your thinking, feeling, sensing experience of interpersonal violence?

Combination: Gallery Artwork and Making Your Responsive Artwork

- How did the combined interaction with gallery artworks and the process of making your responsive artwork in the Open Studio influence your thinking about the Clothesline Project?
- How did the combined interaction with gallery artworks and the process of making your responsive artwork in the Open Studio influence your thinking about interpersonal violence?
- How did the combined interaction with gallery artworks and the process of making your responsive artwork in the Open Studio influence where you placed your artwork within the installation?

Interaction with Others

- How was your Open Studio experience influenced by the presence of and/or interaction with other participants in the group?
- How was your Open Studio experience influenced by the presence of and/or interaction with the artist-researcher?

Other

- What else you would like to share about your experience with the gallery installation and Open Studio?

Example 7.2: Women and Meth Renderings

www.womenandmeth.com

The Women and Meth project took place from 2007-2016. It was a cross-disciplinary project blending nursing science and various humanities' disciplines in the interpretation of the life stories of methamphetamine addicts in recovery. This section provides examples of the various ekphrastic interpretations undertaken over the course of the study. More information on the project can be attained at www.womenandmeth.com.

The research study originated at Washington State University, USA, and culminated at Lakehead University, Canada. It was funded by the Social Sciences and Humanities Research Council of Canada, Lakehead University, American Nurses' Foundation, and Washington State University.

Research Teams

Original Team at Washington State University (2007-2012):

Dr. Roxanne Vandermause, College of Nursing

Dr. Pauline Sameshima, Education

Stephen Chalmers, Visual Arts

Dr. Sheila Kearney Converse, School of Music

Dr. Linda Kittell, Department of English

Dr. Laurilyn J. Harris, Former Theatre Department, History and Dramaturgy

Dr. Carrie Miller, College of Nursing

Dr. Carrie Santucci, College of Nursing

Team at Lakehead University (2012-2016)

Dr. Pauline Sameshima, Canada Research Chair in Arts Integrated Studies, PhD

Dr. Patricia Maarhuis, Washington State University, Health & Wellness Services, PhD

John-Paul Chalykoff, Graduate Student, Musician, BEd

Victoria Bolduc, Graduate Student, Visual Artist, MEd

Dayna Slingerland, Graduate Student, Multimedia Artist, MEd

About the Artists

Dr. Pauline Sameshima is a Canada Research Chair in Arts Integrated Studies at Lakehead University.

Dr. Patricia Maarhuis is a researcher, program designer, and artist in Health & Wellness Services at Washington State University

Stephen Chalmers teaches photography at Youngstown State University in Ohio.

Victoria Bolduc is a Metis artist born and raised in Thunder Bay.

John-Paul Chalykoff is a Michipicoten First Nation member, born in Wawa, Ontario, and raised in Sault Ste-Marie, Ontario.

Background

The problem of methamphetamine addiction prompted the initiation of this research project. The intent to stimulate a broader understanding of the experience of addiction and recovery was to advance clinical, methodological, and social changes.

Drug Rehab and Addiction Services in Canada (DRS, 2017) describes methamphetamine as an instant addiction, meaning that addiction can occur after only one use. The Drug Prevention Network of Canada (DPNC, 2016) reports that meth is so addictive that it has a relapse rate of 92%. The Network also states that the World Health Organization "*estimates over 34,000,000 people use crystal meth daily, more than crack cocaine and heroin users combined*" (DPNC, p. 1).

The question that is commonly asked and for which our team was concerned with was,

> *What does it mean to experience methamphetamine addiction?*
>
> *What does it mean to recover?*

Answers to these social questions were sorely desired. An in depth examination, through multiple lenses, provides a way to an understanding that has eluded science and society. Our study was designed to move deeper into methodological technique while, at the same time, opening possibilities for interpretive representation of meaning.

Sharing Findings

Over the course of the project, the teams used three sets of interview transcripts by Gabriel, Gilda and Jill (pseudonyms) to better understand the experiences of methamphetamine addiction and recovery. The full collection of artefacts created can be accessed at www.womenandmeth.com. Various dissemination processes were used with this project including peer-reviewed journal articles, chapters, lay articles, a book, presentations, and exhibitions.

A knowledge mobilization event in the form of an art exhibition at the Baggage Arts Building at Marina Park, Thunder Bay, took place in Fall, 2015. The culminating exhibition included three participant life stories in nine art translations by five artists. A video of photos can be found https://youtu.be/Yah34TDVbXU.

The benefits of a parallaxic praxis are the use of the ekphrastic artefacts as pedagogic tools for sharing experience and interpretation. It is our belief that "*the sharing of stories encourages reflexive inquires in ethical self-consciousness, enlarges paradigms of the 'normative,' and develops pedagogical practice of liberation and acceptance of diversity*" (Sameshima 2007, p. xi).

The following anonymous comments were collected in response to the exhibit:

- Meaningful displays. Life changing stories. Beautifully displayed and easy to absorb the emotions, hardships and journeys. Great displays and presentations, and a pleasure to attend the gallery show.
- I enjoyed looking at the project. I thought that the subject matter and the different artists' interpretations of the women's stories was very compelling. I like the pottery the best and the watercolours as well.
- Very powerful combination of the words of the drug users and the visual expression of the artists.
- Very interesting. Seeing the same 'words' evoke different art forms was also interesting. It did so addictions is about pain not about the 'badness' of individuals.
- This was an excellent reminder that addiction can strike anyone, that the forces of addiction are powerful and controlling and that we, as a society, need to show support and compassion to all who struggle. Thank you.
- It was a wonderfully informative talk about the exhibitions and the paintings really grabbed me (especially the crow and the wolf dog. The writing that went with the pictures were very real. I am so glad I forced myself out of my cocoon to come here. Thank you for your time.
- Beautiful + fascinating + startling! The art/photos/paintings are incredibly enhanced by the accompanying words. [____] that what you thought you were looking at and when you read the words. Fascinating! Thank you!
- Very interesting – phenomenal interpretations. 'One day at a time.'
- The exhibit is visually fascinating and very moving. I was arrested by some of the images/ text/ images + text. A wonderful exhibit – and nicely laid out.

- Thank you for your exceptional work, Dr. Sameshima. You are an inspiration to many with your grounded and important research. The coordination of your team developed the work into something even more ground-breaking. It was a pleasure to be here. Best wishes.
- Wonderful exhibit, Crystal meth is a wicked drug to overcome, and her story was quite the story. Glad I came, wonderful paintings and displayed perfectly.
- I thoroughly enjoyed all of the different pieces. I especially enjoyed Victoria's works, they were very insightful and thought provoking.
- Powerful images that help hit deeply about what this addiction means and who can be impacted by it.
- Very interesting . . . great to have something like this open to the public.
- So beautifully talented artists. Thank you for the unique display. Please keep this going in our city (Thunder Bay).
- Powerful, creative and insightful.
- All the series come wonderfully together to create a whole, from the despair of using to the [____] of recovery, having been a long time [recover]. The quotes [absorb] all, add thickness to the artistic renderings. What comes out of it is a person rather than a user and the stories behind that person. It is beautiful and at times made me feel like crying.
- This is a fabulous exhibit – would like to see a project where addicts actually do the art. Thank you so much.
- Greatness.
- Really important to connect arts with research and community. Engaging presentations and artworks. Congratulations!
- I truly did not know what to expect, but wow! The movies posters were especially powerful to me. Thank you.
- I am filling out this card as I do not want to become the subject of one of Victoria's next series of media. Beautiful art.

- The exhibition was very helpful in giving a better idea of meth addiction and the recovery process of people who have never used. It gives a bit of a deeper understanding into the motivations and struggles of still-using and recovering drug addicts. The art was not only beautiful, but thought provoking, even with its focus on what is generally a taboo/unsettling topic.

Renderings

Found poetry and photographs

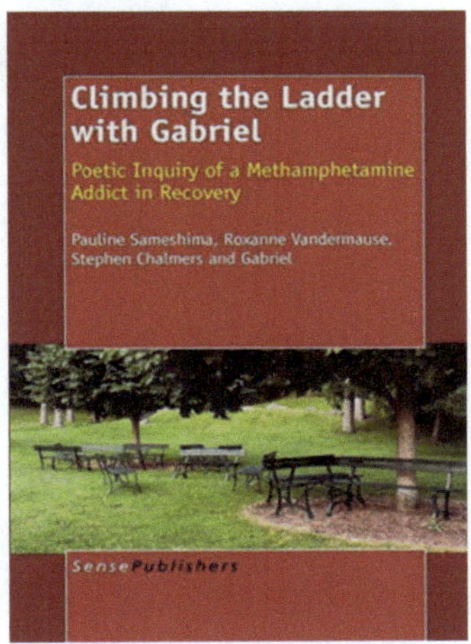

Figure 7.2.1. Gabriel's Book.

Analysis of Gabriel's transcript resulted in a book outlining the research model and Gabriel's story in the form of found poetry. The book is titled: *Climbing the Ladder with Gabriel* (Brill, 2009) by Pauline Sameshima, Roxanne Vandermause, Stephen Chalmers, and Gabriel. The book includes Stephen Chalmers' photographs of significant sites in Gabriel's experience and Gabriel's text about these sites. Please see Chapter 7.8 for a reprint of the introduction to this book which included the early envisionings of parallaxic praxis.

Climbing the Ladder with Gabriel is an example of residual and reparative research (Sameshima, Miyakawa & Lockett, 2017; Sameshima & Slingerland, 2015). Gabriel, who is now a counsellor in the site of her recovery space, uses the book as a dialogic tool as she facilitates recovery for others. The work is residual research in that it continues to 'work' without the researchers present. The research is also reparative in that the research has been returned to the community from which it emerged.

Gabriel: Critical Sites of Recovery

By Stephen Chalmers (Researcher Photographer) and Gabriel (Participant)

10 Images

http://www.womenandmeth.com/chalmers-photographs.html

Figure 7.2.2. Critical Sites of Recovery. Photograph by Stephen Chalmers. *Climbing the Ladder with Gabriel,* p. 34.

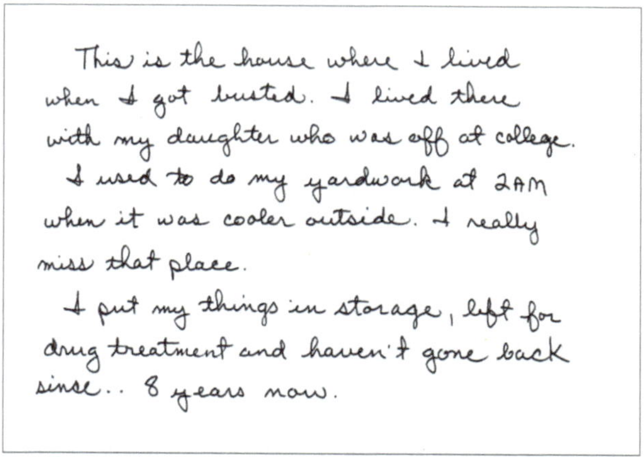

This is the house where I lived
when I got busted. I lived there
with my daughter who was off at college.
I used to do my yardwork at 2AM
when it was cooler outside. I really
miss that place.
I put my things in storage, left for
drug treatment and haven't gone back
since.. 8 years now.

Figure 7.2.3. Critical Sites of Recovery. Text by Gabriel. *Climbing the Ladder with Gabriel,* p. 34.

This series depicts the journey of a methamphetamine addict from her addiction into her recovery. The images show "facts" of the story, told via snapshots of real-life locations, those places that make up pieces of Gabriel's story, yet tell a story of paradox, one that is incomprehensible even its everydayness. (From Climbing the Ladder with Gabriel, 2009)

Figure 7.2.4. Exhibition of "Critical Sites of Recovery Series" and "Me and My Kids Series." Baggage Arts Building, Thunder Bay, 2016.

Gilda's Vessels

By Pauline Sameshima

22 Raku ware pottery bowls

http://www.womenandmeth.com/sameshima-response.html

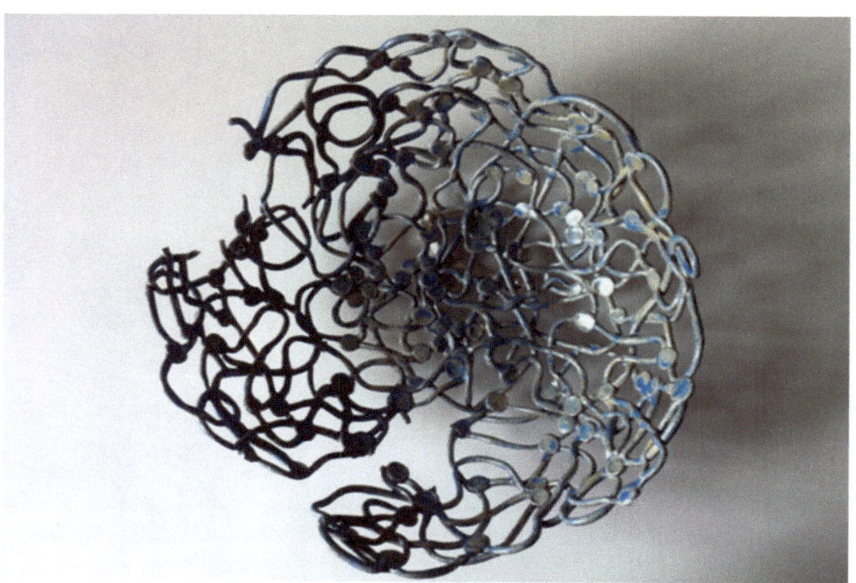

Figure 7.2.5. Gilda: Learning to live with the breakage. P. Sameshima, 2012.

Raku ware or raku-yaki, is a Japanese pottery style usually used in creating tea bowls for the Japanese tea ceremony. Raku ware is traditionally hand thrown and porous because of the low firing temperature. Very often the pieces are removed from the kiln while still hot and allowed to cool in a container filled with combustible material. Raku ware is closely integrated into Japanese culture and literature.

The word raku means 'enjoyment, comfort, or ease' and was originally derived from the name of a palace. Raku was the first ceramic ware to use a seal mark that was presented to the recipient and is the first pottery style to focus on the connection between potter and patron (Branfman, 2001).

I chose raku clay because of its high tensile strength when unfired. The airy pieces were extremely fragile while dying and even after the first firing. This work is titled 'Vessels," referring both to movement on the surface and movement within the body. Gilda's transcripts glitter with moments of euphoria which she tries to control—blissfully eating candy or using amphetamines to control weight. Her free movement is monitored by "stops" and pills. I began by playing with the notions of freedom and control, playing with control taking over.

I played with manic-ness through the different thicknesses of the vessels. I also played with fissures. In one of the very fine vesselled pieces, I noticed that one section of the bowl had separated, not broken, but the stops had not held the pieces properly, and the fissure not only pulled apart but the plane of connection was also separated. Art-making informed me that no matter how dedicated Glida is to repairing her life, she can never bridge the fissures that are permanently there. Her new way of living must be not an attempt to go back to life before addiction, but to create a way to live with the consequences of addiction.

I was most excited about the layered vessels, multi-layered palimpsests of repetition, echoing Glida's recovery endurance.

Figure 7.2.6. Vessels. P. Sameshima. 2012.

Gilda: Windows and Doors

By Patricia Maarhuis

Installation

Maarhuis Interpretation.

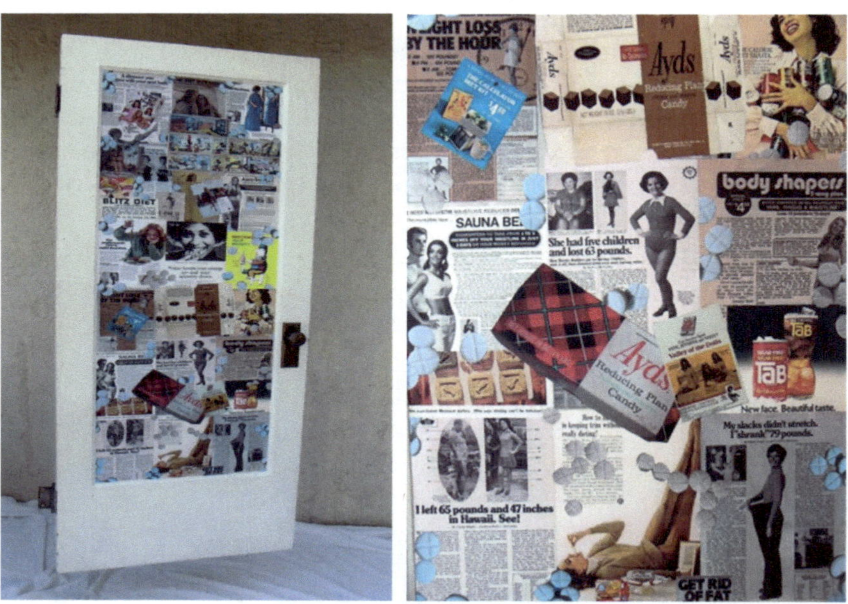

Figures 7.2.7 – 7.2.8. Gilda: Bedroom.
[Found object sculpture, 7' x 4', Series: 1 of 5, 2012]. P. Maarhuis, 2012.

My analysis focused on Gilda's description of her childhood/early adulthood relationships and cultural influences she identified that impacted her addiction. The interpretive artwork consists of six found object sculptures. Each piece in the series depicts relationships and everyday events described by Gilda. Popular culture print images and advertisements, personal messages and notes, and administrative forms from the 1970s are combined with Gilda's narrative to represent the experience of relationships and the cultural influences. Through ekphrastic research practices, aesthetic links are created between Gilda's statements, graphic cultural discourse in the 70s, and the expression of substance abuse in everyday life and relationships.

The works focus on Gilda, her family & friends, dialogue, and the 'doors and windows' of their relationships, which deeply impacted her substance use. The creative inspiration to use actual doors and window as the base for this series came about very suddenly, during my initial reading of Gilda's narratives. In one narrative I read a passage in which Gilda describes a realization that she had:

> *"I didn't get that knowledge until I went into drug recovery. . .To understand that was just like a whole door opening for me. I loved recovery"* (Interview 2, Lines 30-36).

To this, I had an immediate 'first thoughts' response: 'Gilda... You've been going through doors your whole life'. Gilda moved around a lot, especially in her youth due to family instability, addiction, and divorce. Her narratives point out that in her everyday life, no matter where she was or who she was with (father's home, grandmother's home, appointments with the doctor, married with husband and children, out with friends, etc.), Gilda went through doors and windows (physically and psychologically) that impacted her substance use.

Figure 7.2.9. Gilda: Bedroom. P. Maarhuis, 2012.

In Figure 7.2.16, the viewer can see the excited and happy faces of the two friends on one side of the window, but on the other side the viewer can read Gilda's description:

> *I can think back as a child with candy. A girlfriend and I going to the candy store and just eating tons of candy. I can remember being about 8 years old and just sitting there in a kind of euphoria (Interview 1, Lines 14-16.) Because it starts at a young age. I was doing that sugar thing to get away from that hateful chaotic household of mine (Interview 1, Lines 468-469). And the escape of taking a friend who wasn't one of those icky creatures I lived with in a house. And going and getting a sugar high and sitting out in the sun. We'd just get gigglin' and laughin'...*
>
> *So – it was an escape.* (Interview 1, Lines 471-473)

A story about running to the neighborhood store with a friend and buying candy is something most people can relate to and have done in their own childhood. It is something most of us have in common with Gilda and, in the chain of discourse, it has shared cultural codes or signs (Hall, 1997). The ekphrastic representation is a translation that is encoded with specific messages about childhood, going to the candy store and an addict. When the viewer understands or decodes the full context of this ordinary activity for Gilda, that it was an act of escape from abuse, he/she is challenged to re-imagine addiction and the addict. While the reception of this particular message is never guaranteed, the viewer may shift in how he/she makes meaning of addiction and shift his/her social practices. If this shift occurs, the 'production of knowledge through language' or a change of cultural discourse is complete and successful (Hall, 1997).

For extended description and discussion of the interpretive artwork created by Maarhuis for the Women & Meth research project go to:

http://www.womenandmeth.com/maarhuis-response.html

https://www.inbricolage.com/gilda-doors--windows.html

https://www.inbricolage.com/gilda-addiction.html

Figure 7.2.10. Gilda: Bedroom. P. Maarhuis, 2012.

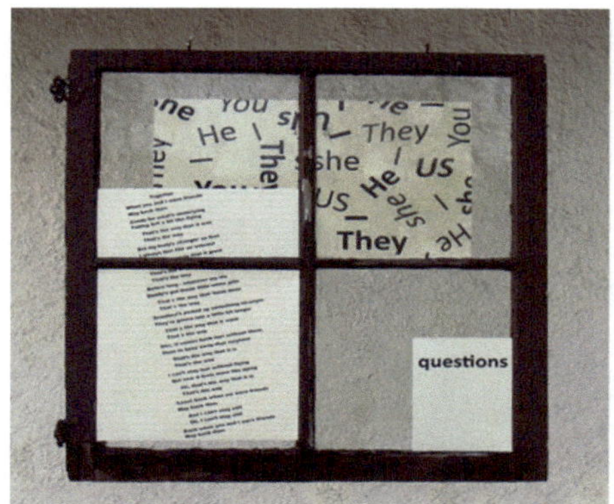

Figures 7.2.11 – 7.2.13. Gilda: Together.
[Found object sculpture with poetry, 4' x 3', Series: 2 of 5, 2013].
From *The Women and Meth Project* [2007-2016].

Figure 7.2.14 – 7.2.15. Gilda: Eviction.
[Found object sculpture, 7' x 4', Series: 3 of 5, 2013].
From *The Women and Meth Project* [2007-2016].

Figure 7.2.16. Gilda: Five and Dime. [Found object sculpture, 5' x 4', Series: 4 of 5, 2013]. From *The Women and Meth Project* [2007-2016].

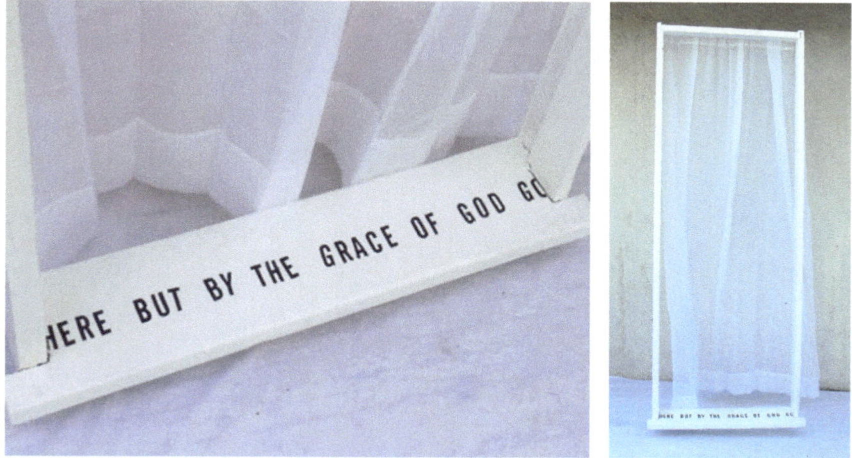

Figure 7.2.17. Gilda: Grace. [Found object sculpture, 7' x 4', Series: 5 of 5, 2013]. From *The Women and Meth Project* [2007-2016].

Jill: Frosted Glass

By Victoria Bolduc

6 Paintings

http://www.womenandmeth.com/bolduc-response.html

Figure 7.2.18. Dogbite, 18" x 24" [Watercolour and ink on paper]. V. Bolduc. 2012.

In her interview, Jill tells a story of an acquaintance shooting a police dog and then being shot himself. The piece depicts the chaos of this story as a man is cornered like an animal and lashes out. It equates the primal impulses of man and dog for fight or flight.

Anonymous Hate–Tribute
John-Paul Chalykoff
http://picosong.com/uvwT

Inspired by Bolduc's painting Dogbite. The song is divided into three different sections, exploring themes of chaos, harsh judgments, and feelings of loss. This sound collage creates a cinematic soundscape that incorporates direct quotes from the interview. These words depict a cruelness in blogs and internet comments, as people respond to the news from the comfort of their computer chairs.

Figure 7.2.19. Mother, 18" x 24" [Watercolour and ink on paper]. V. Bolduc, 2012.

This work uses the image of the 'Madonna' to approach norms and ideal representations of what a mother should be. This image is comparable to how Jill's children may have perceived her as she showered them with luxurious gifts to distract them from her drug use. This piece places the concept of the Madonna in contrast with Jill's reality.

Figure 7.2.20. *Of a Feather,* 18" x 24" [Watercolour and ink on paper]. V. Bolduc, 2012.

The crow represents the image of a social pariah, and the skulls represent the risks of addiction. A harsh reality of addiction is that not everyone reaches sobriety. This piece considers the social context of addiction, and questions the potential harmfulness of relationships between addicts.

Jill: Music Interpretation

By John-Paul Chalykoff

8 Songs with QR Codes

http://www.womenandmeth.com/chalykoff-response.html

Figure 7.2.21. Jill's Music. JP. Chalykoff, 2013.

The website offers access to Chalykoff's music and text.

Figure 7.2.22. Online music. JP. Challykoff, 2013.

Challykoff's interpretations accessed with a QR Reader.

Women & Meth (Intro)

Beginning with a simple drum and bass line, layers of sound are added to the piece. Dreamy sounding strings symbolic of the surreal life Jill felt she was living while using meth. This piece presents tension and danger reflecting the destructive patterns Jill found herself embracing.

Women and Meth (Reprise)

http://picosong.com/uvna

Women & Meth (Reprise)

This piece experiments with the Women & Meth (Intro) recording (http://picosong.com/uWp5), by adding new layers, altering foundations, making extensions and changing the key of the bass. It brings an uplifting tone to the musical journey taken with Jill and her story without abandoning the original musical arrangement.

Redemption

http://picosong.com/uvFR

In her interviews, Jill spoke of hurting others. She spoke of having a second chance at life, and at becoming a mother. This piece highlights second chances and reconciliation. This song incorporates female vocals by Tausha Esquegaa as a tribute to Jill.

The bargaining game

http://picosong.com/uWiB/

This piece represents a progression of Jill's meth use which she describes as "a bargaining game with herself." Every two measures of the song, a new instrumental part is introduced to create an ever-changing soundscape, symbolic of the changes in Jill's life.

Reflections (Of Life and Death)
http://picosong.com/uvs8/

Guitars are used as the only instruments for this piece to create a more intimate, bare-bones, stripped down feeling, to keep that human element alive, to see the person not only the addiction. There is a sense of melancholy throughout this piece, without a grand feeling of joy it maintains hopefulness.

Anger and Sorrow
http://picosong.com/uv3Z

In her interviews, Jill described how she was feeling as she was getting clean. During this time she felt only anger and sadness. This piece brings together two songs reflective of those feelings as a demonstration that although anger and sadness are distinct emotions/songs, they are both part of the same experience.

Fragility
http://picosong.com/uv3v

This piece addresses that addiction can never truly go away, it maintains its presence lurking in the background. The song speaks to cravings, feelings of wanting to let go and give in, knowledge of what could happen in a downward spiral. This is also a piece on self-awareness and strength, a strength that if it were handled roughly, the balance would break.

Jill: Constructing Control

By Pauline Sameshima

A 4-Part Series in Plexiglass & Fishing Line with culled text from the transcripts.

http://www.womenandmeth.com/uploads/2/8/6/5/2865716/reflections_on_jilldraft1.pdf

An explicit part of making this series was that from a distance, the frames looked empty. With light, the designs became visible. So it is with addictions.

Figures 7.2.23. Jill: Constructing Control. P. Sameshima, 2013.

Reflections on Jill's Transcripts

Figure 7.2.24. Constructing Control: One Step at a Time. P. Sameshima, 2013.

1:30-34

from the outside looking in
my life looked pretty put together for a long time
I came from an upper middle class family
my dad was the captain of the Police Department
my mom was a prominent school teacher
I just always looked pretty put together

1:45-47

I had this whole professional life
on one side of me
and this whole drug-cultured side on the other
I held that together pretty well for a while

1:123-128

the one thing that I liked about church
was when I was there
my mom treated me really well
she was so nice to me
when we were there
and the minute we left
it was just the opposite
I remember thinking
I don't want anything to do with a hypocrite
if that's what Jesus and the Bible is all about
I'm going the other way
and I'm going to be the best of that kind of person
It could be that was a real conscious choice that I made early, early on

1:165-170

people see drug addicts and alcoholics as bad people
I believed that about myself for a really long time
and it took some intense treatment
and working with people who were really committed with me
to realize that I wasn't a bad person
I just did bad things.

Jill's construction of good and bad, right and wrong, and other dichotomous perceptions of the world led me to work in a medium that intentionally is both a front and a back. Jill's actions are controlled and calculated and "wild." There is a hardness to this medium, a tautness that is demanded, and a danger. When pulling the fishing gut taught, it can easily abrade the skin when wrapped tightly around the fingers. When too much pressure on a knot is applied, the 10lb fishing line easily gives way and snaps.

Jill sees two opaque sides to her identities, the professional on one side and the drug-cultured side on the other. The plexiglass and fishing line medium represent a transparency – the interconnectedness of each side is reliant and dependent on the other. While I determined that the drilled side (rougher surface) would be the back, and where I placed the knots while working on the pieces, the "back side" was actually the focal view when I created the works. The front and the back are arbitrary choices. Similarly, in Jill's life, the drug-cultured lifestyle was integrally part of her professional life whether she admitted it or not. The image that also spurred the medium was Jill's story about her dry cotton mouth.

1:551-556

someone said to me the other day
"wow, you have pretty healthy teeth for
using meth that much"
my mouth was always so dry
and I always had cotton-mouth
so I had a toothbrush
if I wasn't smoking a cigarette
I had a toothbrush in my mouth
and I was brushing my teeth
trying to get the cotton-mouth to go away

I wanted to create something that represented the web-like cotton covering that implies a tangledness and entrapment. Jill also used the word "shroud" and "cloud of protection' in her interview.

2:26-49

I tried to shroud my kids with this cloud
of protection
they knew what was going on
even if I didn't get loaded in front of them
I was loaded in front of them
ninety percent of the time

Plexiglass 1: Constructing Control: Filling the Void (Circle)

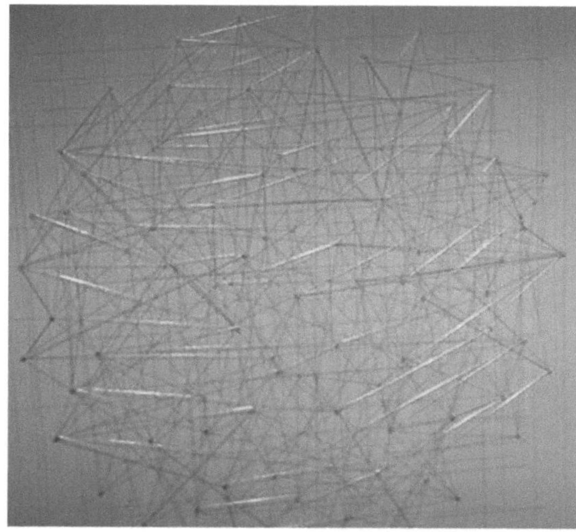

Figure 7.2.25. Constructing Control: Filling the Void. P. Sameshima, 2013.

1:152-155

my addiction
took that pain away and it made me feel different
filled that huge hole that was inside me
I felt pretty in control
so from there on out
I drank or used drugs
to feel different
to keep that void full

The medium and random patterns attempt to express the bitterness, anger, and confusion shared in Jill's story. Her efforts to control and maintain are calculated efforts to fill the void she perceived.

1:129-145

I have an aunt and an uncle who lived about sixty miles away
my mom's brother was an eye doctor
they had a great home and a great relationship
I used to spend a lot of time with them
in the summers at their lake cabin

they drank
they weren't alcoholic drinkers by any means
they would have a glass of wine or a beer here and there
to their face, my mom was so sweet to them
when we were away from them
they were going to hell
heathens, you know, because they drank
I remember thinking in my young little mind
that if that's what drinking does to you
I want to drink and be like my aunt and uncle
and not like my mom
I had gone over to spend the weekend
and they had a wine cellar in their basement
I intentionally went down to the wine cellar
put a bottle of their wine in my backpack
and took it home with me
I thought, you know, I'm going to be like them
and so at ten years old
I drank this bottle of wine in my bedroom
and got drunker than I ever remember feeling
passed out – got sick, passed out
and I woke up the next morning
and I thought
oh, my gosh
this is the answer
to all my problems

The fishing line develops the sense of continuity in the struggle in recovery—the tension in maintaining the "recovery mode" is ever vigilant and demanding.

3:94-100

it doesn't matter if you've been clean a month or twenty years
when you start using, your addiction picks up right where you left off
my disease doesn't go back to square one
it stops and stays where it was when the drugs ceased to be used

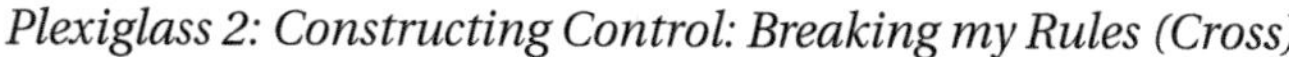

Plexiglass 2: Constructing Control: Breaking my Rules (Cross)

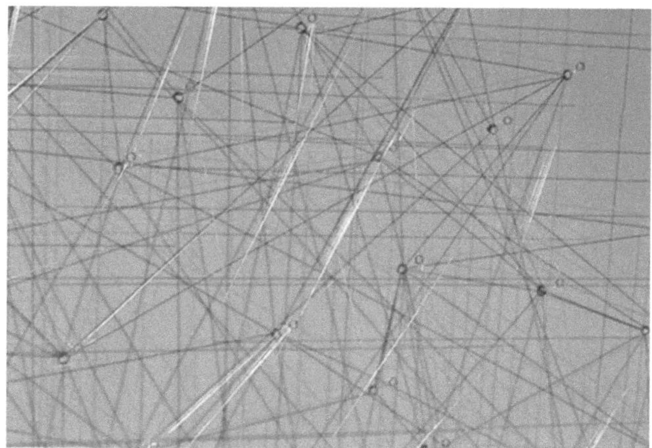

Figure 7.2.26. Constructing Control: Breaking My Rules. P. Sameshima, 2013.

1:193-217

I started doing this bargaining game with myself
I would only use after I got off work
and then only at home
just a little bit before I went to work
I would never use it in my car or at work
then it got to the point where
I said never on the premises
I lived a mile or two away from the medical lab
so I would fly to my house at lunchtime
and get high and then come back
all this bargaining thing in my mind was
telling me I'm still okay
I'm not breaking my rules
but my rules always changed
and then it got to be
not in my office
so I'd go out to my car
and then pretty soon
I had stashes all over my office
a pen on a necklace
that I used to carry around
you could open up the pen

and it was full of methamphetamine
people would say, “Can I use your pen?”
“No!” I guarded it with my life
meth breaks down all the barriers
that process probably took nine months or so
a year maybe
once I started this whole bargaining with myself
my mind was just playing all these games with me
and because I had this good job
I convinced myself that I was okay

Plexiglass 3: Constructing Control: One Step at a Time (Diagonal)

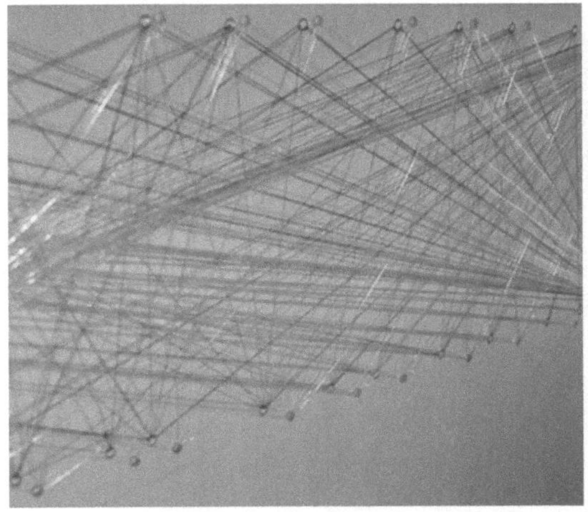

Figure 7.2.27. Constructing Control: One Step at a Time. P. Sameshima, 2013.

1:398-412

they say the only thing that you have to do
is to change one thing in order to get clean and stay clean
and I thought, wow, I can do that
they told me the one thing was everything
that just terrified me
I have to change everything in my life?
I can’t do it
I heard a speaker
When I was about four or five months clean

he said, "You know, it was really helpful to me
when someone told me that you can't change everything
but you can work on one thing all the time."
I could wrap my mind around that
so that's what I started doing
just working on one thing
all the time in order to get better

1: 415-432

they say, "Don't ask what; ask how."
and the how is learning how to be honest
open-minded, and willing
I don't know how to be honest
my whole life was a lie
I was pretty convincing
one thing about drug addicts and alcoholics
is we're really smart people
I could convince you that I love your blue sweater
and you're saying, "this is black"
I could twist it up
and make you think you're wearing blue
when you're really wearing black
I'm just this convincing – convincing liar
my whole life was a lie
I lied even when I didn't need to
and so here's the principle of learning
how to be honest in order to get healthy
and I said, "You know, I don't know how to be honest."

There is disarray. There are images of cutting and slicing with anger in many parts of the transcripts. Imagery of lines and emphasis on certain lines are evident throughout the transcripts.

2:406-413

my daughter looked at my picture
and cut it up with some scissors
it just crushed me
"you know, my mom might be fat now
but she could never not do drugs
and I don't want to see her again."
and she just sliced the picture in half

Plexiglass 4: Constructing Control: Tangling Thoughts (Synapse)

Figure 7.2.28. Constructing Control: Tangling Thoughts. P. Sameshima, 2013.

1:513-542

at six feet tall and a hundred pounds
my legs looked like my arms
I could barely hold myself up
I was about at the end of my rope
my heart was under so much strain
trying to keep me alive
it had been months and months and months
since I had put food in my body
or actually chewed or eaten any kind of food
my brain never told my body that it was hungry
I remember the last thing that I put in my body
one of my friends make me this rice dish
that had butter and cinnamon
and sugar
it was kind of sweet
that was the last thing that I could actually eat
I literally could not make myself swallow
there was nothing firing in my brain
to tell me to swallow

This piece attempts to express the tangled constructions in the neural pathways. There is structure and yet, the workings are open and lose. The ends are not tied off.

3:434-461

I had to start listening to totally different radio stations
because everything in my life reminded me of using
people talk about triggers
if I'm awake, I'm triggered
there wasn't, for a really long time
a day that went by if I was awake
that I wasn't high or in the process of trying to get high
you've got to learn how to live life
because just being awake is a trigger
changing my whole mindset
I really started to believe in the
what goes in is what comes out

Jill: Not So Hollywood

by Patricia Maarhuis

10 posters with accompanying poems

http://www.womenandmeth.com/maarhuis-response1.html

Often, when doing interpretive artwork, I take basic themes, forms, and medium from initial thoughts that float up while I'm reading through the narrative for the first time. For this series, the phrase that almost immediately came to me was: That's just so Hollywood... On the surface, Jill's narrative has some of the same elements used by the movie and media industry to 'sex up' a story and sell theater tickets-guns, violence, drugs, money, and intrigue. But, when it comes to women, their families, and meth addiction, the representations sold by the movie industry in films are never the whole story and living meth addiction is not that glamorous.

This poetry and poster series chronicles the deeper issues in Jill's experience of addiction and her relationships, loss, leaving, and pain. The poetry is taken directly from the interview narratives, edited into poetic form (Prendergast, 2009), each paired with an interpretive poster. A few of the posters are plays—visual and narrative—on actual films such as Home Alone (Hughes & Columbus, 1990), Romancing the Stone (Douglas & Zemeckis, 1984), and Scarface (Bregman & De Palma, 1982) that were popular during the 1980s & 1990s. Coincidentally, during that same time, use of stimulants—cocaine, crack, crystal, amphetamine, and methamphetamine—peaked in the U.S. (NIDA, 2016) as did the rise and dominance of Mexican drug cartel trafficking (Beittel, 2013). The posters are not meant to be sarcastic or a parody. Rather, the works are a deliberate overstatement—juxtaposed and exaggerated representations—of how Jill's full experience is just so not Hollywood when explored in depth and with compassion.

Each of the 10 posters has similar design elements. The movie credits are made up of the Women & Meth research collaborators, literally giving credit to the whole research team for the project. The graphics and font type were chosen based on the themes or events depicted in the poster and the type of movie represented, such as children's animation, action drama, horror, romance, and documentary. The "movie star" featured in the faux films, Jill Spoke is an extension of the pseudonym (Jill) used in the research interview. I chose a consistent look for Jill Spoke, often used in the film industry: pretty, white, tall, and blonde. Additionally, the movie titles and much of the poster narrative are made up of direct quotes from the interview transcripts. This trace within the artwork establishes a direct connection to Jill's own voice present in my interpretations of her story.

For extended description and discussion of the interpretive artwork created by Maarhuis for the Women & Meth research project go to: http://www.womenandmeth.com/maarhuis-response1.htmlv

Jill Spoke Movie Posters

Figure 7.2.29. Jill: Find Another Way. [Digital image on paper, faux movie poster, 11 x 17, Series: 1 of 10, 2014]. From *The Women and Meth Project* [2007-2016].

Find Another Way

This first piece depicts the beginning of Jill's substance abuse and addiction process at age 10. The first experience she has with alcohol is striking. Though her response appears illogical, there is a rationale that is quite reasonable to her young mind. Despite the nausea, vomiting, and loss of consciousness, Jill desires to 'get more' and have the control to take away her pain. Even at the beginning of her substance use, there isn't any of the fun or relaxation, usually associated with having a drink. Using is about trying to be pain-free, to feel in control. Somewhat understandably, most popular children's films don't explore this wounded interior, the headwaters of addiction.

Find Another Way

I went down to the wine cellar
put a bottle of their wine in my backpack
and took it home with me.

I thought
I'm going to be like them.

At ten years old,
I drank this bottle of wine
in my bedroom and got drunker
than I ever remember feeling
passed out – got sick - passed out.

I woke up the next morning
and I thought, Oh My Gosh.
This is the answer to all my problems.

There wasn't ever just a social drink –
I mean, at ten years old –
who drinks socially at ten years old?

But I remember thinking,
I have to find another way to get more
so I can feel that way again.

I felt in control.
It just took the pain –
that huge hole that was inside me
It just took that pain away
It made me feel different.

So from there on out
I drank or used drugs
to feel different
to keep that void full.

Figure 7.2.30. Jill: Romancing the Smoke. [Digital image on paper, faux movie poster, 11 x 17, Series: 2 of 10, 2014]. From The Women and Meth Project [2007-2016].

Romancing the Smoke

The second piece portrays Jill's first use of meth and its intense emotional quality. Often, her descriptions of meth addiction and struggle toward recovery are characterized as being in an intense emotional relationship with an entity—a type of being, rather than an object or a substance. Similarly, through my experience in working with people who are addicted, I have heard clients refer to the powerful connection or even love that they felt when first using and being around others that use. Like the trope played out in the film *Romancing the Stone* (Douglas & Zemeckis, 1984), this poster points to the "mis-matched couple on a romantic adventure," but without the happy ending. Later on, her feeling shifts to horror, as illustrated in the piece, *The Crystal.*

Romancing the Smoke

I was twenty-three or twenty-four
the first time I tried methamphetamine.
I tried it because - you know -
some friends I was with
we were getting ready to get high
but no one had any cocaine.

And this friend said, "Here. Try this."
I remember trying it....
Thinking - Oh My Gosh - I think
I just found the love of my life.

And from that point on
it was pretty intense for
the last six or seven years
of my addiction.

Figure 7.2.31. Jill: Double Trouble. [Digital image on paper, faux movie poster, 11 x 17, Series: 3 of 10, 2014]. From *The Women and Meth Project* [2007-2016].

Double Trouble

This third poster characterizes the short time in Jill's life when she is transitioning from a quickly disintegrating family and professional life to the chaos of dealing and deeper addiction. Again using a familiar metaphor, Jill has a secret double life, concealed from those around her. She works in health care 'by day' but deals drugs 'by night,' but meth is quickly encroaching on every aspect of her life. Few of the harsh consequences of meth addiction have set in yet and dealing for the Mexican Mafia feels powerful and exciting.

Double Trouble

I worked full-time.
I had a great job at a medical lab.

Again, from the outside looking in,
I had a pretty put-together life.
We had a nice home, nice car.
My kids always looked clean,
healthy, and didn't miss school.

So I had this whole professional life
on one side of me
and this whole drug-culture
on the other side of me.
I worked four days on and four days off.
My weekends got longer.
So that was helpful.

Then I started doing this bargaining game.
I would use only, after I got off work.
Then only at home – just a little bit
before I went to work.
Later, I would never use it
in my car or at work.

But then it got to the point where
I never used on the premises.
I lived, a mile or two away from the lab.
So I would fly to my house at lunchtime,
get high, and then come back to work.

This whole bargaining thing in my mind
was a way to say, I'm still okay.
I'm not breaking my rules.
But my rules always changed.
Meth just breaks down all the barriers.

By that time, I had gotten
hooked up with the Mafia.
I was dealing drugs the four days I was off.
Then I was working, four days a week.
So, I started off as this naïve,
professional dope fiend.

You know, people see drug addicts
and alcoholics as these bad people.
I believed that about myself for a really long time
It took some intense treatment to realize

I wasn't a bad person.
I just did bad things.

So it was pretty fraying once shame
and guilt were peeled away.
But I could realize,
I wasn't born a bad person.
This disease is treatable.
I'm not going to be cured from it,
but I can go on to live
a full, productive life.

Figure 7.2.32. Jill: No One at Home. [Digital image on paper, faux movie poster, 11 x 17, Series: 4 of 10, 2014]. From *The Women and Meth Project* [2007-2016].

No One at Home

The fourth poster is one of the first pieces completed in the series but one of the most difficult to create. It is a takeoff on the movie, *Home Alone* (Hughes & Columbus, 1990), a comedy which plays on every parent's fear of accidentally forgetting their child somewhere. In this case, however, it's the children, who leave on vacation and the mom, who purposely moves out before they return. In the juxtaposed telling I, like Jill, struggled with separating out the harmful and traumatizing actions of addiction from the person who commits them.

No One at Home

Well, I – I just walked away.
They were on vacation with their dad
and I moved – packed up our house.
Moved to another place.

It was a couple of years,
during my first few months clean,
before I was able to see them again.

I remember towards the end
before my kids were gone,
they became a nuisance.
They became a problem.

It was like, you know,
how do I get out and
do what I want to do and party?
How do I deal these drugs
with my kids around?

Everything was gone.
I gave it all up because of meth.
For a long time, I tried to convince myself
– especially about my children –
I tried to convince myself that
I was being a good mom.
Letting them go so they didn't have to go
Through the horrors of my addiction.

But when I first got clean and
started working with a sponsor,
he was pretty adamant:
"You know, Jill, there's nothing

about being a good mom.
You were a self-centered dope fiend
that chose dope every time.
You put dope in front of your kids,
and they were going to lose every single time."

Jill Spoke is in....
Room 3
Don't ask this girl any questions...
Just give her a room.
IMBRICOLAGE PICTURES PRESENTS A Jill Spoke PRODUCTION A FILM BY PATRICIA MAARHUIS "Room 3"
MUSIC BY SHEILA KEARNEY CONVERSE COSTUME DESIGNER CARRIE SANTUCCI EDITED BY LAURILNY J. HARRIS PRODUCTION DESIGNER LINDA KITTELL
EXECUTIVE PRODUCER ROXANNE VANDERMAUSE STORY BY JILL SPOKE DIRECTOR OF PHOTOGRAPHY STEPHEN CHALMERS PRODUCED BY CARRIE MILLER SCREEN PLAY BY VICTORIA BOLDUC DIRECTED BY PAULINE SAMESHIMA
Room3.com
SONY PICTURES
UNIVERSAL
R RESTRICTED

Figures 7.2.33 – 7.2.35. Jill: La Rubia, Room 3, and Big time. [Digital image on paper, faux movie poster, 11 x 17, Series: 5, 6, 7 of 10, 2014]. From *The Women and Meth Project* [2007-2016].

La Rubia, Room 3, Big Time

This trilogy of posters portrays Jill's rise as a successful dealer, then her sudden fall from power, and the fast escape from the Mexican Mafia. *Big Time* is a takeoff on the movie Scarface (Bregman & De Palma, 1982) in its cold, calculating drive for power and money. 'A Big Timer' is how Jill's children, with misguided admiration, describe her life as a dealer. *La Rubia* focuses on the intrigue of her set-up and betrayal by her running partner and the need to escape. Hiding in *Room 3*, Jill slowly shifts from plotting murder and revenge to realizing what her life has become. Through kindnesses of many—the hotel manager to strangers to homeless shelter staff—she slowly approaches recovery. Often, in popular culture media, this is when the heroic story of dealing, addiction, and redemption comes to a hopeful conclusion, leaving the audience to assume the perpetual American notion of having "a happy fresh start and new beginning."

Big Time

When I lost my job at the medical lab,
I was so far into dealing with the Mafia
that I took this as a sign from God:
I was supposed to be a drug dealer.

I fell into it and was pretty naive.
I had this friend who had good drugs
and sold them to me for a good price.
He was wealthy and drove nice cars.
I never put two and two together
that he was a drug dealer.

But later he left. After five or six days
I wonder what happened to him.
Then I got a phone call.
It was him and he was in jail.
He said, "I need to talk to you.
Come – will you come visit me?
And so I went to visit him.
It turns out he was the top dog in the
Mexican Mafia for the whole region.

He told me who he was and what he did.
Then he said, "I know you're smart
enough to run my business.
It supports my family in Mexico.
And, I need you to run my business.
I'm getting deported."

And I just remember thinking,
Holy cow! This is great!

I just jumped into the business
and did a really good job.

He had his grandpa, a couple uncles,
and a cousin come up to meet
this tall little white girl, who was
runnin' their family business.
They couldn't believe how well
it was going without him there.

It was fast-paced. It was a lot of money.
He spent it on cars and guns and bodyguards.
I made good money at the lab.
But I was making thousands of dollars
a day - on a bad day - dealing for the Mafia.
I just got sucked into the whole lifestyle of it.

Figure 7.2.36. The Crystal [Digital image on paper, faux movie poster, 11 x 17, Series: 8 of 10, 2014]. From *The Women and Meth Project* [2007-2016].

Crystal

Strangely, both addiction and recovery are about loss. The Crystal addresses the haunting depth of loss in Jill's life: her children and family, a good job and home, her physical and mental health, the love of the first high, her rich and fast-paced life of dealing. As she begins her recovery, the realization of these losses starts to pile up. Like in the movie poster *Romancing the Smoke,* Jill feels intense emotion, but this time it is anger and horror. Meth has betrayed her! After giving everything, the love of her life ends up turning on her. The addiction and loss is so deep; Jill can only describe it as something outside of herself - a rapacious evil entity that takes everything and wants more.

The Crystal

It was just like this evil
in the back of my mind –
always wanting more,
wanting to find ways to get
more - to use more.

By the end,
it got to the point where
I couldn't function without it.
It was the all-consuming
motivator of my life.

It took everything from me, too.
I lost my job at the medical lab
Four beautiful children were gone
My home. My cars.
Everything was gone.

I was really angry because,
I had given everything up
that meant anything to me
to use that drug.
And, it ended up turning on me.

By the end of my addiction,
there was no amount of meth
that would give me the first high
I felt, from years before.
But my mind just kept trying.
It just wanted more.

It was this infectious evil,
I couldn't control.

Figure 7.2.37. Chew. [Digital image on paper, faux movie poster, 11 x 17, Series: 9 of 10, 2014]. From *The Women and Meth Project* [2007-2016].

The Chew

The work, *CHEW: Relearning to eat* is a documentary film and points to the need to relearn many of the most basic functions of life during Jill's recovery from meth addiction. This is one of the most poignant points in her story. Jill has been entirely consumed – in body, heart, and mind – by meth use and, consequently, can't take in enough sustenance. This description opens up the experience of recovery from meth addiction through an everyday experience – eating breakfast. Most people can fully relate to Jill's fully embodied experience: a steaming plate of warm pancakes, feeling hunger and wanting to eat. Then, there is the sorrow and the realization of an emaciated and broken condition. But next, there comes the kind touch of another wanting to care and the awkwardness of relearning a basic human function - chewing.

Chew

The very first morning I was there
it was my first day clean.
I can still see the plate of pancakes
they had for breakfast that morning.
It was the best plate of pancakes
I've ever seen before or since.

I went and sat down at the table.
There were utensils on each side of the plate.
I remember looking at the fork and the knife
looking at other people, and thinking,
I know I'm supposed to use these -
to get that food into my mouth -
but I had no recollection of how to do it.

Tears just started streaming out of my eyes.
The girl sitting across from me said,
"I suppose you're going to tell me
you don't know how to eat."
I thought it's not even worth answering
because I don't.

The cook at the time was this
short little round lady who waddled out
to the table and she leaned over.
She put her arm around me and she said,
"You don't know how to eat, do you, honey?"
I just shook my head.

And she said, "I'm going to fatten you up while you're here."
She cut into that pancake and she put it on a fork
She put it in my month and closed it.
And she just kind of, moved my jaw up and down.
Then she held a glass of milk up
and said, "Swallow it.
OK. That's enough for now."

Figure 7.2.38. The Choice. [Digital image on paper, faux movie poster, 11 x 17, Series: 10 of 10, 2014]. From *The Women and Meth Project* [2007-2016].

The Choice

The tenth piece in the series, *The Choice,* captures Jill's sense of recovery. Unlike the finality of a typically happy and heroic ending, the series closes with an image that has a perennial feeling of recurrent choice. Jill speaks on a number of occasions in the interviews about what she feels her choices—or the lack of choices—are in addiction and recovery. And, Jill is clear: if she could, she would use meth but, then, addiction would completely take over and her ability to choose would be gone. Then again, once fully into her recovery, Jill feels she does have an active choice to practice recovery and to not relapse, but with ever-present vigilance.

The Choice

People say that you can just choose not to use.
I think that works for some people.
But if I had a choice, I would be loaded.

If I could use just on the weekends,
you know, have a line or two of meth,
I would use.

But when I get loaded, bad things happen.
So, there wasn't a choice for me.
Because, once the addiction gets kicked in,
it just goes into overdrive.
There's no stopping it.

Once I got into my recovery and
knew there was a different way to live,
then I have a choice.

Relapse is a definite choice.
It would be a very conscious choice
for me to go back to using again.
I have a choice now.

Me and My Kids Project

By Pauline Sameshima

6 posters - 3 included here: Photos taken at recovery home.

See http://www.womenandmeth.com/me-and-my-kids.html

You're diagnosed with a fatal disease
your doctor says, go to the hospital, talk
about your disease for an hour a day
and it will go into remission
COURAGE
Would you do that?
Women and Meth Transcript 81: 202-205
A Washington State University research study
Supported by the American Nurses' Foundation
meth

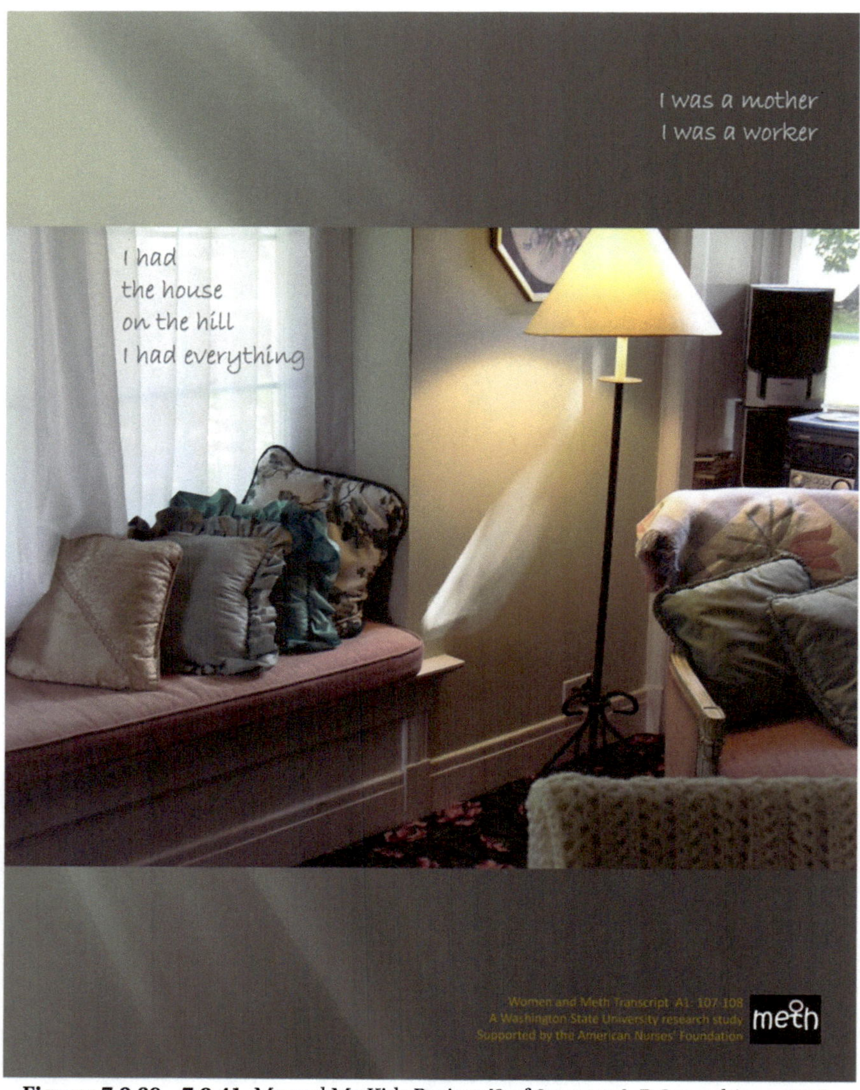

Figures 7.2.39 – 7.2.41. Me and My Kids Project [3 of 6 posters]. P. Sameshima, 2011.

Interview Observations

By Patricia Maarhuis

Arts integrated observation about the interview transcript questions and answers

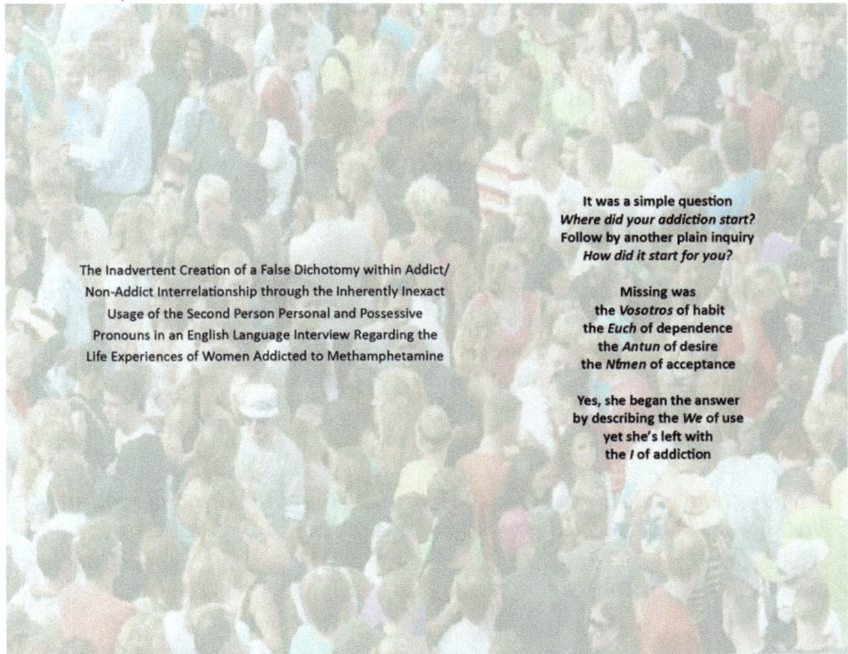

Figure 7.2.42. The Interview. [Poetry and digital image on paper, 8.5 x 11, 2014]. From *The Women and Meth Project* [2007-2016].

Reprinted Examples

7.3 This article offers a procedural example for engaging with ideas.

Sameshima, P., Miyakawa, M., & Lockett, M. (2017, Dec.). Scholarly engagement through making: A response to Arts-Based and Contemplative Practices in Research and Teaching. *Revista VIS, 16*(2), 45-67.

7.4 This article demonstrates knowledge production through making.

Wiebe, S., & Sameshima, P. (2017, Dec.). Generating self: Catechizations in poetry. *Revista VIS, 16*(2). 140-155.

7.5 This article offers an example of three analyses using different modalities examining the same data set.

Stock, R. V., Sameshima, P., & Slingerland, D. (2016, July). Constructing pre-service teacher identities through processes of parallax. Special Issue: Artful inquiry: Transforming understanding through creative engagement. *LEARNing Landscapes, 9*(2), 489-512.

7.6 This article explains the idea of ekphrasis (the translation of modality) through multiliteracies theory in a single participant case study.

Wiebe, S., & Caseley Smith, C. (2016). A/r/t/ography and teacher education in the 21st century. *McGill Journal of Education, 51*(3). 1163-1178.

7.7 This article explicates the liminal studio space—a generative locale for performing the data analysis in a parallaxic praxis model.

Wiebe, S., & Sameshima, P. (2018, January). Sympathizing with social justice, poetry of invitation and generation. *Art/Research International, 3*(1)7-29.

Grateful acknowledgement is made for permission to reprint the following article:

7.8 This article is an early descriptor of the model used with an interdisciplinary team.

Sameshima, P., Vandermause, R., Chalmers, S., & Gabriel. (2009). Introduction. *Climbing the ladder with Gabriel: Poetic inquiry of a methamphetamine addict in recovery* (pp. 3-16). Rotterdam, The Netherlands: Sense.

Example 7.3: Scholarly Engagement Through Making

A Response to Arts-Based and Contemplative Practices in Research and Teaching[2]

By Pauline Sameshima, Muga Miyakawa & Michael Lockett

Abstract

This paper reimagines the scholarly book review while responding to *Arts-based Contemplative Practices in Research and Teaching* (edited by Walsh, Bickel, & Leggo, 2014), a rich, sagaciously curated text that will inform the future of the symbiotic field of arts and contemplative practice in curriculum. The authors respond to the anthology through Parallaxic Praxis, a research model that enacts a contemplative artful approach which the team specifically used to address the contemporary challenges of time, attention, and connection. Their review reframes the learning possibilities within the interactive space between self and experience and, in turn, illustrates scholarly engagement through making as a sustainable, deliberate practice of contemplative practice with critical attention.

Keywords

arts integrated research; parallaxic praxis; catechization process; arts-based research; contemplative practices; mindfulness; reparative research; fibre arts research.

Introduction

With growing interest in mindfulness and other contemplative forms of learning and research in education, new ways of knowing and being have emerged from the incorporation of embodied and spiritual ways of engaging in human development. On the frontier of this exciting exploration into mindfulness in education is a symbiosis between contemplative inquiry and arts integrated research. Working in tandem, these two forms of inquiry promise additional interpretive directions that delve into epistemological and collaborative

---

2 Reprint. Sameshima, P., Miyakawa, M., & Lockett, M. (2017, Dec.). Scholarly engagement through making: A response to Arts-Based and Contemplative Practices in Research and Teaching. *Revista VIS, 16*(2), 45-67.

investigations. In this paper, we present an exploration of mindfulness and "making" through a review of the book, *Arts-Based and Contemplative Practices in Research and Teaching: Honouring Presence*, edited by Susan Walsh, Barbara Bickel, and Carl Leggo (2014). The methodology offers an alternative to the traditional book review product, demanding researchers attend to time, attention, and connection in their engagement with a text.

Mindfulness is a practice that allows individuals to increase attentional awareness, focus, and open monitoring of thoughts and emotions without engaging instantaneously and habitually to them. The ability to center awareness to greater levels has the potential to allow humans to access new ways of perceiving the world and the relationships they engage in (Davidson and Kaszniak, 2015; Ericson, Kjonstad, and Barstad, 2014). The book review response involved "making" through the conceptualization of theory and the construction of knowledge through material design. The making in this instance represents a process-oriented practice that explicates methodological curriculum constructions of understanding. This making process is an example of Aokian aligned curriculum-making, far from notions on management systems, inputs, and outputs (see Aoki, 2005: 271), far from the procedural steps of writing a traditional book review.

The book *Arts-Based and Contemplative Practices in Research and Teaching* is a welcome addition to the growing field of mindfulness and contemplative practice. Macintyre Latta's (2015) review succinctly describes the focus of the book as "how arts-based and contemplative practices in research and teaching draw attention to the ability to see, and concomitantly act, on the potentiality of the present" (2015: 1). Binder (2016), in her review, notes how the 10 authors intimately bring together arts-based research and contemplative practice. She highlights the remarkable "insights rendered by [the] experienced researchers, who explore the liminal spaces of practice where intention, presence and co-creation unfold" (2016: 227). Guiney Yallop (2016), who also praises the book, insightfully points to Walsh and Bai's (2014) description of the variation possible in creating meditative and contemplative states of consciousness within a multitude of everyday activities.

While this rich, edited book depicts and extends the burgeoning field of contemplative practices in higher education (Barbezat and Bush, 2013; Bush, 2011; Shapiro, Brown and Austin, 2008), the intents and processes for contemplative practices using arts integrated approaches remain less understood and specific explications of how these practices can be practically engaged is helpful. This review and process-explanation of contemplative arts integrated methodology offers one example for imagining possibilities for scholarly review and engagement. This work follows in the tradition of

Canadian curriculum scholarship of holding a complex coherence of differing voices (Pinar, 2014) as counterpointed compositions (Ng-A-Fook, 2014).

In overview, we will situate mindfulness and contemplative practice to clarify our concerns around intent, offer possibilities for how metaphors play a central role in this practice, and detail the "making" process. The paper concludes with questions generated with the co-editors of the book, born out of their responses to the products of the making process. The research team is made up of Pauline Sameshima, with a focus on contemplative arts-integrated research; Muga Miyakawa, with a focus on mindfulness; and Michael Lockett, with a focus on metaphor constructions. The team also dialogued with the co-editors of the book to generate new knowledge and additional questions impelled from the artefacts Pauline created as responses to the book.

Situating mindfulness

Mindfulness is growing in popularity. Contemporary mindfulness, or what many in North America consider to be mindfulness, is often mindfulness-based stress reduction (MBSR) or some derivative of it. Mindfulness appears in diverse contexts, from clinical psychology to education, to business, to the military, and so on (Hyland, 2015; Paulson et al., 2013). It has worked its way into the mainstream, spread on magazine covers, purporting to improve life in a trope of calm, peaceful, centeredness, and being *at one with the universe.* As a strategy to increase attentional awareness and focus, mindfulness has the possibility to be a powerful catalyst to improve the human condition through various psychological and social avenues.

Jon Kabat-Zinn (2003), known for his work at the University of Massachusetts Medical School as the founder of MBSR, claims that mindfulness is a state of being aware and focused on the present moment, with complete acceptance and recognition of the experience without attachment to thoughts or emotions that would otherwise regulate the experience (also see Paulson, Davidson, Jha, and Kabat-Zinn, 2013).

Mindfulness, in its original conceptualization is derived from Buddhist ethics and philosophy (Kabat-Zinn, 2011; Khong, 2009; Marx, 2015; Orr, 2014; Thayer-Bacon, 2003), specifically The Eightfold Path, which is itself a part of Buddhist ontology as described by The Four Noble Truths (DeMoss, 2011; Khong, 2009). Mindfulness in the context of The Eightfold Path is formally referred to as 'right mindfulness' in its English translation, where the word 'right' refers to a quality of wholesomeness and wisdom, and the word "mindfulness" describes a myriad of qualities, including: reflexivity, thoughtfulness, sensitivity, empathy, and awareness. The Eightfold Path is divided into three categories, of which mindfulness falls into the category of concentration and meditation, denoting its connection to praxis.

Mindfulness provides a means of mediating interaction between the self and experience by disrupting automatic mental processes, and instead inserting a 'stop' (Applebaum, 1995; Fels, 2010) wherein the individual may observe and hold the experience in awareness non-judgmentally, thereby using all of the senses and cognitive awareness to experience the present moment as it is. Wiebe (2016) describes this Levisanian aporic moment wherein the researcher is at an irresolvable internal disjunction, face to face with a need to create a re-presentation of the encounter to establish an alternate prepositional position. Mindfulness, as such, has the possibility to be a powerful catalyst to enable researchers to suspend assumptions or to purposefully delay conclusions.

This process of cultivated awareness allows one to inhabit the relationship with self and others in a more open and accepting way (Paulson et al., 2013). To illustrate this acceptance, there is evidence to suggest that mindfulness has positive correlations to empathy, compassion, connectedness, and pro-social behaviour (Mabsout, 2015)—all of which are beneficial for education, teaching, and research. Therefore, it is suggested that mindfulness allows for the space (psychological, temporal, and physical) to allow for multiple ways of knowing and understanding through various modalities of experience (Khong, 2009), illustrated by the process undertaken by this research team.

The good and the bad

Kabat-Zinn's original motivation was to use mindfulness as a method to change patients' relationship to pain and stress in clinical contexts such as hospitals. Scientific study of the effects of mindfulness has demonstrated a large suite of positive benefits for personal well-being, including: "increased effective functioning including academic performance, concentration, perceptual sensitivity, reaction time, memory, self-control, empathy, and self-esteem" (Oman et al., 2008, p. 570). Given these benefits, the popularity of mindfulness has increased and a plethora of similar treatments have emerged. Some examples are: mindfulness-based cognitive therapy (MBCT), mindfulness-based relapse prevention (MBRP), mindfulness-based childbirth and parenting (MBClothesline Project), mindfulness-based eating awareness training (MB-EAT), and mindfulness-based elder care (MBEC) (Kabat-Zinn, 2011).

Due to the success of MBSR and its analogues, primarily in clinical contexts, there is a scientific leaning to the inquiry of mindfulness. The impetus pushing mindfulness from its original conception as *one component* in a *system* rooted in Buddhist ethics towards a prescriptive intervention for personal well-being can be attributed to the study of mindfulness from a North American perspective, demonstrably in neuropsychology and health sciences that have driven the entire field towards quantitative, positivist, and instrumental interpretations of mindfulness. The result is a privileging of quantitative research on mindfulness, perpetuating the primacy of Western positivism, effectively minimizing the holistic and embodied effects of mindfulness.

Applying mindfulness in curricula has demonstrated benefits of increasing academic performance and decreasing anti-social behaviour (Orr, 2014). As institutions and administrators fixate on these positive effects of mindfulness, the reason for implementing it in curricula becomes prescriptive and instrumental. As MBSR and similar programs are secularized, devoid of overt connection to Buddhism, there is no longer any ethical framework to ground mindfulness to remain connected to its foundational principles, namely the Buddhist precepts of non-harm, impermanence, undifferentiated compassion, interconnectedness, and working towards the cessation of suffering for all beings. "Such a colonization of mindfulness . . . has an instrumentalizing effect, reorienting the practice to the needs of the market, rather than to a critical reflection on the causes of our collective suffering" (Purser & Loy, 2013). Thus, we close this section on the Good and the Bad with wonderings about the intent of researchers' use of these practices.

Making scholarly research

For this book review, three silk and merino wool scares (Figure 2.3.1) were created by Sameshima as a mindful and contemplative research practice into the book themes. The central purpose of this inquiry process is not in the end product but, rather, the act of making which facilitates access to deeper and untapped ways of knowing and the transformation of the self in relation to the other. The making is much like a self-autonomous vehicle that transports the researcher to novel and new associations that arise from the immersion of the sub-consciousness into a process that frees the mind from the usual entrapments of ego and self-identity. The process of making for the other is a process of constructing relation and connection. Each scarf was gifted to a specific co-editor, as a form of reparative pedagogical research.

> *Reparative pedagogy is guided by perspectives of balance and offering. . . . [resting] on the belief that developing skills and knowledge bases are not enough and that transformational learning requires intentional dynamic development of imagination, creativity, flexibility, holistic thinking, interdisciplinary perspectives, and deep mindfulness.* (Sameshima & Slingerland, 2015: 9-10)

Figure 7.3.1. Nuno Felted Silk and Merino Wool Scarves. Artist: P. Sameshima, 2016.

When the maker (also named the 'creative,' used as a noun) is reparatively positioned, there is an expectation for rupture to occur (Sameshima & Slingerland, 2015). Sedgwick (1997) explains this outlook as, "*the position from which it is possible to turn to use one's own resources to assemble or 'repair'... the part-objects into something like a whole – though not, and may I emphasize this, not necessarily like any preexisting whole*" (p. 8). Reparative research is activism, *"a reparation to community"* (Sameshima & Slingerland, 2015, p. 21). In the making, the creative builds a relation with the receiver. Although constructed and uni-directional, it is through gifting and sustained time in making that fabricates a softened and loving relation with the other, changing the possibilities for new communal relationships.

Constructed Studio Spaces: Metaphoric Landscapes to Traverse

The conceptual model of *Parallaxic Praxis* offers a pragmatic working frame. The research model involves the analysis of data through play, assemblage, rebuilding, translations, and juxtaposition (Sameshima & Vandermause, 2008; see http://www.solspire.com/research-model.html). For example, researchers might translate text data (interview transcripts) into an artful modality (i.e., poetry, visual art, etc.) as a means to interrogate, play with, or dislodge automatic associations. These rendered, functional artefacts materially reveal, question, and convey researcher inquiries and interpretations in aesthetic forms. They are artworks imbued with meaning and created for the sake of provocation, intended to be used to induce dialogue and trouble assumptions. The renderings (created pieces) are then used to press dialogue forward and generate new thinking. The model incorporates a direct team analysis using a Catechization Process (questioning technique) to generate meaning from the renderings. To catechize, etymologically, is *to sound out*, to press knowledge forward through questioning. Catechizations are sets of questions used to determine knowledge, to question searchingly (Merriam-Webster, 2017).

To better understand the liminal studio space (Wiebe & Sameshima, 2018), we invite you into the metaphoric maker-space. Re-occuring foci that were threaded through the book were: self, place, relationship, play, falling, time, the ordinary, preparation/practice, humility, and offering. Sameshima used these building blocks to construct metaphoric 'stories' constructed landscapes for wandering through—an imagined ground that allowed traversing through the questions raised in her engagement with the book. The metaphoric story enables the investigator to 'enter' the rendering as if it were a landscape. A short divergence into the world of metaphors will help understand how metaphors work, as investigative landscapes, and thus how scarves can be used to review a book on contemplative educational research.

Living and dead metaphors: a brief overview

Metaphors can be sorted, grossly, through a paradigm of live versus dead. Our work engages primarily with live metaphors, an important distinction. A dead metaphor is one with which we no longer linger, no longer pause to consider its metaphoricity. Often these are the figures of speech that have become idiomatic and expected and so we rarely notice their metaphoric origins. For example, *ponytail*—presumably this metaphor was once nascent. At some point in the history of hairstyles, some human might have said to another something like, 'the back of your head looks like the backside of a pony.' And thus, a neologistic metaphor was born because it was apt and convenient. Certainly, more convenient than a literal alternative, than something like, "I like the way you've collected all the long strands of hair on your scalp and bound them close to their roots at the longitudinal centre and lower latitudinal hemisphere of your head so they flow outwards in a bundle splaying from its binding." Because the initial metaphor has been lexicalized, we rarely recall the association with a pony's backside and thus we declare the metaphor dead.

In cases such as the *ponytail,* it could be argued that the *time of death* coincides with lexicalization when those responsible for our dictionaries acknowledge the term in their collections. In other cases, it might be a matter of personal proximity—a matter of an individual declaring cliché. For instance, imagine a poem depicting a flower sprouting through a crack in a sidewalk, an image symbolizing the tenacity of life, for flourishing amidst arduous circumstance. If we have encountered the image before, we might recognize it as cliché. But this is not a lexicalized metaphor. So, although this metaphor is dead to us, it might be alive for some. This aspect of the death process, because it is determined by the proximity of cliché, is more explicitly a cultural than a lexicalized death and therefore we can never be entirely sure when these metaphors die. Many of these dying or dead metaphors can be resurrected through mindful play if we ponder them through new perspectives. Furthermore, if metaphor and thought are inseparable, as Zwicky (2008) and Frost (1972/1930) suspect, then our thought is likely swayed by living and dead metaphors in much the same way that our reality is shaped by time and historicity. As the *ponytail* example suggests, etymological attention, or looking back or below, might reveal an appellation's analogical origins.

Metaphors can be expressed in literature through structures and forms unavailable in other forms. Literature can hold sequential connected events like the story of *Jack and the Beanstalk*; whereas, in the following section, as the reader will see, a scarf with a vine could simply be a representation of foliage or much more if the reader knows it is Jack's beanstalk. Grossly, the structural differences are partly a product of genre and partly a product of approaches to truth. This knowledge reminds us that literature has structures which the non-literary has not, and therefore literature can express metaphor in ways the non-literary cannot; and it reminds us that metaphor and literature share an ability to invent—exactly what the creative wishes for.

Metaphor's ability to invent, or deceive, is particularly important. If the statement *A is B* is metaphoric, then the statement *A is B* must also be false. Yet, through that falsehood, metaphors can point to greater truths, to "wider natural laws" (Punter, 2007, p. 35). McKay (2001) expounds this idea by examining some striking parallels between metaphor and trickster figures from Indigenous myths; consequently, he likens metaphor to the trickster of a language system. Literature, with its possible fictive ability, is comparably tricky and honestly dishonest. Frye (1968), for example, considers literature a specialized form of language, defined and empowered by its ability to lie:

> *The apparently unique privilege of ignoring facts has given the poet his traditional reputation as a licensed liar, and explains why so many words denoting literary structure, "fable," "fiction," "myth," and the like, have a secondary sense of untruth, like the Norwegian word digter which is said to mean liar as well as poet. But, as Sir Philip Sydney remarked, "the poet never affirmeth," and therefore does not lie any more than he tells the truth.* (pp. 75-76)

Although the discursive divide between literary and non-literary metaphor might seem self-evident, it does have some use, even if that use is limited to two reminders: that metaphor can be expressed in ways which partly depend on genre conventions; and that metaphor, like literature, lies.

> *To paraphrase Heidegger, when we set out "to reveal the real," if we were to change "our mode of ordering," the real reveals itself to us (Heidegger, 1977, p. 20). The openness to revelation is simply the acknowledgment that there are possibilities that exist beyond our current frameworks. Such acknowledgment is the basis of research, that there is knowledge yet to be discovered, that we do not and cannot yet completely and fully understand. We add too, that this aporic view leaves all revelations, findings, and knowings ongoingly incomplete.* (Wiebe & Sameshima, 2018, p. 11)

Just as an aporia (an irresolvable disjunction) requires alternate route-taking, the metaphors require flexibility of mind. In returning to the ponytail, Frost (1972) encourages us to treat metaphors like horses, a matter of appreciating their grace and swiftness while respecting their limits in terms of reach and terrain. In other words, as the metaphoric storied landscapes are constructed in the scarves, we acknowledge that metaphors can take us to new perspectives, but those vantages might preclude or eclipse other perspectives; like horses, they can take us to some places but never all places.

Constructing the metaphoric landscape

The above considerations informed the creative process in important ways. The making of three silk and wool nuno felted scarves in response to the book represents a process-oriented contemplative practice that supported Sameshima in better understanding the themes in the book. In this form of contemplative data analysis, metaphor is prominent. This example attempts to illustrate the Buddhist concept of dependent origination, or *Pratītyasamutpāda* in Sanskrit, which describes the way in which all life, beings, and existence, are interdependent. The metaphoric landscape is a constructed space the creative generates through stories. For example, in the first artefact, the space of investigation takes place within a fairytale. The creative compares the character's actions to the actions of a researcher using a contemplative research method. Within the fairytale landscape, the creative traverses the juxtapositions or structural aporias encountered in the constructed landscape to generate questions, the basis of knowledge production in this research methodology. While this is a co-created project, the following section is written from Sameshima's perspective, based on her journals during the making process. In this article, the focus is predominantly on the first scarf titled "Jack," to demonstrate the use of metaphor.

Figure 7.3.2. Artefact 1: Jack's Singularity. Artist: P. Sameshima, 2016.

'*Jack*' (Figures 7.3.2 & 7.3.3) is the scarf gifted to the book co-editor, Susan Walsh. It is a representation of the beanstalk in the popular children's story *Jack and the Beanstalk* (Jacobs, 1890). In the story, Jack has been told to sell the family cow. Instead of returning with coins, he returns with magic bean seeds. His frustrated mother throws them out the window and the next morning, a large beanstalk appears reaching into the clouds. Jack begins his ascent of the beanstalk to another world.

Contemplative Practice as Challenging Tradition. My initial interest in the beanstalk was my wonderings about Jack's mindset. Why did Jack buy the beans? Is he enchanted by the imaginary? Is he taken by the promise of the beans and is seeking a story that is other than the economic-based story-line? Is he seeking something other than? Like his mother, many researchers may think Jack's beans are a waste of money and time. In terms of value and time, is contemplative inquiry possible in academia? How has the value of time been influenced by its worth economically? What motivates researchers to become involved in contemplative methodologies that take more time and are perceived of as less valuable?

What is Jack thinking as he climbs? Is he weighed by his mother's disappointment and is seeking to get the most out of a bad situation? Or is he simply climbing because the stalk is there? As Jack climbs, hand over hand, foot over foot—a slow, methodical, meditative motion seeking steady holds, he finds presence, being in the moment. Similar to how one might walk carefully on a steep hike on loose shale, climbing the beanstalk would require being in the moment. How might routines and methods for growing a contemplative practice support this methodology? This is a methodology that requires dedication to process, a commitment to intention. The commitment and risks are high. If the stalk were small, it would not reach the sky or support Jack's weight. Undertaking the climb is significant.

Ontological and Epistemological Views. Jack notices the vistas from above. He sees Gadamer's (1975/2004) horizon anew. Is he afraid, brave, courageous, daring, or foolish? What is he expecting? What lies beyond the cloud cover? Is there an end and what will the end yield? What happens when he reaches his goal? In addition to a Foucauldian (1969) perspective of surveying the landscape from the beanstalk, does Jack metaphysically embody a somatic disposition to experiencing? In other words, epistemologically, is he able to justify the truth of the beanstalk through his bodily experience of it, through his "living body (soma) as a site of sensory-aesthetic appreciation (aesthesis) and creative self-fashioning" (Shusterman, 2008, p. 1)?

Figure 7.3.3. Jack's Palimpsest. P. Sameshima, 2016.

Integration of Routine. The beanstalk vine is created on both sides of the scarf to recall Jack's multiple travels. He traverses up and down the beanstalk, each time bringing back something from the other world until he finally returns with the means to sustain that which he was searching for (the golden egg-laying hen). How does one create sustained contemplative practices when these are based on mindful practices of presence in the moment?

The beadings represent the touchstone jewels (or treasures he takes home) of learning along the way—some so significant that they pierce through to the other side of the scarf as experiences are integrated and learned, becoming a part of the permanent, albeit, constructed landscape. The translucent palimpsest of the stalk showing through from the other side of the scarf offers climbing scaffolds based on previous experience—with time and intention, integrative practices can become routine.

Journeying. The purple striping points to the color of the crown chakra, the seventh stage at the top of the chakra ladder. In Eastern thought, there are seven spiritual energy sites on the body (Ferretti, 2014). The crown chakra is grounded in the earth and reaches upward in connection to the universe. The chakra is considered an energy node of pure consciousness where there is neither object nor subject. My intent for using the purple ladder is to demonstrate the condensing of levels, or shortening of the journey of climbing when the aligning energies and intentions are created. The sole flower attached to this scarf represents the individuality, ownership, and independent process of the journey.

Figure 7.3.4. Artefact 2: Intention. P. Sameshima, 2016.

Intention (Figure 7.3.4) is the scarf gifted to co-editor, Barbara Bickel. Nuno felting was a fibre technique first developed in New South Wales, Australia, around 1992 (Ziek, 2004). The technique bonds loose wool fibre onto silk gauze. The word *nuno* means cloth in Japanese. In the physical making process, to integrate the fibres of silk and wool, aggressive agitation must occur.

Figure 7.3.5. Bubble Solar Wrap. P. Sameshima, 2016.

To integrate the wool with the silk, the design is abraded with a wooden tool while the silk sits on an uneven surface (swimming pool cover similar to bubble wrap; see Figure 7.3.5). I use an alkaline, soapy solution to help open up the silk weave to allow for the wool fibres to inset themselves. To enable the insetting, I rub the wool fibres into the silk with a wooden tool. I then apply pressure through rolling within the solar pool cover nub material 100 times, then hitting and banging the rolled scarf 100 times, and finally throwing the scarf 100 times onto a solid surface. This process is completed for each layer of colour and pattern separately, for each side of the scarf. The physicality of the integrative processing is a reminder of how change requires distress, strain, and stretching.

As the wool shrinks during the process of agitation, the silk is drawn in, creating the wrinkled effect. My use of the 100 rolls and 100 throws for each layer of integration is considered standard practice in nuno felting. For me, the number 100 is a reference to 100%—a fullness in effort and authentic intention. While working with this green scarf (see Figure 7.3.4), I explored the layered tensions in the miasma of freedom, wildness, and discovery within meditative contemplative studies. Variations of green wool were placed organically on the silk without any structured patterns. As a gardener, I am also very aware of the disciplined cultivation of nurturing a garden through weeding, care, and vigilant discipline. The practice of contemplative work may seem loose and unstructured to some but involves intense dedication.

Figures 7.3.6 – 7.3.7. Artefact 3: Journey - Scarf for Carl Leggo.
Artist: P. Sameshima, 2016.

"*Journey*" (Figures 7.3.6 & 7.3.7) is the scarf gifted to co-editor Carl Leggo. This scarf is much thicker than the other two scarves in this series. The multi-layers were added individually with abrading and rolling over each layer on each side to create a topographic effect. The variation in relief also creates a difference in the way the silk is gathered between the merino wool. The depressions and elevations represent relative highs and lows in a journey, a mimetic exaggeration of journeying in the present. It is only in looking back, in overview, when one might conflate or name a time as particularly smooth or difficult. In the heightened moment of the present, every noticeable high and low is exaggerated.

In this scarf, I stitched "walking lines," imagining the way we seek to break from following pre-constructed paths but always returning to the path. The attempt to break from the familiar requires mindfulness, attention, and intention. In the following section, the Catechization Process, or the analytic questioning process that directed the dialogue between the researchers and participants is explained. Further details of this research process are offered in Chapter 7.4 (Wiebe and Sameshima, this issue).

Catechizations in the Parallaxic Praxis Model

In addition to exploration with making, the team engaged with the co-editors of the book to bring forth collective interpretations of each other's processes. In co-creating and co-discovering, the process of sharing has an element of reciprocation in that we are giving back to the co-editors a response to what they have given to us through the book. A focus group interview was conducted using the rendered makings (scarves) as conversation prompts to allow the opportunity for additional understanding and reciprocation to occur and to keep avenues open to the full experiencing of the process.

As a means of inquiry, a mindful and artful method to investigate pedagogical and curricular questions involves an engagement that is at its root a relationship or conversation with self and with others. Using mindfulness and art as foundational pillars, we invited multiple perspectives and voices, and ways of gaining access to information and knowing, in which we envisioned the possibilities in addressing our relationships with our research, ourselves, our colleagues, and our students. To fully absorb and practice this way of research and teaching, it is necessary to acknowledge the way we can embody our work and communicate with one another. In a dialogue with the co-editors of the book, we sought to explicate the nuances of inviting mindfulness and art into the process of conducting research. We framed our review with the overarching questions: 'What does contemplative and arts-based research look like?' and 'What processes are involved in contemplative and arts-based research?'

Significant discussions about contemplative arts-based research arose from the dialogue session with the co-editors when using the scarves as provocateurs. In the Parallaxic Praxis model, the analysis of artworks involves discussion structured by the Catechization Process (Maarhuis, Sameshima & Chalykoff, 2014; Sameshima & Maarhuis, 2013). As briefly described previously, this process uses questions to move ideas forward, spark new thinkings in the moment of discussion, and generate discussion and knowledge production. Initial questions are generated from the Catechization terms:

> *Mimesis*: In looking at the scarves, how are ideas or authors' works in your book re-created or mirrored? In what ways are the artefacts mirrors of your thinkings? What do you see in the scarves that echo themes in the book?

> *Poesis*: How do you, as teachers, researchers, learners, and creatives respond to these artefacts now, in this moment? What do you take from the work that was created? What do you notice about the artefacts?

What has changed in speaking together about the scarves compared to individual experiences in thinking about your own scarf?

Palimpsest: Consider how both the participant and the researcher can be present at once. How or when were you present as an editor with the authors? What traces are coming through from the artefacts in your lives as teachers, researchers, learners and creatives? What are the layers underneath that are more complex beyond the surface of what has been made? How does the material speak to you? In what way does your artefact echo or trace the work in the book?

Intertextuality: How do the artefacts or chapters work in combination with one another? What commonalities do they have?

Antiphona: Now that we know the commonalities, how do they work together to teach you something new? What did you learn from these commonalities? In what ways do the materials, the model, or the discussions teach?

Sorites: How do you frame or value particular aspects of the phenomenon we are studying? What themes appear to be significant? Why? What specific quotes or ideas from the book do you see expressed in the artefacts?

Aporia: What puzzles you, or challenges you when thinking about the artefacts created? How do the artefacts play with or against one another? (For more information on the Catechization process, please see Stock, Sameshima & Slingerland, 2016).

Select Learnings from the Interview Dialogue

The parallaxic praxis model is generative because of the acute personalization that is possible through the catechization process. The translative analysis is based solely on the skills and capacities of the research team and the catechization process has the most meaning to the group involved. The following are select, culled sharings.

Holistic Integration of Research and Researcher, Research and World. *Even with mindful attention to my (Sameshima) body alignment to the height of the table and the mechanics of my motions, I knew I would feel the making in my body in following days. The physical exertion and embodied nature of the making, particularly through the repetitive 100* *throws and rolls for each layer, leaves trace in the body, a proprioceptive knowing that becomes memory, the building blocks of future meaning making. These traces, a layered palimpsest of autobiography become part of me. My insertion into the fibres of the co-editors' lives become me. Barbara Bickel likens the "friction that creates that interconnection [as]... a tactile, bodied" merging of researcher and research. Correspondingly, Susan Walsh (co-editor) expresses the synergy, synchronicity, and serendipitous evolution of the book and Carl Leggo describes the "intersections among diverse kinds of projects" and layering, the continuation of the integrative expansion of knowledge production as mimetic yet morphing echo. This work researches in ways that are antithetical to current dominant narratives that signal the neoliberal encroachment on higher education; and represents understandings of dependent origination, the Buddhist concept that posits the interconnectedness of everyone and everything, nothing exists in isolation, and that in research contexts, all ideas are co-generated because of the inherent holistic, embodied, and relational ways in which knowledge is produced.*

Risk. Susan Walsh continues the discussion on risk—*her resonations on Jack's climbing. She explains that for her, risk took place on two levels: "the kind of work (i.e. bringing the contemplative and arts-based together in the research context) [and] integrating this aspect of [her] personal journey with [her] professional work." Additionally, Walsh points out that the commodification of spiritual practices (like mindfulness) is problematic, but that if you push past the superficial and commit to the practice, it has tremendous potential. As researchers, we are reminded of how closely the personal is impacted in the research choices we make—"that is part of the ongoing process of becoming that we are engaged in, in creative work, in scholarly work, and in our own lives." Carl Leggo continues, likening a catechizing term palimpsest to a form of becoming. The layers of the past inform who we have become; the traces remain as evidence of development and change, a haunting, honoring presence.*

Organic Nature of Contemplative Work. The co-editors talk about their work as organic, how the *"art is part of the organic processes that we have engaged in. . . . this process is organic. That's it, that's where I'm drawn, that's where I've been trying to get to. . . This whole project, book . . . it is living and continues to live" (Carl Leggo).* The colours of the scarves remind the co-editors of the "connection to the world." Barbara Bickel, in looking at the three scarves together suggests that they remind her of layerings and cartographic mappings that give a sense of embeddedness and anchoring.

Historicity. Carl, in thinking about the catechization word "sorites" shares: *I think the significance of the book lies in something that emerges when a reader interacts with the text . . . the text is not complete . . . you can't read our text and believe that this is the definitive word on anything. What this text is, again like the scarves, it is a particular composition, created in a particular historical time. . . . The longevity [is] beautifully stunning. So the book emerged out of something beautiful . . . .and I don't mean beautiful in just a traditional sense ... like a fire ... like a light ... hard hopes ... and it's offered in those ways and then we hope, trust that readers, viewers, seekers, spiritual seekers will come and be moved by parts of the book, by what's not in the book . . . sit with the book like sitting at a fire . . . I want them to sit with it like a fire . . . I was camping this summer and sitting around the campfire for four nights with two granddaughters and their parents and just being together, just enjoying the fire, the shapes, the colours, the music of the fire, but also realizing that thousands and tens of thousands of years ago, people were sitting around fires.*

Closing with opening questions

Examining the book *Arts-Based and Contemplative Practices in Research and Teaching,* we present the idea that arts-based and contemplative perspectives and approaches to research and teaching require that which is seemingly in short supply in industrialized, modern cultures: time, attention, and connection. Arts-based and contemplative practices may provide pathways to new and more inclusive ways of knowing that add to our collective knowledge. And yet, despite its contributions, arts-based and contemplative practices frequently encounter resistance and friction, especially when pushed up against the established order of academia. Viewed as non-traditional and lacking in empirical (read: positivist and post-positivist) qualities, arts-based and contemplative practices suffer the stigma of not being 'real' research. Nevertheless, the collective voice of researchers and academics who employ arts-based and contemplative practice grows, and perhaps offers a glimpse of a gradual change to the research (and in this case, educational) landscape that has been labelled a "contemplative turn in education" (Ergas & Todd, 2016).

The Parallaxic Praxis model is a cyclical process. The constructed renderings are intended to derive new investigative directions. As a closing, we draw from our discussion with the co-editors and the questions that arose from the scarf makings:

- As academics, how do we do this kind of practice with regards to time?
- What are the constraints of doing this type of research?
- How do the values of contemplative research align with the values of academia?
- How are contemplative practices, when intentionally not tied to any Eastern root, situated in relation to morality?
- How is morality a driving force behind Western conceptions and interest in Eastern wisdom traditions?
- Can research be gifting?
- How might art for economic growth impact the value of art?
- Do we need social innovation on new ways to experience art?
- What is the value of art? Are economic translations too fixed to capture the inestimable?
- Can we theorize the value of art in non-economic ways?

This paper presents the argument for the greater inclusion of contemplative and arts integrated research in the academy through an examination of metaphors and making. Mindfulness presents the opportunity for teachers/researchers to give value to the possibilities that time, attention, and connection, through making processes, can enrich the traversal process towards greater understanding. Contemplative making and arts-based contemplative practices demonstrated by the editors and authors in this book are born out of a divergence from the traditional research path. Contemplative practices seek out the generation of possibility, the creation of the not yet.

Like Guiney Yallop (2016), we point to William Pinar's foreword in the book asking "How shall I live?" (xviii). Contemplative arts-based research can provide valuable insight into educational philosophy and curriculum implementation. The addition of reparative making further contributes to relational community building. We believe reparative gifting "makes" love and hope for the world (Sameshima, Wiebe & Hayes, in press).

References

Barbezat, D. P., & Bush, M. (2013). *Contemplative practices in higher education: Powerful methods to transform teaching and learning.* San Francisco, CA: Jossey-Bass.

Binder, M. (2016). Review. *Arts-Based and Contemplative Practices in Research and Teaching: Honouring Presence.* International Journal of Education through Art, 12(2), Volume 12 doi: 10.1386/eta.12.2.227_5

Bush, M. (2011). Mindfulness in higher education. *Contemporary Buddhism, 12*(01), 183-197.

Davidson, R. J., & Kaszniak, A. W. (2015). Conceptual and methodological issues in research on mindfulness and meditation. *American Psychologist, 70*(7), 581-592.

DeMoss, D. (2011). Empty and extended craving: An application of the extended mind thesis to the four noble truths. *Contemporary Buddhism, 12*(2), 309-325.

Ergas, O., & Todd, S. (2016). *Philosophy East/West: Exploring intersections between educational and contemplative practices.* Hoboken, NJ: Wiley-Blackwell.

Ericson, T., Kjønstad, B. G., & Barstad, A. (2014). Mindfulness and sustainability. *Ecological Economics,* 104, 73-79.

Fels, L. (2010). Coming into presence: The unfolding of a moment. *Journal of Educational Controversy, 5*(10). Available at: http://cedar.wwu.edu/jec/vol5/iss1/8

Ferretti, A. (2014, June 30). A beginner's guide to the Chakras. *Yoga Journal.* Retrieved from http://www.yogajournal.com/article/chakras-yoga-for-beginners/beginners-guide-chakras/

Foucault, M. (1969). *The archeology of knowledge and the discourse on language.* (A. M. S. Smith, Trans. New York, NY: Pantheon Books.

Frost, R. (1972/1930). Education by poetry. In E. Lathem & L. Thompson (Eds.). *Robert Frost: poetry and prose.* (pp. 329-340). New York, NY: Holt, Rinehart & Winston.

Frye, N. (1968). *The educated imagination.* Toronto, ON: Anansi.

Gadamer, H. G. (1975/2004). *Truth and method.* (D. Marshall & J. Weinsheimer, Trans.). (2nd revised ed.). New York, NY: Continuum. (Original work published 1960)

Guiney Yallop, J. (2016). A book review of Arts-based and contemplative practices in research and teaching: Honoring presence. *Art/Research International, 1*(1), 283-291.

Hyland, T. (2015). The commodification of spirituality: Education, mindfulness and the marketisation of the present moment. *Prospero, 21*(2). 11-17.

Jacobs, J. (1890). Jack and the Beanstalk. *English fairy tales* (pp. 59-67). London, UK: David Nutt.

Kabat-Zinn, J. (2003). Mindfulness-based interventions in context: past, present, and future. *Clinical Psychology: Science and Practice, 10*(2), 144-156.

Kabat-Zinn, J. (2011). Some reflections on the origins of MBSR, skillful means, and the trouble with maps. *Contemporary Buddhism, 12*(1). 281-306.

Khong, B. S. L. (2009). Expanding the understanding of mindfulness: Seeing the tree and the forest. *The Humanistic Psychologist, 37*(2), 117-136.

Macintyre Latta, M. (2015). Book review. Arts-based and contemplative practices in research and teaching: Honoring presence. *Canadian Journal of Education, 38*(3), 1-3.

McKay, D. (2001). *Vis à vis: Field notes on poetry and wilderness.* Kentville, NS: Gaspereau Press.

Marx, R. (2015). Accessibility versus integrity in secular mindfulness: A Buddhist commentary. *Mindfulness, 6*(5), 1153-1160.

Merriam-Webster. (2017). Catechize. Available from https://www.merriam-webster.com/dictionary/catechize

Oman, D., Shapiro, S. L., Thoresen, C. E., Plante, T. G., & Flinders, T. (2008). Meditation lowers stress and supports forgiveness among college students: A randomized controlled trial. *Journal of American College Health, 56*(5), 569-578.

Orr, D. (2014). In a mindful moral voice: Mindful compassion, the ethic of care and education. *Philosophical Inquiry in Education, 21*(2), 42-54.

Paulson, S., Davidson, R., Jha, A., & Kabat-Zinn, J. (2013). Becoming conscious: The science of mindfulness. *Annals of the New York Academy of Sciences, 1303*(1), 87-104.

Punter, D. (2007). *Metaphor.* New York, NY: Routledge.

Purser, R., & Loy, D. (2013, July 1). Beyond McMindfulness. *Huffington Post.* Retrieved from: http://www.huffingtonpost.com/ron-purser/beyond-mcmindfulness_b_3519289.html

Sedgwick, E. (1997). Paranoid reading and reparative reading; Or, you're so paranoid, you probably think this introduction is about you. In E. Sedgwick (Ed.), *Navel gazing: Queer readings in fiction* (pp. 1-40). Durham and London: Duke University Press.

Shapiro, S., Brown, K. W., & Astin, J. A. (2008, October). *Toward the integration of meditation into higher education: A review of research.* Northampton, MA: Contemplative Mind in Society. Retrieved from http://prsinstitute.org/downloads/related/spiritual-sciences/meditation/TowardtheIntegrationofMeditationintoHigherEducation.pdf

Shusterman, R. (2008). Body consciousness: A philosophy of mindfulness and somaesthetics. New York, NY: Cambridge University Press.

Thayer-Bacon, B. J. (2003). Buddhism as an example of a holistic, relational epistemology. *Encounter: Education for Meaning and Social Justice, 16*(3), 27-38.

Wiebe, S. (2016). Rock 'em sock 'em poetry. In M. McLarnon et al. (Authors), The school bus symposium: A poetic journey of co-created conference space. Art Research International: A transdisciplinary Journal, 1(1), 141-173.

Wiebe, S., & Sameshima, P. (2018, February). Sympathizing with social justice, poetry of invitation and generation. Art/Research International, 3(1)7-29. Walsh, S., Bickel, B., & Leggo, C. (2014). Arts-based contemplative practices in research and teaching: Honoring presence. New York, NY: Routledge.

Walsh, S., & Bai, H. (2014). Writing witness conscious. In S. Walsh, B. Bickel, and C. Leggo (Eds.), Arts-based contemplative practices in research and teaching: Honoring presence. (p. 24). New York, NY: Routledge.

Ziek, B. (2004). The felt frontier: I: Polly Stirling: Contemporary feltmaker. Surface Design Journal, 28(4), 35-38

Zwicky, J. (2008). *Wisdom and metaphor.* Kentville, NS: Gaspereau Press.

Example 7.4: Generating Self

Catechizations in Poetry[3]

By Sean Wiebe & Pauline Sameshima

Abstract

In this paper, the authors illustrate how creatives might use a specific aspect of Sameshima's Parallaxic Praxis Model, the Catechization Process. They outline the procedural steps and possibilities of *catechization*, a process Sameshima has co-developed to advance meaning and creativity generation in research. The process benefits creatives in multiple fields and can be applied wherever investigations take place through arts-making. In this explication, the authors share seven response poems created in the *Catechization Process* to theorize the imaginative space of producing knowledge through research. When researchers can imagine themselves as creatives and experiment with more strategies for generating new ideas, their work will open novel possibilities for understanding.

Keywords

poetic inquiry; parallaxic praxis; catechization process; arts integrated research; creativity propulsion

Catechizations in Poetry

With a foundational position that creativity can be learned, Sternberg, Kaufman, and Pretz (2001; 2002; 2003) have synthesized a vast literature on creativity and developed eight creativity propulsion strategies. Creativity propulsion recognizes that some activities are high yield and therefore worth engaging in. In considering creativity pedagogy, Sternberg et al. start with generating a creative outlook, and the technique they advance for this is *Conceptual Replication*, which means repetition with a variation. An example might be students rewriting parts of the lyrics to a song. The other propulsion strategies include: *Redefinition*—overlaying an idea in a different context; *Forward Incrementation*—developing the next step in a sequence; *Advance*

---

[3] Reprint: Wiebe, S., & Sameshima, P. (2017, Dec.). Generating self: Catechizations in poetry. *Revista VIS, 16*(2).140-155.

Forward Incrementation—making a significant leap in a forward direction; *Redirection*—redirecting the field to a new way of thinking; *Regressive Redirection*—uptaking a discarded idea; *Reinitiation*—starting the field again; and *Synthesis*—collating divergent ideas.

Similar to Sternberg et al.'s, (2002) creativity propulsion theories is Sameshima's *Parallaxic Praxis Model* (Sameshima & Vandermause, 2008), which provides consistent language for understanding how creatives work and advance knowledge. *The Parallaxic Praxis Model* enables interdisciplinary teams to frame their arts-integrated research methods and better articulate their creative processes of making. The *Parallaxic Praxis Model* was first developed in a methamphetamine addiction study by an interdisciplinary team of researchers at Washington State University in 2007 (Sameshima, Vandermause, Chalmers, & Gabriel, 2009). The model has since been used in various disciplines and for a range of research projects. For example: HIV research (Defechereux, 2017), violence against women (Maarhuis, 2016), Aboriginal mental health care (Saunders 2015); learner-centred pedagogy (Ingalls Vanada, 2017); cervical cancer screening (Sameshima et al., 2017); dementia studies (Wiersma et al., 2015); identity studies (Stock et al., 2016), and technology (Marino et al., 2008). The model is research/researcher centered, leveraging the researchers' personal strengths and talents.

Bringing together the languages, purposes, and philosophical underpinning of the *Parallaxic Praxis Model* and *Creativity Propulsion Theories*, in this paper, the authors used the propulsion theories of *Redefinition, Forward Incrementation, Advance Forward Incrementation, and Redirection* to define the processes within the model. By employing these propulsion theories, they achieved a more robust understanding of the Parallaxic Praxis Model (Sameshima & Vandermause, 2008) and specifically how the Catechization Process (Maarhuis, Sameshima, Chalykoff, 2014; Sameshima & Maarhuis, 2013) within the model might be used in research contexts where the data to be analyzed are multiple, varied, fragmented, and rendered via disparate creative traditions and discourses.

This research project began when Sameshima created a nuno wet felted scarf for Wiebe as part of a reparative research investigation (Sameshima & Slingerland, 2015). The scarf-making project grew from Sameshima's collaborative-poetry writing investigation with Wiebe and another poet, John Guiney Yallop (Sameshima, in review). She created a scarf for each poet in preparation for co-writing with each of them. Through making, she sought to better understand her conceptions of their poetic voices and styles. Then, using the scarf as a prompt, Wiebe was asked to consider the seven catechization categories: Mimesis, Poiesis, Palimpsest, Intertextuality, Antiphona, Sorites, and Aporia (definitions provided below).

Figure 7.4.1. Nuno Scarf 1. P. Sameshima, 2016.

Thinking through how creativity propulsion and parallaxic practice inform one another, first, in the making of the scarf, Sameshima redefined the data, the scarf being a material creation of them, as such her making/investigation of data can be understood as a *Redefinition* creativity propulsion strategy. Second, Sameshima and Wiebe then used the *Forward Incrementation* propulsion strategy—which involves inventing, altering, and/ or employing a new step in a sequence. In this case, Sameshima's Catechization Process (Maarhuis, Sameshima, & Chalykoff, 2014; Sameshima & Maarhuis, 2013) served as the next step in the sequence, and Wiebe's response poetry is the rendering that resulted from that step. As a new rendering of the data and an illustration of the Catechization Process, Sameshima and Wiebe see both the *Redirection* propulsion strategy and the *Advance Forward Incrementation* propulsion strategy at work; in redirection the field is oriented to a new way of thinking (changing modalities from textile to poetry); and in *Advance Forward Incrementation* there is a significant leap forward in theorizing, positioning, and pedagogy. This progression can be seen as:

Our Process	**Creativity Propulsion Strategy**
Scarf making (redefine data from thought to textile)	Redefinition Strategy
Catechization Questioning (inventing/altering)	Forward Incrementation
Poem making (textile to poetry/theorizing)	Redirection & Advance Forward Incrementation

For those who analyze multimodal or non-text based work, the guided dialogue of the Catechization Process enables participants and researchers to trouble their ontological suppositions and rethink the genesis of their findings; in traditional qualitative work, for example, there is a looking back orientation, while in post-qualitative work researchers look forward to the not yet. The philosophical differences of these contrasting ways of seeing are vast, so orienting research one way or the other is never easy. Located in the post-qualitative paradigm, Wiebe and Sameshima's research is illustrative of a not-yet orientation. Because there are few examples that describe exactly how not-yet data analysis is done, the detailed account that follows will help those who employ art-making in their research better articulate and justify their methodologies.

To that end, in the *Parallaxic Praxis Model*, procedurally, the researchers transmediate data (interview transcripts, journal entries, numerical data, etc.) into artworks (material artefacts, poems, stories, etc.) as a way to trouble conventional ways of coding and to include alternate semantic fields to frame the data. These renderings are then used to provoke discussions and new ideas through a guided questioning analysis technique called the *Catechization Process*. This paper presents the Catechization response of the participant (Wiebe) after the researcher (Sameshima) created a nuno wet felted scarf for him as part of a reparative research investigation. The use of reparative research (returning created artefacts to the data contributors) and the act of making as theorizing mediator is part of the Parallaxic Praxis model. The scarf-making process was used to investigate the building-blocks of Weibe's poetry, his humour, playfulness, word play, and joy that evidenced itself through his collections. Sameshima also used the scarf-making to query her perceptions of his navigation between the private and public, concealment and revelation, surrender and acceptance, nostalgia and wanderlust, and other wanderings from reading his poetry.

As previously introduced, in the Parallaxic Praxis model, artworks (artefacts) are made as translations of the original data as a means to reveal, convey, or inform researcher investigations. The Catechization Process is an analysis process whereby researchers use the artworks (transmediated data) as prompts in dialogic situations to generate new knowledge. To catechize is "to question or examine closely or methodically; to teach or examine by means of questions and answers; to put questions to (someone)" (Farlex Dictionary, 2017). Understood in terms of Sternberg et al.'s, (2002) creativity propulsion theories, the making of the scarf or material creation of the investigation of data is a *Redefinition* creativity propulsion strategy. This is followed by the *Forward Incrementation* propulsion strategy—taking the next step in the sequence (beginning the Catechization Process), the *Redirection* propulsion strategy—redirecting the field to a new way of thinking (changing modalities from textile to poetry), and *Advance Forward Incrementation* propulsion strategy—to take a significant leap forward. Using the scarf as a prompt, Wiebe wrote poetry that was constrained by and elicited from the catechization categories: Mimesis, Poiesis, Palimpsest, Intertextuality, Antiphona, Sorites, and Aporia. The poems below are what he has written in response to the scarf; he also used the catechization categories as nucleate pivots to illustrate how these categories are a means of creativity propulsion.

Mimesis

In looking at the scarf, in what ways does the scarf echo or mirror your thinking?

Originally a Greek word, it has been used in aesthetic or artistic theory to refer to the attempt to imitate or reproduce reality since Plato and Aristotle. "Mimesis" is derived from the Greek verb mimeisthai, which means "to imitate" and which itself comes from mimos, meaning 'mime.' The English word mime also descends from 'mimos' as do 'mimic' and 'mimicry.' (Merriam-Webster, 2017)

That's a Great Scarf. Thank you.

Yes, I have a shelf in my closet
for scarves, and this one refuses
to settle there, invisible with the others,
laid out in a schedule to match
my suits of various winter shades: black,
charcoal, obsidian, sable,
and a navy, that, I admit, is basically black.
The way this one curves under
my jacket collar is wild and unexpected.

I have walked office towers at night,
carrying the allegorical stones in my briefcase
whilst I search hallways for more impressive
doors to glue my name and title to,
mostly failing to get a wider window
designed specially for the view.
Can you see me there, leveraging my knee
into a crevice of another promotion,
daring to tenure myself? This one

wants to go out into the world,
stretching its merino wool along my neck,
floating in a light gesture, an arc flush on skin,
settling warm, untroubled, nuzzled under my chin
and close to mind, crowds out thoughts
other than itself, released after months
of incubation, as if, wrapped around me,
what was once utterly invisible
becomes a shower of meteors,

flashes of light seeds of other stars
within them. Maybe, I even realize
it would be okay to take the elevator down.
Waving good luck to those who notice
subtle changes in my wardrobe.

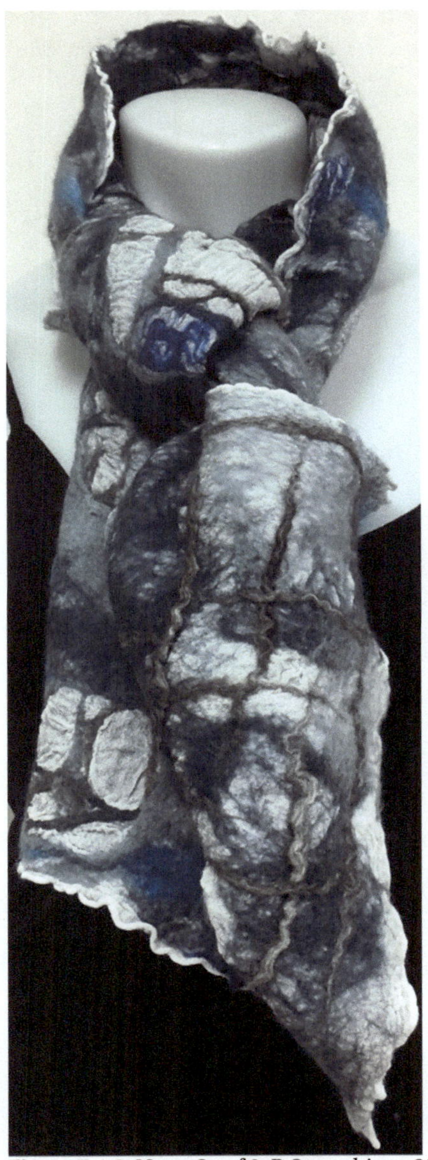

Figure 7.4.2. Nuno Scarf 2. P. Sameshima, 2016.

Poiesis

What do you notice about the scarf at this moment?

Poïesis (Ancient Greek: ποίησις) is etymologically derived from the ancient Greek term Ποιέω, which means "to make". This word, the root of our modern 'poetry,' was first a verb, an action that transforms and continues the world. . . Heidegger refers to it as a 'bringing-forth' (phusis as emergence), using this term in its widest sense. He explained poiesis as the blooming of the blossom. (Wikipedia, 2017)

Is Faith

Is faith a door
or window, both
can be open, closed,
go fuzzy
with old growth
new spores
of moss, morning
promises broken
open in rain.

On the back
of my bathroom door
are two pegs,
what is the other
one for? Through
the kitchen window
two squirrels chase
each other along
the neighbour's eaves.

Maybe faith is
the hinge that squeaks
in the middle
of the night
while I'm trying
to sleep?

Palimpsest

In terms of your life as a teacher, researcher, creative, what traces come through the scarf for you? What are the under layers?

A parchment or the like from which writing has been partially or completely erased to make room for another text (Dictionary.com, 2017). Writing material (as a parchment or tablet) used one or more times after earlier writing has been erased; something having usually diverse layers or aspects apparent beneath the surface. (Merriam-Webster, 2017)

The New Door

The old douglas held,
among the fir trees, leaning

not yet broken, last night's
spring storm exceeding

Environment Canada's warning,
to find a shelter,

maybe even go to church,
if it had a good supply

of candles, cans,
and answered prayers.

In little more than an hour
everything lasting wasn't

the horizon miles and miles
of fallen. As he walked

the lost greeted him,
among them, the douglas fir,

even now offering its trunk
for the new door.

Intertextuality

How does the scarf work in combination with your ideas to generate a new text?

The complex interrelationship between a text and other texts taken as basic to the creation or interpretation of the text (Merriam-Webster, 2017). *The interrelationship between texts especially works of literature; the way that similar or related texts influence, reflect, or differ from each other: the intertextuality between two novels with the same setting. (Dictionary.com, 2017)*

Trapping Air

I make the same mistake
curving this scarf around my neck

too tightly, not wanting any skin
to be exposed. When winter

begins to green, I learn
how to trap the air in loose layers,

folding in my own heat
against another freeze.

To be fair, it is not my only mistake,
an upturned kayak

testifies of my negligence
to an ancient, underwater tribe

that has survived the worst
for millions of years. Everything

that has sunk to their depths
is an ornament of joy, a life vest

that keeps them from floating
to a dangerous surface.

Antiphona

In what ways do the materials, processes, or commonalities teach?

From the root, antiphon: a verse or song to be chanted or sung in response; a psalm, hymn, or prayer sung in alternate parts; a verse or a series of verses sung as a prelude or conclusion. (Dictionary.com, 2017)

Items Regifted or Returned

Bugs Bunny tie,
Mickey Mouse hat,
purple dinosaur socks,
take one snap,
then send it all back.

Sheepskin vest,
long underwear, overalls,
too itchy, too warm,
too lumberjack.

Bic pen, Bic lighter,
Bic shaver, Bic chocolate,
Bic backpack.
Hasn't anyone heard of Swiss?

Wool scarf. Wait.
I think I'd like that.

Sorites

What themes appear to be significant? Are there specific quotes or ideas that come to mind?

A form of argument having several premises and one conclusion, capable of being resolved into a chain of syllogisms, the conclusion of each of which is a premise of the next. (Dictionary.com, 2017)

The Third Adam

"I decided to paint the image of a locomotive . . . In order for its mystery to be evoked" (Rene Magritte, 1988, p. 135)

If you had to make a man
out of three objects,
I would start with the chimney
its mantle already a suitable waist
to hold up whatever body
might be placed on top.

Coming down from the mantle
are the wide legs,
on either side, like pilings
driven into the ground,
his feet unseen, unmoved
and skeptical. Between them,
where a fire might be lit,
is the charring and residue of history.

With only a clock
and a mirror to choose from
as the last two objects,
the careful reader will intuit
that the man being made is more
a projection of the creator.

The trouble is the mirror belongs nowhere,
who would dare lean in to kiss lips
that pouted and pursed
in sequence to one's own?
And who would have a heart
made of mimicry, a soldier
encouraged in his pursuit,

his aim only as the other does,
obedient to a fault,
changeless and void.

At last the dice are thrown
and the clock is chosen as the head
so that the man's thoughts
will be consumed with time,
a pitiable end to an exercise
in signification.

And what if there were a pity,
if, in the looking on,
an unbridgeable gap did not separate
the gazer from the gaze,
and, instead, there was a language
where he might say you belong to me.

Ah, shame I cannot create
such a garden for you and I,
in belonging longing is lost
in possessives, and language slips
into the chimney, choking itself
with smoke for lack of kindling.

What is, is only smoke after all,
the heralding of a fire,
that never quite arrives.
Here, let us use a fourth object
in our image of the ideal man,
let there be a locomotive
shooting out from his legs
offering pleasure as distraction
from what would be a pitiable life.

Aporia

Are there challenges that come to mind? What puzzles you? How might ideas play against one another?

The expression of a simulated or real doubt, as about where to begin or what to do or say; a difficulty encountered in establishing the theoretical truth of a proposition, created by the presence of evidence both for and against it. (Dictionary.com, 2017)

Prometheus Lights a Marlboro

From ankle to chin it's cold.
He stoops to light a fire
but is not a natural Prometheus,
so drapes a scarf around his neck
like a shawl, waiting
for the wood to catch.

Going back to bed,
would recover the warmth
not yet drained from his blankets,
the alternating smell of sweat
and cleanliness, but here he is,
a part of the tedium.

The only way to endure
is to make lists
the day made less pointless
in increments, 30 minute habits
forged into a fist, a stone,
a paper weight,
a thing to hold down time.

His heart wrenched
in nostalgia, by a fire
swapping stories in an old Western
a six shooter the solution
to any conflict he might have had,
playacting scenes
of a forgotten violence, sanity,
as real as Marlboro Man.

He is trying to grow old gently
or not gently, mostly confusing

them in the early light,
lightheaded, the panic of being
lost in the lonely hallways
of memory, himself. These flames
finally leaping about
a temporary indulgence
to fill existential space.

What Do These Responses Mean? Wiebe Explains

Mimesis: In this category, in "*That's a Great Scarf. Thank you,*" I addressed the scarf as a tangible object. It was a gift, and so I used first-person, wanting to tell the story of my experience with wardrobes. In 25 years of education, the dark suit, at least in the employment contexts that I have worked in, is still the gold standard for professionalism. In the political games of public and policy significance, the dark suit holds the same weight as large-scale quantitative data.

Poiesis: The poem, "*Is Faith,*" extends my first response. As such, there is no direct mention of the scarf. Instead, I wanted to explore the idea that changing one's wardrobe is not necessarily about clothes, though changing one's clothes is sometimes the invitation to change one's thinking as well. With Sameshima's prompt to respond with my own making, I introduce the imagery of windows and doors. What I find intriguing with windows and doors is that they are sometimes, conventionally, seen as opposites, and yet *both* are thresholds to a new space.

Palimpsest: In "*The New Door,*" the challenge was adding an additional layer of text, a layer that might have existed before the poem, "Is Faith." Keeping with the imagery of windows and doors, one thing that I discovered in the writing process was the word *offering.* In the context of research, particularly when working with human participants, I seek experiences that are absorbing, enough so that I lose track of time, or lose myself in the process. When I write, I want to discover something that I did not know before, that I did not know existed within me.

Intertextuality: It turns out that I actually don't know how to wear a scarf. This one seemed too short, then too long, then too stiff. I tried looping it, and making a single knot, and then just draping it over the back of my neck. For a while I stopped wearing it. It seemed destined to be one of those gifts that was beautiful but not all that practical. When Sameshima taught me to wrap it loosely so that there would be airflow, it was so opposite to my expectations it was like being told that if I put on a life vest it would keep me safely underwater where I could live for thousands of years. Intertextuality is like the multiple ways that a scarf can be draped.

Antiphona: Christmases, birthdays, anniversaries. Are some people simply better than others at selecting the perfect gift? Recently, visiting my parents, I put on a pair of slippers that my brother had knit for me years ago. They fit perfectly. My feet are small and it is difficult to find slippers in a size 5. For years I've been looking for some black leather slippers that would go with my collection of suits. Just in case. I realized that what I've wanted all along were these slippers my brother knit. In their bright Hawaiian colors they went with everything. In the poem, "*Items regifted or returned*" I found the prompt of antiphona difficult. While I set out to write a serious poem, a prayer, or something equivalent, what came out was playful and ironic. The effort hasn't been a complete loss, when it comes time to read this poem out loud, I will likely chant it.

Sorites: In the poem, "*The Third Adam,*" there are a series of images that act like premises in the argument for the ideal man. When writing poems that belong in a series, I don't know in advance the imagery that will be carried forward from poem to poem. Because the scarf is the focus that I've been working with, if there has been any intention regarding an image that is carried forward, it has been to think about style and presentation of the body in relation to clothing. In this poem, language and intentions slip into the chimney, and it is the imagery of fire that is carried forward.

Aporia: In the final poem of this series there is once again fire. It has been interesting to notice how the imagery of windows and doors has shifted to that of chimneys, smoke, and campfires. Aporia is the method of bringing these together to see what kind of meaning might be made from them. A dear friend of mine keeps a candle in the window. His door is always open.

Aporetic Openings

The word *aporia* is the closing catechization category and refers to an impasse, indecision, or particular point of doubt. It can also be imagined as a good way to keep a fire going when all the doors and windows appear closed. When encountering a wondering moment, a good idea is to dwell in the space and to anticipate the possibilities of multiple solutions. We conclude with wonderings: How do the Catechizations serve to generate freedom yet within a frame? In our study of creativity theories for better understanding and theorizing processes for imagination and knowledge generation, we see the tension between freedom and rigidity as critical for growth to occur. The Catechization categories, while structured, provide intentional focus and supported growth. Closed doors and windows will direct the fire toward oxygen. A framework allows for concentrated energies to be funneled in a particular direction. A framework allows for a conceptual safety to explore freely.

How does the catechization process, using Wiebe's poem responses, lead to new learning? And what do all the poems mean in the context of knowledge generation? This paper began with Sternberg et al.'s (2001; 2002; 2003) eight creativity propulsion theories providing example through the Parallaxic Praxis Model and Catechization Process. Wiebe offered a response poem to the scarf within each catechization category and subsequently provided an artist statement for each poem. "*The assemblage of heterogeneous components*" (Lee & Denshire, 2013, p. 222), what Sternberg et al., (2003) describe as the creativity propulsion theory of *Synthesis*—collating divergent ideas, is also supported by other post qualitative researchers as generative construction (Barad, 2007; Deleuze & Guattari, 1987; O'Sullivan, 2006). "*The 'emergence of the new*" (MacLure, 2013, p. 659) is built on a base foundation that is not sequential unidirectional constructivism but multi-level, multi-planed, dimensional, and contingent on place, time, and histories (Sameshima, Wiebe & Hayes, in review). The poem responses, the very beauty of creative construction and generation of knowledge is the unknown. As Sameshima makes the scarf, she does not know exactly how the final product will look when the wool shrinks and crinkles the silk from the rolling and throwing process. As Wiebe begins his poems, he does not know where they will lead. When expectations for something powerful to sync, or merge into anticipated meaning are suspended, new possibilities arise.

The scarf Sameshima makes helps to materialize how she conceives of Wiebe's poetry (see Sameshima, Miyakawa & Lockett, this issue). Her making and Wiebe's poetry are the symbolic interaction of self-construction and reconstruction (Denzin, 2002), the "*reorganization of experience which adds to the meaning of experience, and which increases ability to direct the course of subsequent experience*" (Dewey, 1916, p. 76). Through the Parallaxic Praxis Model and the Catechization Process, they demonstrate a means of self-learning and self-change that has the possibility of social change (Kumar, 2011). As researchers use the investigative renderings to prompt discussions, inspire ideas, and generate questions and trajectories, they are intentionally engaging in strategies for advancing possibilities of thinking differently and producing new knowledge.

References

Barad, K. (2007). *Meeting the universe halfway: Quantum physics and the entanglement of matter and meaning.* Durham, NC: Duke University Press.

Defechereux, P. (2017, March 24). *The DaVinci paradigm: Arts and sciences building community. Paper presentation at the* 2017 Annual Bay Area HIV Health Disparities Symposium. San Francisco, CA.

Deleuze, G., & Guattari, F. (1987). *A thousand plateaus: Capitalism and schizophrenia.* Minneapolis, MN: University Press.

Denzin, N. K. (2002). *Interpretive interactionism.* London, UK: Sage.

Dewey, J. (1916/2011). *Democracy and education.* New York, NY: Macmillan.

Dictionary.com. (2017). Antiphon. Available at http://www.dictionary.com/browse/antiphon

Dictionary.com. (2017). Aporia. Available at http://www.dictionary.com/browse/aporia?s=t

Dictionary.com (2017). Intertextuality. Available at http://www.dictionary.com/browse/intertextuality?s=t

Dictionary.com. (2017). Palimpsest. Available at http://www.dictionary.com/browse/palimpsest

Dictionary.com (2017). Sorites. Available at http://www.dictionary.com/browse/sorites?s=t

Farlax Dictionary. (2017). Catechize. Available from http://www.thefreedictionary.com/catechize

Ingalls Vanada, D. (2017). Teaching for the ambiguous, creative, and practical: Daring to be A/R/Tography. *Art/Research International: A Transdisciplinary Journal, 2*(10), 110-135.

Lee, A., & Denshire, S. (2013). Conceptualizing autoethnography as assemblage: Accounts of occupational therapy practice. *International Journal of Qualitative Methods, 12,* 221-236.

Kumar, A. (2011). *Understanding curriculum as meditative inquiry: A study of the ideas of Jiddu Krishnamurti and James MacDonald.* Unpublished dissertation. University of British Columbia, Canada. Available at https://open.library.ubc.ca/cIRcle/collections/ubctheses/24/items/1.0055327

MacLure, M. (2013). Researching without representation? Language and materiality in post-qualitative methodology. *International Journal of Qualitative Studies in Education, 26*(6), pp. 658-667. doi: 10.1080/09518398.2013.788755

Magritte, R. (1988). Modern and contemporary paintings. In S. F. Rossen, R. V. Sharp, E. Stepina & S. Weidemeyer (Eds.), *Master paintings.* The Art Institute of Chicago. Chicago, IL.

Maarhuis, P. (2016). Replies to wounds: *Meaning across multiple ekphrasic interpretations of interpersonal violence and the clothesline project* (Doctoral dissertation) Proquest, #11770. Retrieved from Washington State University Research Libraries: https://research.libraries.wsu.edu:8443/xmlui/bitstream/handle/2376/12049/Maarhuis_wsu_0251E_11770.pdf?sequence=1

Maarhuis, P., Sameshima, P., & Chalykoff, J. P. (2014, May 25). Research-antiphona: One transcript, four responses, and five catechizations. *Arts, Researchers & Teachers Society, Canadian Society for the Study of Education,* St. Catharines, Ontario.

Marino, M. T., Sameshima, P., & Beecher, C. C. (2009). Enhancing TPACK with assistive technology: Promoting inclusive practices in preservice teacher education. *Contemporary Issues in Technology and Teacher Education, 9*(2). Retrieved from http://www.citejournal.org/vol9/iss2/general/article1.cfm

Merriam-Webster. (2017). Intertextuality. Available from https://www.merriam-webster.com/dictionary/intertextuality

Merriam-Webster. (2017). Mimesis. Available from https://www.merriam-webster.com/dictionary/mimesis

Merriam-Webster. (2017). Palimpsest. Available from https://www.merriam-webster.com/dictionary/palimpsest

O'Sullivan, S. (2006). *Art encounters Deleuze and Guattari: Thought beyond representation.* New York, NY: Palgrave Macmillan.

Poiesis (2017). Wikipedia. Retrieved from https://en.wikipedia.org/wiki/Poiesis

Sameshima, P. (in review). Designing imaginative processes: Making the world. *Canadian Journal of Education.*

Sameshima, P., & Maarhuis, P. (2013, June 5). *Ekphrastic catechization: Arts-integrated, collaborative, and multimodal research techniques.* Presentation for the Canadian Society for the Study of Women in Education, Canadian Society for the Study of Education, Victoria, BC.

Sameshima, P., Miyakawa, M., & Lockett, M. (2017). Scholarly engagement through making: A response to *arts-based and contemplative practices in research and teaching. REVISTA VIS 16*(2), 45-67.

Sameshima P., & Slingerland, D. (2015, Aug.). Reparative pedagogy: Empathic aesthetic learning. *Canadian Review of Art Education, 42*(1), 1-21.

Sameshima, P., Slingerland, D., Wakewich, P., Morrisseau, K., & Zehbe, I. (2017, February). Growing wellbeing through community participatory arts: The Anishinaabek cervical cancer screening study (ACCSS). In G. Barton & M. Baguley (Eds.), The Palgrave handbook of global arts education (pp. 399-416). Brisbane, Australia: Palgrave. doi: 10.1057/978-1-137-55585-4

Sameshima, P., Wiebe, S., & Hayes, M. (in review). Imagination: The generation of possibility. In B. Andrews (Ed.), *Perspectives on arts education research in Canada.*

Sameshima, P., & Vandermause, R. (2008). Parallaxic praxis: An artful interdisciplinary collaborative research methodology. In B. Kožuh, R. Kahn & A Kozlowska (Eds.), *The practical science of society* (pp. 141-152). Grand Forks, Nottingham, Krakow: The College of Education and Human Development & Slovenian Research Agency (AARS).

Sameshima, P., Vandermause, R., Chalmers, S., & Gabriel. (2009). *Climbing the ladder with Gabriel: Poetic inquiry of a methamphetamine addict in recovery.* Rotterdam, The Netherlands: Sense.

Saunders, V (2015) *". . . ": Using a non-bracketed narrative to story recovery in Aboriginal mental health care.* Unpublished thesis. Townsville, Australia:

Nursing, Midwifery & Nutrition, College of Healthcare Sciences, Division of Tropical Health and Medicine, James Cook University.

Sternberg, R. J., Kaufman, J. C., & Pretz, J. E. (2001). The propulsion model of creative contributions applied to the arts and letters. *Journal of Creative Behavior, 35,* 75-101.

Sternberg, R. J., Kaufman, J. C., & Pretz, J. E. (2002). *The creativity conundrum: A propulsion model of kinds of creative contributions.* New York, NY: Psychology Press.

Sternberg, R. J., Kaufman, J. C., & Pretz, J. E. (2003). A propulsion model of creative leadership. *Leadership Quarterly, 14,* 455-473.

Stock, R. V., Sameshima, P., & Slingerland, D. (2016, July). Constructing pre-service teacher identities through processes of parallax. Special Issue: Artful inquiry: Transforming understanding through creative engagement. *LEARNing Landscapes, 9*(2), 489-512.

Universities Canada (2016, November). *Mobilizing people and ideas: Supporting the creative economy and fostering Canadian culture in the digital world.* Available from https://www.univcan.ca/wp-content/uploads/2016/12/universities-canada-submission-fed-govt-review-on-canadian-content-in-digital-world-dec-2016.pdf

Wiersma, E., Sameshima, P., Dupuis, S., Caffery, P., & Harvey, D. (2015, July 3). Visually depicting the dementia journey. *44th Annual British Society of Gerontology Conference 2015.* Newcastle Upon Tyne, England.

Example 7.5: Constructing Pre-Service Teacher Identities

Through Processes of Parallax[4]

By R. Varainja Stock, Pauline Sameshima & Dayna Slingerland

Abstract

This paper presents an arts-integrated process for teacher educators to engage their students in critical thinking, meaning-making, and knowledge construction in order to enable pre-service teachers to analyze metanarratives that inform their teacher identities. The research team used the Parallaxic Praxis research model to frame its art-making investigations in a practice-based research process. The three researchers each created an artefact as part of their individual inquiry of the data set, comprising 90 material cloaks created by pre-service teachers, to enter into dialogue addressing the prevailing metanarratives expressed by the pre-service teacher participants.

Keywords

parallaxic praxis; teacher education; teacher identity; arts integrated research; pre-service teachers

Pre-service teacher (PST) self-identity, which underpins and drives the construction of teaching philosophies and practice, is arguably one of the most essential components for PSTs to investigate in their teacher preparation programs. High numbers of new teachers continue to leave the teaching profession in Canada (Clandinin et al., 2012; Clark & Antonelli, 2009; Gambhir, Broad, Evans, & Gaskell, 2008), echoing ongoing concern with attrition rates in the United States (Barnes, Crowe, & Schaefer, 2007; Boe, Cook, & Sunderland, 2008; Liu & Ramsay, 2008; NCES, 2011). Many teachers who leave the profession in the early years do so partially because their teacher education programs lack "*systematic efforts to provide pre-service*

---

[4] Reprint: Stock, R. V., Sameshima, P., & Slingerland, D. (2016, July). Constructing pre-service teacher identities through processes of parallax. Special Issue: Artful inquiry: Transforming understanding through creative engagement. *LEARNing Landscapes, 9*(2), 489-512.

teachers with a realistic understanding of teachers' emotional experiences and developmental stages" (Hong, 2010, p. 1540). We "*acknowledge that the teacher-identity is continually shaping and morphing with experience*" (Sameshima, 2007b, p. 6); however, in practice, some teachers remain locked in preconceived idealistic notions of the K-12 environment (Cheng, Chan, Tang, & Cheng, 2009) that are unchallenged until these PSTs enter the profession. This research seeks to better understand PSTs' conceptions of their teacher identities and to offer teacher educators a process for enabling thought-provoking, critical, and dialogic discussions on teacher identity development in their programs.

This paper presents an arts-engaged process for teacher educators to move beyond reflection-writing assignments and discussion methods with their students to processes of critical thinking, meaning-making, and knowledge construction in order to enable PSTs to relook at the metanarratives that inform the development of their personal teacher identities. Understanding personal narratives, often built on established metanarratives, can enable PSTs to construct more meaningful professional identities and, in turn, reduce teacher attrition (see Izadinia, 2013, pp. 695–696). This paper presents the first phase of analysis from one of three sites involved in a multi-site research project spanning three Canadian universities.

Figure. 7.5.1. Clockwise from top left: Cloaks by 'Grace,' 'Chloe,' and 'Olivia.'

The research team of three artist-researchers used the Parallaxic Praxis research model (Sameshima & Vandermause, 2008) to frame their art-making investigations in a practice-based research process. The three researchers each created an artefact as part of their individual inquiry of the data set, comprising 90 material cloaks (see Figure 7.5.1) created by pre-service teachers. Similarly, White and Lemieux (2015), co-researchers at one of the other project sites, use the creation of artefacts, in their case 'identity-boxes,' to examine pre-service teacher identity and the teaching self.

The Parallaxic Praxis model involves the translation of data into artistic mediums that are used by the research team to provoke collaborative engagement, knowledge production, and further questionings. These artefacts are also used to generate discussions with participants and broader audiences. The range of modal translations can include numeric data presented in the form of a graph; or interview transcripts rendered through translations of poetry and photographs (Sameshima, Vandermause, Chalmers, & Gabriel, 2009); or music, graphic experiments, and watercolour paintings (Maarhuis, Sameshima, & Chalykoff, 2014).

As a collaborative research model, parallaxic praxis encourages critical thinking in order to "*understand core, underlying truths, not simply that superficial truth that may be most obviously visible*" (hooks, 2010, p. 9). These translative practices resulting in artefacts can offer concrete means to better challenge and understand how preconceived, clichéd notions of teacher identity affect pre-service teachers' ongoing professional identity formation. We provide a process, called Ekphrastic Catechization, for engaging pre-service teachers in dialogue to move beyond the constructed clichés.

PST Teacher Identity Development

Much research has been done which reveals a naiveté in PSTs' expectations for their future roles. The use of reflection, art, and metaphor have consistently revealed a disconnect between what PSTs envision their future roles to be and what their future roles will actually be. This disconnect may be setting PSTs up for unnecessary negative experiences early in their careers due to unrealistic expectations. The 90 PST participants in this study consistently presented idealistic images on their cloaks and in their reflection writings of their future roles as teachers. The data in our study revealed a variety of utopian narratives focused on establishing classroom families and communities; being beholders of inspiration and encouragement to their students, and caring for each student as an individual. While these goals are wholesome, prior research purports that unrealistic expectations by new teachers may negatively affect their decision to stay in the profession (Barnes et al., 2007; Hong, 2010; Liu & Ramsey, 2008;

Schafer, 2013); how they teach; and how successful they become as teachers (Carlyle & Woods, 2002; Cheng et al., 2009; Head, 1992; Hong, 2010).

Developing a professional identity is an ongoing process as identities are constantly navigated through interactions, in context, and over time (Gee, 2000, see p. 99). Geijsel and Meijers (2005) contend that teacher identity formation is informed by "*interpretations [emphasis in original] of concepts as they exist in the culturally constructed worlds in which the person participates*" (p. 425). Further, identity formation involves an emotional element as meanings are developed through a relationship with culture and events. "*Identity construction is seen to be a circular learning process, in which experiences and self-concept are related through using concepts and endowing them with personal sense*" (p. 425). To further explain this connection, Geijsel and Meijers found that "concepts and meanings that are available . . . but cannot be related to experiences and thus are not given a personal sense, will not become a part of the identity configuration" (p. 425). Thus, although many teacher education programs may already include identity development programming, unless teacher educators are able to encourage PSTs' personal connections to teaching philosophies, little change will occur.

Previous research has identified links between teacher identity and attrition (Hong, 2010) and a lack of a connection between PST teacher identity and the actual demands of the profession (Beltman, Glass, Dinham, Chalk, & Nguyen, 2015; Buchanan, 2015; Geisel & Meijers, 2005; Hong, 2010; Thomas & Beauchamp, 2011). Hong's (2010) US study involving 84 teachers and PST participants identified a naiveté and idealism associated with PST professional identities. Similarly, a Canadian study that asked PSTs to explain their teacher identity through metaphor demonstrated a marked difference between the metaphors used by PSTs and those used after participants had begun teaching (Thomas & Beauchamp, 2011). The metaphors employed by PSTs "*focused on supporting future students, nurturing, protecting and helping them find their way*" (p. 765) whereas the metaphors used after entering the teaching profession focused heavily on personal survival and meeting the challenges in the classroom. Building on previous research (Eren & Tekinarslan, 2013; Northcote & Featherstone, 2006; Pinnegar, Mangelson, Reed, & Groves, 2011; Thomas & Beauchamp, 2011), Buchanan (2015) explored the use of metaphors to further understand the shift in identities from PSTs to practising teachers and how this shift affects the profession and teacher attrition. The metaphors in Buchanan's study were consistent with previous studies of PSTs as the majority of PST participants created metaphors that were "*positive and optimistic*" (p. 44). Buchanan also found that PSTs presented "*inflated views of the control a teacher exercises*" (p. 44) demonstrating a naïve or uninformed vision of themselves as future teachers. This idyllic outlook is problematic as it increases the likelihood they will "*be confronted with the reality of little control and, at times, even hostility and resistance from a source they might not suspect*" (p. 44).

Studies of PSTs' identity development have foregrounded the use of activities that involve reflection "*as a way of questioning taken-for-granted assumptions and teaching practices stabilized in early stages of a teacher's career*" (Izadinia, 2013, p. 697). Art-making and reflection have been used as effective processes for self-exploration in teacher identity development (Boulton-Funke, 2014; Sinner, Wicks, & Rak, 2015; Weber & Mitchell, 1996; White & Lemieux, 2015). Beltman and collaborators (2015) studied 125 pre-service teachers at a university in Australia. Participants were asked to draw a picture based on the question: What kind of teacher do you hope to become? The drawings overwhelmingly presented positive expectations for their future identities as teachers. The PSTs' "*drawings indicated a confidence in their capacity to become the teacher and to do the work of teaching in an engaging and caring manner. Much of what is relevant to teaching, however, was not addressed*" (p. 238). A Canadian study in Quebec with 64 university students enrolled in undergraduate and graduate programs in education explored their professional identities through drawing and written reflection (Weber & Mitchell, 1996). Students were instructed to draw an image of a teacher and write a reflection based on their drawings, which they then presented to their classmates. "*In reflecting and commenting on the pictures, they became aware of the incredible power that past experience and stereotypes seemed to have on them*" (p. 307). The researchers affirmed that this process provided space for students to "articulate previously unexamined ambivalences and tensions around their identity and work as teachers" (p. 306).

Methodology

Parallaxic Praxis Research Model

The Parallaxic Praxis model (see Figure 7.5.2) was developed by an interdisciplinary research team (Sameshima & Vandermause, 2008) and has since been used in various ways to provoke dialogic discussions on a diverse range of topics including interpersonal violence (Maarhuis & Sameshima, 2013); assistive technology (Marino, Sameshima, & Beecher, 2009); teacher education (Sameshima, 2009), Aboriginal mental health care (Saunders, 2015), and empowering older persons (Neumiller, Corbett, Gates, & Vandermause, 2015).

Parallaxic Praxis is a research model for conducting collaborative arts-integrated research that furthers understanding and provokes new questions, never settling on a conclusion, rather opening up the dialogue for unbounded, spiralling inquiry (Saunders, 2015).

The concept of parallax comes from astronomy and "*is the apparent change of location of an object against a background due to a change in observer position or perspective shift*" (Sameshima, 2007a, p. 293). As a collaborative method, parallax helps to understand how an object will look different depending on the vantage point or line of sight of the viewer. In effect, different people will see different things based upon where they stand, and therefore, researchers from different fields will interpret the same data differently, not only through the words they use, but also through the discourse of their fields, and varying funds of knowledge. Additionally, using artistic renderings, or modal translations (text to art, numbers to graphs, etc.), creates energetic space for multiple interpretations, which "affords the audience to think more critically about the content from a personal meaning-making perspective" (Sameshima et al., 2009, p. 10). These functional artefacts, in that they are artworks imbued with meaning or created for the sake of generating meaning, can be created in any artistic medium—including narratives or stories, performance, poetry, and visual arts—and are intended to be used to provoke dialogue. Eisner (2008) explained that "*something that mediates the researchers' observations and culminates in a form that provides the analogous structure*" (p. 7) can be the avenue to articulating the unsaid.

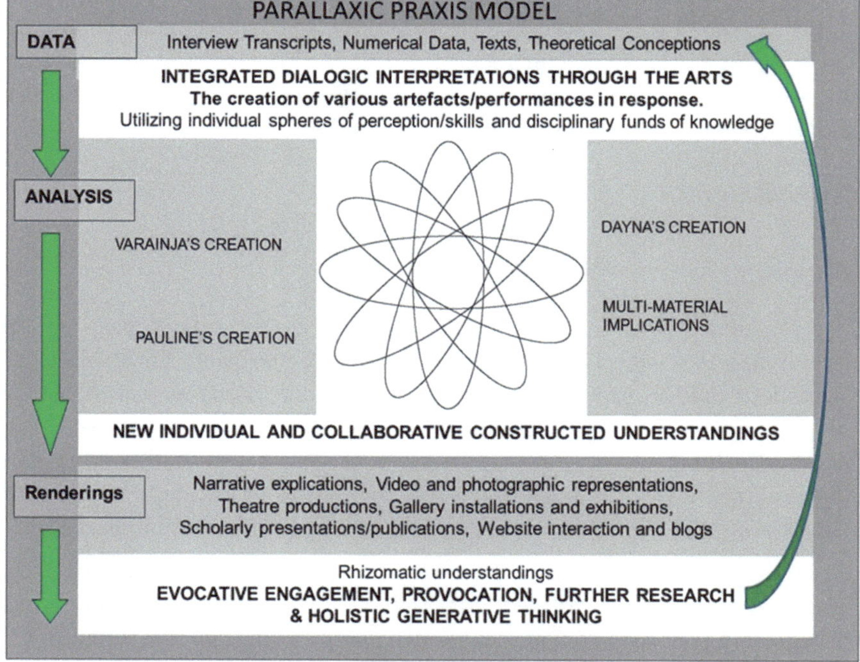

Figure 7.5.2. Parallaxic Praxis Framework. P. Sameshima. 2016.

In the process of creation, questions will arise which begin an inertial movement toward knowledge generation. As well, in bringing together the artist-researchers' created artefacts, not only can the juxtaposition of artefacts offer provocative spaces of exchange between mode and meaning, and challenge normativity inherent in social constructs, but also "*systems of analysis and interactions in the hybrid nexus spaces can be discussed*" (Sameshima et al., 2009, p. 10).

Ekphrastic Catechizations

Parallaxic praxis research uses ekphrastic catechizations, or questioning within specific themes, to guide analytic processes of the data visualizations. "*Ekphrasis is a rhetorical device where one medium tries to re-create an object's essence and form in another medium in the hopes of relating more directly with the audience.*" (Maarhuis, Sameshima, & Chalykoff, 2014, n.p.). To catechize is to question systematically. In this framework, catechizations are used to direct conversations when looking at collections of artefacts in order to move the dialogue forward and to further inspire questions from investigators and audiences. For example, instead of only describing 'what' each artefact is, the seven catechization categories interrogate how the artefacts work together and what they do as artefacts of analysis. The ekphrastic catechizations are mimesis, poiesis, palimpsest, intertextuality, antiphona, sorites, and aporia. Importantly, the catechizations offer a means for researchers to theorize and discuss the artefacts constructed from the original data.

Mimesis "*is the relational, ecstatic re-presentation*" of a previous work. In this model, mimesis is the act of translating data in order to relate it to a larger audience. "*Mimetic works are not static copies or an imitation but rather ecstatic formations that unfold ontologically, fluidly, temporally, and referentially*" (Maarhuis et al., 2014, np). In the context of this research, the research team created mimetic art works to reveal the participant metanarratives to audiences. The researcher-generated artefacts are "*active and dialectical*" (Lotz, 2012, p. 93) and contribute to clarification of ideas. A possible question in this category in relation to the artefacts could be: How have we rendered similar metanarratives in our three artefacts?

Poiesis is an event in parallaxic praxis research when the mimetic work comes to life through interpretation, dialogue, bearing witness, or reflection. The mimetic work provides the opportunity for an interaction, an event, for the researcher(s), participants, and audiences to respond to the work of art as it is "*recreated every time it is aesthetically experienced*" (Dewey, 1934/2005, p. 113). A question used here may be: What similarities and differences do we notice today between the three artworks?

A **palimpsest** is used to describe something that has been reused or altered but still bears visible traces of its earlier form. In parallaxic praxis the mimetic work is already a palimpsest, presenting new ideas built on older ones in a new form. The artefact is the dialogic in physical form, reaching back and reciprocally changing meaning of the data and the artefact through the interchange of creation and construction (see Bakhtin, 1981). The PSTs' cloaks and reflection writings are the original texts that form the basis for the research team's mimetic works to create new understandings and provide opportunity for poiesis. Palimpsest provides the depth and layers to allow both the participant and the researcher to be present at once. Ensuring the participant perspectives are present is "*critical in an arts-based text*" (Barone & Eisner, 2012, p. 134). The relationship between the multiple layers creates an ongoing dialogue where the artworks are viewed by different audiences, in different contexts, and at different times. The questions used here could be: What inspired you to use that particular material? In what way does your artefact echo or trace the data?

Intertextuality adds breadth to interpretations by creating a relationship between the various texts—the mimetic works and participant data—and meaning is derived from seeing or unpacking the researcher-generated artworks in reference to each other and in reference to the participant-generated artwork. The question here could be: How do the three artefacts work in combination to teach us something anew?

Antiphona expands on the concept of intertextuality in parallaxic praxis. Antiphona is a harmony, "*a versicle or sentence sung by one choir in response to another*" (Oxford English Dictionary, 2016, n.p.). Each researcher created a separate response to the participant-generated artworks and writings. Once these pieces were created, we brought them together to create dialogue between the pieces and the meaning infused in them individually and as a collective. The choral response allows for a fuller resounding response to our inquiry question. Here, a question could be: In what ways do the materials we used and the responses we made echo one another?

Sorites refers to the collaborative process of analysis in parallaxic praxis research. The combination of researcher, participant, and audience interpretation is an act of *cumulation* or a heaping of pertinent phenomenal elements, language, and interpretations before one crosses a decision line or threshold that may be indistinct but, in the final analysis, is recognized as a process that answers research questions (Maarhuis et al., 2014, n.p.).

The practice of sorites in research interpretation is therefore contextually bound and "*requires acceptance by and interaction with the audience as well as participants and the community of those who have a stake in the particular cultural phenomena*" (n.p.). A question we might ask here is: What specific quotes pushed us to integrate the phenomenon into our final rendering?

Aporia means "*an impasse or puzzlement*" and philosophically is a "*puzzle or a seemingly insoluble impasse in an inquiry, often arising as a result of equally plausible yet inconsistent premises. . . the state of being perplexed or at a loss*" (Collins English Dictionary, 2011). "*To embrace aporia, the researcher, viewer, and participant must sit in the dissonance of simultaneous and seemingly contradictory life circumstances that do not fit into familiar cultural narratives and 'truths' (Dewey, 1934/2005; Spivak, 2013).*" (Maarhuis et al., 2014, n.p.). Our question here could be: How do the artefacts play with or against one another? By using the catechizations to guide discussion, researchers can intentionally attempt to approach the artefacts from original, revelatory, and more critical perspectives.

Method

Members of the research team each created an artefact to re-present the combined essence of 90 PSTs' material cloaks. All the researchers familiarized themselves with the previously collected PST data (material cloaks and written reflection pieces) in ATLAS ti, a qualitative analysis program. The researchers also worked together in analyzing the data and discussed prevailing themes, connections, and issues that stood out in the PST data. Concurrently, the researchers worked independently on creating their artefact. With the belief that "*it is through the making, both in the midst of construction and in reflection, that new understandings and knowledge are acknowledged*" (Sameshima, 2007b, p. 5), the researcher-generated artefacts then became points of dialogue for analyzing PST identity development.

Participants

This analysis draws on previously collected data from 90 PSTs from a teacher education program at a university in the United States. Student composition in the teacher education program was predominantly female and the participant sample reflected this. PSTs were recruited from three sections of a mandatory course called K-8 Arts Integration. Participants voluntarily provided written consent for their course assignment to be used as research. University ethics approval was granted to carry out this project at the data collection site, as well as the current researchers' university, and all ethical protocols were followed in the use, processing, and dissemination of findings in this study.

Data

As part of their course, students were instructed to create a material representation of their developing teacher identity in the form of a cloak that was then presented to their respective classes. Students used a myriad of materials including photographs of family and friends, patterned prints, iron-on transfers, paints, and markers (see Figure 8.3.1). To accompany their cloaks and their presentations, the students were required to write a reflection paper describing their process and learning. The cloaks were photographed, capturing as much detail as possible, and then digitized. The reflection writings were submitted electronically. To process the data, participants were assigned pseudonyms. All images and reflection writings were de-identified before being entered into ATLAS.ti.

Teacher-created artefacts

The following section shares individual reflections on the three artist-researcher-created artefacts.

Tranquility by Dayna Slingerland

Figure 7.5.3. Model: Dayna Slingerland (2016). *Tranquility.* Wool needle felting and wet felting.

The material and aesthetic composition of my piece was inspired by the encouraging air within the PSTs' writing. I wanted to create a piece that would be pleasing to wear by using a wool blanket and merino fleece for a feeling, soft to the touch as well as warm to the body. This piece covers and comforts as do the PSTs' idealistic visions for student learning. One participant described, "*It is essential that my classroom be a warm and inviting place, one that both my students and myself feel comfortable in so that in turn, we will all be able to work better*" (Alexa). Another participant explained, "*I truly value each student's uniqueness, and that I would hope that they can respect one another for their differences so my classroom will be a warm, positive, nonjudgmental place for them to learn and grow*" (Laura).

While working on the finer details of the cloak, I integrated materials and patterns to reflect a deeper complexity. The felted spiralling and climbing lines that cover the piece remain separated and broken apart from one another. I felted on lace and yarn that twisted and tangled together. I wondered while reading the teacher identity reflections if the students had given consideration to the complexities of personal identities as well as teaching identities. Student teaching identities are based on knowledge of teaching rather than direct experience. Because students "*have outsider as opposed to insider knowledge, they expect to teach as they were taught and they are largely unprepared for the realities of teaching in today's classroom*" (Beattie, 1997, p. 115). I wanted the art piece to speak to the comfort and feelings of security in this outsider knowledge. A participant noted:

> *All of us either want to replicate a teaching style that impacted us so strongly from our past, or improve the classroom experience because of a bad teacher they once had. Either way, all of our past experiences in education have shaped who we are and why we want to become teachers.* (Jasmine)

While reading through the PST reflections, I considered the challenges of engaging in self-reflection and how this skill might affect the process of creating an identity. Lauren wrote: "*I have never really reflected on my experiences that have shaped my teaching identity. I really enjoyed thinking of past memories that have inspired me to become a teacher.*" Additionally, another participant described a reflective process, "*The part of this experience that I found most valuable was taking the time to process and reflect on what was truly important to me and to my students*" (Alicia). In authentic inquiry:

> *individuals must choose to pursue their own questions and to engage in the issues. For those who do, it is entirely possible for them to come to see and understand themselves in new ways, to liberate themselves from old*

> *and binding visions of themselves, and to imagine themselves as professionals who can create emancipatory, transformative settings and experiences for the students they teach.* (Beattie, 1997, p. 124)

I wanted my artefact to speak to being comforted in the 'known.' Difficulties in possessing a critical consciousness in self-reflection may stem from "*the fact that many prospective teachers do not clearly understand what constitutes self-reflection, or how to do it. They confuse reflection with describing issues, ideas, and events*" (Gay & Neftali Kirkland, 2003, p. 182). My art piece shows a comforting, safe, warm ideal, yet the fibres tear away at the seams and the complexity is revealed upon closer examination. Each layer in this piece is bound to the one beneath through the needle-felting technique. I question the depth to which PTSs are bound to the ideal representation—are the idealisms a protective layer, or are they helping to build foundations for creating an identity that has yet to take on form?

Entwined Storying by Varainja Stock

Figure 7.5.4. Varainja Stock (2016). *Entwined storying.* Canvas, twine, and mixed media. Model: Mina Stock.

Thomas King (2003) stated: "*the truth about stories is that that's all we are" (p. 2).* The importance of storying King explained is that the stories that we tell ourselves, that we are told, and those that make up and construct our lives *"can control our lives"* (p. 9), *"so you have to be careful with the stories you tell. And you have to watch out for the stories that you are told"* (p. 10). I was struck by the stories that the PSTs shared about their lives and how these stories had influenced their teacher identities. For some, these identities were embodied in popular cultural icons such as Disney characters and superheroes. One participant wrote:

> *If you get to know me, you know I love Disney, children's books, and playing games. I am all about being able to have fun and be creative. I put Tinkerbell on my cloak to symbolize this. I am a child at heart. I want my students to know that and know I understand them and have been where they are. I also want to be able to identify with my students and through my ability to see through a child's eyes allows me to do so.* (Layla)

Another participant stated, *"Disney is a theme that means a lot to me, and I hope that I can incorporate that within my classroom and my cloak I believe helped me show this"* (Amari).

Figure 7.5.5. Scanned cover of The New Basic Readers: The New Friends and Neighbours.

For Entwined Storying I worked with canvas, storybook images, gesso, twine, and white glue. I began with images from The New Basic Readers: The New

Friends and Neighbours (1952) (see Figure 7.5.5), a collection of stories for teaching reading. I then found second-hand Disney children's books including: Peter Pan, My Very First Winnie the Pooh, Sleeping Beauty, and Snow White and the Seven Dwarfs. I wanted the images from the storybooks to appear faded and worn away, present but not obvious so that the observer needs to look closely. I used a method of reverse image transfer—first painting a section of the canvas with gesso and then placing the paper image-side-down against the gesso to dry. Once dry, the back of the paper was gently removed by dampening it with a wet paintbrush and rolling the paper off with my finger.

There were two sides to many of the participant cloaks. Some students chose to represent their personal lives on the inside and their professional lives on the outside, while in their reflection writings they acknowledged that the two were separate, yet connected. A participant stated, "I also learned that I cannot separate my family from my teacher identity, but I don't think that I should have to. I want my students to view me as another person, one who makes mistakes, learns every day, and has a family" (Erin). The personal and professional were connected and entangled. I created twine balls that rest against the body, keeping the cloak separate from, but connected to the body in some places, distorting the appearance of the figure underneath as the outward appearance is an imperfect translation of the collection of life experiences and stories that make up the individual.

I wanted my cloak to be rough, stiff in some places, and be reminiscent of fantastical/otherworldly images. Many of the participants recognized that their teacher identity was an unfinished piece that they would continue to develop throughout their lives, especially in the first few years of teaching. This realization often happened in the process of making their cloaks: "*A lot of time doing this cloak is reflection time and my fears of not knowing the curriculum or making a few mistakes, my first few years, seem so contrary to what actually matters in the end*" (Lindsay).

***The Amway Apple* by Pauline Sameshima**

I wanted to play with the apple cliché through iconoclastic use of materials. Cassandra sums it up shiningly with "*all teachers love apples.*" Many students referred to the apple as a symbol for teaching, tradition, respect, the future, connection to the love of Mac technology products, love of teaching, and more. Amway Apple was made by knitting and crocheting cassette tape into a covering for an armature in the shape of an apple. The covering is based on a pattern of a cocktail dress. When stretched around the apple and tucked in at the base, the design looks completely transformed. This play with the cocktail dress becoming unrecognizable reflects the disparity between the human form (self) and the expected teacher form (apple). The front has a tightly knitted stitch allowing very little of the armature to be seen. The sides and the back are more exposed. Similarly, the PSTs' constructions of what is public (the face of the identity) received much more energy and consideration than the inside or private side of the cloak.

Figure. 7.5.6. *Amway Apple* [Cassette tape over a poly-propylene film armature]. P. Sameshima, 2016. Model: Cameo Sameshima.

I chose to use Amway motivational training cassettes from the 1990s specifically for their messages. Amway (American Way) is a direct selling / multi-level marketing company which sells home and personal care products and is the 30th largest private company in America (Forbes, 2015). Many of the training tapes are heartfully told motivational stories—narratives of woe ending in financial freedom. The tapes exemplify the perpetuation of the American dream, Disney character jubilance, and superhero unselfishness that surfaced in the PSTs' visions of their future careers. Amelia noted, "*I chose this material because it reflects my excitement and my bright future in my teaching career*" and Avery declared, "*I want my students to know that I love and support each and every one of them.*" Rebecca wrote, "*I have wanted to be a teacher my whole life and this has greatly impacted my decisions throughout my schooling. This is something that defines who I am as a person.*" These beautiful narratives of fairy tale-like desire are driven by innocent intentions, goodness, and cultural metanarratives. In a parallel stream, these comments by an Amway sales rep, remind us how these dreams can play out once PSTs start teaching. He says, the Amway tapes "*get you in [a] frame of mind that you need to feed on the materials in order to survive.*" The rep felt that "*the barrage of motivation aids put him 'in a performance trap' where he obsessed about achieving, but felt mired in failure*" (Morrill & Stancill, 1995).

The armature (structural form) and leaf are made of polypropylene film packing tape. I intentionally used tape to echo bandaging practices. There are many ways of learning how to teach and most programs include practicum training or immersion in the field. This 'baptism by fire' can be likened to 'cut and bandage.' Once assigned a class, teachers are generally completely alone with their students. Whether beneficial or detrimental, numerous layers of bandaging form a solid structure. The protective nature of the cliché apple shields the PST but, without armholes, PSTs have little autonomy.

The notions of mothering and care particularly stood out to me. Amanda stated: "*I plan on taking care of them and nurturing their growth and learning. If they don't have a loving, safe place to go home to, they will always feel safe and taken care of in school.*" Amanda wrote about respect and kindness, "*something a mother would also teach.*" Crystal reminisced,

> *In those small towns everyone cared and loved . . . everyone else. The neighbours looked after neighbors and would bring a casserole or a cake over if someone was sick or needed some help. Someone was always there to care for you and you felt so welcomed. I want my classroom to be a community and I want my students to care for each other as much as I care for them.*

These protective notions, and also intentions of care as expressed by many other participants, point to constructions of teacher identity based on the Florence Nightingale Model of teacher as nurse, healer, caregiver, and conduit of curriculum prescriptions (Sameshima, 2007b). An October 11, 2015 blog in the guardian, an online Teacher Network, offers an anonymous student's post aptly titled, "'*Show us that you care': A student's view on what makes a perfect teacher.*" For PSTs and non-PSTs, it appears, care is the defining characteristic of good teaching. Aligning and concurring strongly with the 2015 research on PSTs by Beltman and colleagues, the PSTs in our study also focus predominantly on care and love with very limited reflection on specific pedagogical strategies, teaching theories, or the actual performance of teaching. As an elementary classroom teacher for 17 years, I do agree that there are nostalgic familial-like moments re-created in the classroom; however, these moments are integrally embedded within a larger pedagogic sequence which does not appear to be considered by the PSTs.

Discussion

Resembling the processes of the creation of a text, art production also considers both critical reflection and meanings made by others. According to Sullivan (2005), artistic thinking embodies "*an ongoing dialogue between, within, and around the artist, artwork, viewer and context, where each has a role in co-constructing meaning*" (p. 9). After working individually on our material cloaks, the research team came together to engage in creating a dialogue generated from our artistic renderings (poiesis). This dialogue becomes an accumulation of our individual analyses to bring attention to shared meaning, places of tension, and of divergence in interpretation and experience. All three artefacts highlighted idealized expectations. The PSTs' cloaks and reflection writings enacted powerful entanglements with Disney narratives and the American dream. This participant shares her values:

The disney phenomena

> *The front left flap of my cloak has the American flag as its background. This is because I love our country and the freedom each individual has. I believe that the foundation of our government and its structure has influenced how I see life and others. . . My goal is for my students to collaborate with each other and myself as valued pieces to our classroom. I think our founding fathers are wonderful role models of this. They stood up for what they thought, fought for it, and then collaborated together to create a democracy for all people.* (Hailey)

While this data was collected at a US university, concerns around attrition rates, disillusionment, and teacher identity offer many commonalities across North American and Australian research. In Canada, we are certainly not immune from Disney, superhero, and American Hollywood tropes.

The 'living the dream' trope is illustrated in the nostalgic images from the 1950s reader that Stock used to create her artefact. We wondered how these tropes affect people's identities, notions of happiness, and expectations about life. In reality, the naïve hopefulness and images of peaceful, safe classroom spaces are in direct opposition to the American dream now fuelled by financialism, greed, and competition (see Haiven & Khasnabish, 2014; Hess, 2011), resulting in high levels of stress (Pope, Brown, & Miles, 2015). Challenging PSTs to interrogate metanarratives that drive their self-identities and teaching philosophies will play a critical role in the development of pedagogical practices grounded in current educational contexts.

Becoming

We noted that the PSTs' teacher identities were informed by their experiences as students, and recollections of "good" teachers from a student perspective. They relied on their experiences as students to inform their professional identities, posing a challenge to teacher educators wishing to help PSTs develop a professional identity.

Is it possible to create an identity before living that identity? Stock's cloak offered a path into this discussion. The storybook images on Entwined Storying are 'veiled' or blurred through the transfer process, and the twine entanglements are visible yet shrouded by the canvas covering. Sameshima's apple armature also offers a screened view into the PST body. The process of becoming and taking on a new identity is complex. How might PSTs merge who they are, into who they are becoming, when who they are becoming is an unknown? Slingerland kept parts of her artefact unembellished, "*I was keeping them open as a way of thinking about students absorbing and being susceptible, and thinking of being open to developing an identity that might not totally be their own, and might be one that's been observed.*"

The private and the public

Participants expressed a tension between their personal and professional identities. For example, one student created a cloak with a double layer; the hidden, inner layer displayed a large cross that was kept from view by another layer of material. Through our discussion it was revealed how each of us had intentionally or inadvertently expressed the relationship between the private and the professional, each expressing different levels of comfort while still emulating ideas from the PST data. Stock used the tangled balls of twine to hide the shape of the body underneath the cloak. Even while trying to hide our personal selves, the artefacts evidenced revelations in unexpected ways. We discussed the difference between hiding who you are and enacting a professional identity. Slingerland identified a rawness in the PST cloaks exercise, noting that each piece she added to her felted cloak helped cover up the nakedness underneath by being wrapped in a warm, soft, and safe cloak. Sameshima's piece predominantly hides the wearer's form, encasing the wearer in a cellophane bubble. This obscuration creates safety as it keeps the individual distanced from her role as a teacher and from the judgment of the students. Sameshima's artefact reflects the idea of the PST protected and dependent inside the idealized, iconic apple image of the teacher. Clichés, in general, have been used as a protective shield or to quell concerns (Lifton, 1989; Arendt, 1978), an explanatory shortcut (dictionary.com, 2016), or even to justify action (Arendt, 1963). The iconic teacher identity has become cliché.

The extent of control we can exercise was a prominent point in our discussion. Debating what we can actually control, what we believe we are controlling, and how this need to control our outward appearance can hamper our development as teachers. For new teachers, this distance can create unnecessary issues with feelings of inadequacy and unwillingness to reach out to colleagues for support. In support of the safety of the cliché, the Amway Apple was reportedly very comfortable to wear, and without armholes the artwork carries the expectations of being cared for, and feelings of warmth encased in a cocoon, waiting to be birthed.

Moving forward

Carl Leggo (2008) recommended, "*we need to know our stories before we can attend to the stories of others with respect and care*" (p. 92). As artist-researchers, this research process has given us a better understanding of not only the constructions of PST identities but also our own negotiated identities. This paper offers some examples of the rich discussion generated from making artefacts to represent developing teaching philosophies as a method for moving PSTs beyond naïve and clichéd notions of teacher identity. The artefact offers a new lens to discuss and deconstruct inchoate topics with aspiring teachers. With artefacts in hand, the use of the Parallaxic Praxis model, and guided by the Ekphrastic Catechization process, new spaces of investigation into teacher identity formation are possible.

Acknowledgement

This research was funded by the Social Sciences and Humanities Research Council of Canada.

References

Antiphon. (2016). *Oxford English Dictionary online.* Retrieved from http://www. oed. com/ view/ Entr y/8760?redirected From=antiphon&

Arendt. H. (1963/2006). *Eichmann in Jerusalem: A report on the banality of evil.* New York: Viking Press.

Arendt, H. (1978). *Life of the mind: Thinking.* San Diego, CA: Harcourt Brace Jovanovich.

Bakhtin, M. (1981). *The dialogic imagination: Four essays.* M. Holquist (Trans.). Austin, Texas: University Press.

Barnes, G., Crowe, E., & Schaefer, B. (2007). The cost of teacher turnover in five school districts: A pilot study. *National Council on Teaching and America's Future.* Retrieved from http:// nctaf.org/wp-content/uploads/ 2012/01/ NCTAF-Cost-of-Teacher-Turnover-2007-full-report.pdf

Barone, T., & Eisner, E. W. (2012). *Arts-based research.* Thousand Oaks, CA: Sage.

Beattie, M. (1997). Fostering reflective practice in teacher education: Inquiry as a frame-work for the construction of a professional knowledge in teaching. *Asia-Pacific Journal of Teacher Education, 25*(2), 111-128. doi:10.1080/1359866970250202

Beltman, S., Glass, C., Dinham, J., Chalk, B., & Nguyen, B. (2015). Drawing identity: Beginning pre-service teachers' professional identities. *Issues in Educational Research, 25*(3), 225-245.

Boe, E., Cook, L., & Sunderland, R. (2008). Teacher turnover: Examining exit attrition, teacher area transfer, and school migration. *Exceptional Children, 75*(1), 7-31.

Boulton-Funke, A. (2014). Narrative form and Yam Lau's Room: The encounter in arts based research. *International Journal of Education & the Arts, 15*(17), 1-17.

Buchanan, J. (2015). Metaphors as two-way mirrors: Illuminating pre-service to in-service teacher identity development. *Australian Journal of Teacher Education, 40*(10), 32-50.

Carlyle, D., & Woods, P. (2002). *Emotions of teacher stress.* Stoke on Trent, UK: Trentham Books.

Cheng, M. M. H., Chan, K.W., Tang, Y. F., & Cheng, A. Y. N. (2009). Pre-service teacher education students' epistemological beliefs and their conceptions of teaching. *Teaching and Teacher Education, 25,* 319–327.

Clandinin, D. J., Schaefer, L., Long, J. S., Steeves, P., McKenzie-Robblee, S., Pinnegar, E., et al. (2012, April 30). *Early career teacher attrition: Problems, possibilities, potentials.* Centre for Research for Teacher Education and Development: University of Alberta. Retrieved from http://www.elementaryed.alberta.ca/en/Centres/CRTED/~/media/ elementaryed/Documents/Centres/CRTED/ ECA_-_FINAL_Report.pdf

Clark, R., & Antonelli, F. (2009). *Why teachers leave: Results of an Ontario survey 2006-08.* Ontario Ministry of Education. Retrieved from http://www.otffeo.on.ca/english/media_room/ briefs/why_teachers_leave.pdf

Cliché. (2016). *Dictionary.com.* Retrieved from http://dictionary.reference.com/brow

Eisner, E. W. (2008). Art and knowledge. In G. Knowles & A. L. Cole (Eds.), *Handbook of the arts in qualitative research* (pp. 3–12). Thousand Oaks: Sage.

Eren, A., & Tekinarslan, E. (2013). Prospective teachers' metaphors: Teacher, teaching, learning, instructional material and evaluation courses. *International Journal of Social Sciences and Education, 3*(2), 345-445.

Forbes. (2015). *Forbe's America's largest private companies.* Retrieved from http://www. forbes.com/companies/amway/

Gambhir, M., Broad, K., Evans, M., & Gaskell, J. (2008, September). *Characterizing initial teacher education in Canada: Themes and issues.* International Alliance of Leading Education Institutes. University of Toronto. Retrieved from http://www.oise.utoronto. ca/ite/UserFiles/ File/CharacterizingITE.pdf

Gay, G., & Neftali Kirkland, K. (2003). Developing cultural critical consciousness and self-reflection in preservice teacher education. *Theory into Practice, 42*(3), 181–187.

Gee, J. P. (2000). Identity as an analytic lens for research in education. *Review of Research in Education, 25,* 99–125. doi:10.3102/0091732 X025001099

Geijsel, F., & Meijers, F. (2005). Identity learning: The core process of educational change. *Educational Studies, 314*), 419-430. doi:10.1080/03055690500237488

Haiven, M., & Khasnabish, A. (2014). The radical imagination. Winnipeg, MB: Fernwood.

Head, F. (1992). Student teaching as initiation into the teaching profession. *Anthropology & Education Quarterly, 23*(2), 89-107.

Hess, Ed. (2011, Feb. 24). The business revolution that's destroying the American Dream. *Forbes.* Retrieved from http://www.forbes. com/2011/ 02/24/destroy-american-dream-leadership-leaders-financialism.html

Hong, J. Y. (2010). Pre-service and beginning teachers' professional identity and its relation to dropping out of the profession. *Teaching and Teacher Education, 26*(8), 1530-1543.

hooks, b. (2010). Teaching critical thinking: Practical wisdom. New York: Routledge.

Izadinia, M. (2013). A review of research on student teachers' professional identity. *British Educational Research Journal, 39*(4), 694-713. doi:10.1080/01411926.2012.679614

King, T. (2003). *The truth about stories, a Native narrative.* Toronto, ON: House of Anansi Press

Leggo, C. (2008). The ecology of personal and professional experience: A poet's view. InM. Cahnmann-Taylor & R. Siegesmund (Eds.) *Arts-based research in education: Foundations for practice* (pp. 89–97). New York, NY: Routledge.

Lifton, R. J. (1989). *Thought reform and the psychology of totalism: A study of brainwashing in China.* Chapel Hill, NC: UNC Press.

Liu, X., & Ramsey, J. (2008). Teachers' job satisfaction: Analyses of the teacher follow-up survey in the United States for 2000-01. *Teaching and Teacher Education, 24,* 1173-1184.

Lotz, C. (2012). Distant presence: Representation, painting and photography in Gerhard Richter's reader. *Symposium: Canadian Journal for Continental Philosophy, 1,* 87-111.

Maarhuis, P., & Sameshima, P. (2013b, June 5). Pedagogy and parallax: The narrative canvasses of a Clothesline Project. Presentation for the *Arts Researchers & Teachers Society special interest group,* Canadian Society for the Study of Education, Victoria, BC.

Maarhuis, P., & Sameshima, P., & Chalykoff, J. P. (2014, May 25). Research antiphona: One transcript, four responses, and five catechizations. *Arts, Researchers & Teachers Society,* Canadian Society for the Study of Education, St. Catharines, ON.

Marino, M. T., Sameshima, P., & Beecher, C. C. (2009). Enhancing TPACK with assistive technology: Promoting inclusive practices in preservice teacher education. *Contemporary Issues in Technology and Teacher Education, 9*(2).

Morrill, J., & Stancill, N. (1995, March 20). Yager motivational tapes reel in cash. The Charlotte Observer. Retrieved from http://www.ex-cult. org/ Groups/Amway/dexter-yager-2.txt

NCES (National Center for Education Statistics). (2011, September). *Beginning teacher attrition and mobility: Results from the first through third waves of the 20007-08 beginning teacher longitudinal study.* Retrieved from http:// nces.ed.gov/pubs2011/2011318/

Neumiller, J., Corbett, C., Gates, B., & Vandermause, R. (2015). *Preserving self: Empowering older persons with multiple chronic medical conditions.* Patient Centered Outcomes Research Institute. Washington State University. Retrieved from https://nursing.wsu.edu/research/funded-projects/preserving-self-empowering-older-persons-with-multiple-chronic-medical-conditions/

Northcote, M., & Featherstone, T. (2006). New metaphors for teaching and learning in a university context. In *Critical visions: Proceedings of the 29th Annual HERDSA Conference,* Perth, WA, 10-12 July (pp. 251-258). Retrieved from http://www.herdsa.org.au/publications/conference-proceedings/ research-and-development-higher-education-critical-visions-33

Pinnegar, S., Mangelson, J., Reed, M., & Groves, S. (2011). Exploring preservice teachers' metaphor plotlines. *Teaching and Teacher Education, 27,* 639-647. doi:10.1016/j. tate.2010.11.002

Pope, D., Brown, M., & Miles, S. (2015). *Overloaded and underprepared: Strategies for stronger schools and healthy, successful kids.* San Francisco, CA: Jossey-Bass.

Sameshima, P. (2007a). *Seeing Red–A pedagogy of parallax: An epistolary bildungsroman on artful scholarly inquiry.* Amherst, NY: Cambria Press.

Sameshima, P. (2007b). Seeing shadows in new light: A procatalepsis on narrative inquiry as professional development. (Special issue: Creativity and education: An international perspective), *New Horizons in Education, 55*(3), 10-21.

Sameshima, P., & Vandermause, R. (2008). Parallaxic praxis: An artful interdisciplinary collaborative research methodology. In B. Kožuh, R. Kahn, & A Kozlowska (Eds.), *The practical science of society* (pp. 141-152). Grand Forks, Nottingham, Krakow: The College of Education and Human Development & Slovenian Research Agency (AARS).

Sameshima, P. (2009). Stop teaching! Hosting an ethical responsibility through a pedagogy of parallax. Journal of Curriculum and Pedagogy, 6(1), 11-18. doi:10.1080/15505170.2009.10411719

Sameshima, P., Vandermause, R., Chalmers, S., & Gabriel (2009). *Climbing the ladder with Gabriel: Poetic inquiry of a methamphetamine addict in recovery.* Boston: Sense.

Sameshima, P., Wiebe, S., & Hayes, M. (in press). Imagination: The generation of possibility. In B. Andrews (Ed.), *Perspectives on arts education research in Canada.*

Saunders, V. (2015) *". . . ": Using a non-bracketed narrative to story recovery in Aboriginal mental health care.* Unpublished thesis. Nursing, Midwifery & Nutrition, College of Healthcare Sciences, Division of Tropical Health and Medicine, James Cook University. Townsville, Australia.

Schafer, L. (2013). Beginning teacher attrition: A question of identity making and identity shifting. *Teachers and Teaching: Theory and Practice. 19*(3), 260-274.

Sinner, A., Wicks, J., & Rak, S. (2015). Minding the gap: Exploring the potential of the teaching portfolios as curricular innovation. *Visual Arts Research, 41*(1), 16-26. doi:10.5406/ visuartsrese.41.1.0016

Spivak, G. (2013). *An aesthetic education in the era of globalization.* Cambridge, MA: Harvard University Press.

Sullivan, G. (2005). *Art practice as research: Inquiry in the visual arts.* Thousand Oaks, CA: Sage.

The Guardian Teacher Network. (2015, October 11). *'Show us that you care': A student's view on what makes a perfect teacher.* Retrieved from http://www.theguardian.com/teacher-network/2015/oct/11/show-care-students-view-what-makes-perfect-teacher

Thomas, L., & Beauchamp, C. (2011). Understanding new teachers' professional identities through metaphor. *Teaching and Teacher Education, 27,* 762-769. doi:10.1016/j. tate.2010.12.007

Weber, S. J., & Mitchell, C. (1996). Drawing ourselves into teaching: Studying the images that shape and distort teacher education. *Teaching & Teacher Education, 12*(3), 303-313.

White, B. E., & Lemieux, A. (2015, Autumn). Reflecting selves: Pre-service teacher identity development explored through material culture. *LEARNing Landscapes 9*(1), 267-283.

Example 7.6: A/r/tography and Teacher Education

in the 21st Century[5]

By Sean Wiebe & Claire Caseley Smith

Abstract

In this article, we summarize research on Prince Edward Island where a Prince Edward Island teacher, identifying as an a/r/tographer, designed a digital and multiliteracies unit, as part of a directed studies course in her Master of Education program. Small in scope, this single participant case study was designed to give a fuller picture to three difficulties teachers often face when teaching new literacies. These are (1) applying multiliteracies theory, (2) thinking across literacies domains, and (3) assessing literacies holistically. Findings are derived from our six research conversations, and our discussion highlights the necessity of artistic ways of being and thinking for teacher education programs in the 21st century.

Keywords

multiliteracies; a/r/tography; new literacies; multiliteracies theory

From 2011-2015, working with Prince Edward Island teachers on a digital and multiliteracies' project, the Digital Economy Research Team (DERT) developed the following threshold concept map (see Figure 7.6.1) to describe the key literacy thresholds teachers would need to understand in order to design effective new literacies instruction, regardless of the medium, mode, or technology they planned to employ in their unit of instruction.[6] The threshold concept map was designed to demonstrate that when one is creating art, one is also in an analytical mode of thinking. Furthermore, as DERT's previous research has confirmed, the threshold between art and research is where teachers' thinking needs to develop (Wiebe, 2013).

---

[5] Reprint. Wiebe, S., & Caseley Smith, C. (2016). A/r/t/ography and teacher education in the 21st century. *McGill Journal of Education, 51*(3). 1163-1178.

[6] This research was funded by a Joint Educational Research Grant and a Social Sciences and Humanities Research grant.

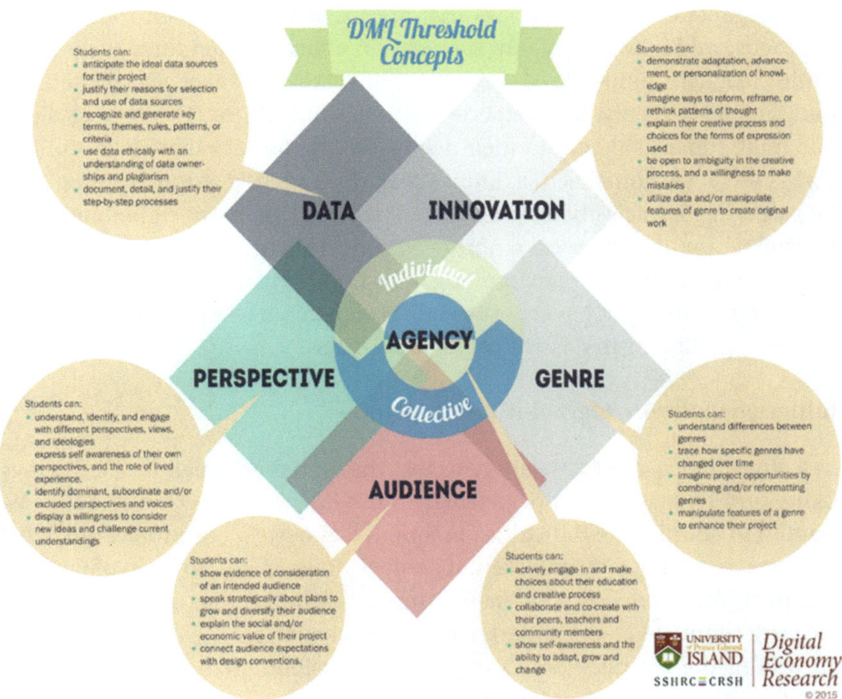

Figure 7.6.1. Digital and multiliteracies threshold concepts

Adapted from the New London Group's (1996) assertion that concept knowledge and technical skills are transferable amongst similar rhetorical contexts (i.e., the underlying thinking in framing a photograph is transferable to framing an argument in an essay), the central premise of the DERT's theoretical mapping of new literacies is that knowledge and skill competencies have multiple intersections, overlaps, and subtle shades of meaning; for this reason, and from these critical competencies, additional subset competencies follow. For teacher education programs, articulation of these subset competencies is an ongoing process, partly because such work is so vast, and partly because doing this work is a means of becoming more aware of how competencies transfer from one rhetorical context to another. Creative and critical thinking depend on these kinds of adaptations and transfers, so while articulation is happening in curriculum development, it should also be happening in all aspects of teaching and teacher education. This encircling of the teacher into the realm of curriculum thinking, particularly with respect to new literacies, is the power and promise of the DERT threshold concept map.

DERT generated three findings that are particularly relevant to advancing the theory and literature of new literacies in education. Findings suggest that while teachers understand key concepts with respect to digital and multiliteracies theory, they experience three difficulties: (1) applying digital and multiliteracies theory in their day-to-day planning teaching; (2) thinking across literacies domains, (i.e., from speaking to writing to representing); and (3) assessing literacies holistically, where separate skills are embedded into a holistic or applied experience of the learning. In teacher education contexts, these three difficulties are limiting questions regarding what constitutes learning, where literacy success can be demonstrated without reference to the underlying thinking that is critical to that success.

Initiation of the A/r/tographic case study

In a single participant case study to test the aforementioned DERT findings, Claire and I began our work together in the last week of October 2014.[7] We wanted to address the difficulties mentioned above, so our project was small in scope, involving only one class of grade 8 students and the two of us as co-planners. This work was a follow-up from a directed studies course Claire had recently completed, and undertaking it was part of her ongoing professional growth. As the teacher, Claire's primary responsibility was to the curriculum, and this important limitation ensured that students' new literacies projects would meet grade 8 English Language Arts curriculum outcomes. My role was to provide support as a co-planner, to document the process, and to take the lead in our research activities.

While having an art practice (blog, music, and poetry writing), Claire describes herself as fairly new to technology and to digital and multiliteracies. She hadn't previously had students using their mobile computing devices (MCDs) in class, whether it was their smartphones, iPods, or iPads. To prepare for our work together and teaching this unit, Claire familiarized herself with using her MCD as a creativity device. She explored digital storytelling apps, music capture and editing apps, video capture and editing apps, and various platforms for collaborative work.

Clarie's work with me also involved learning about a/r/tography, and it was with identities as a/r/tographers that we worked together. A central premise in a/r/tography is that teaching, researching, and art intertwine link a Gordian knot, and that each separate process is really not separate but braided with the others. Having located my own art-making, research, and teaching in

---

[7] A companion article based on the same data examines students' use of smartphones to create cellphilms (see Wiebe & Caseley Smith, 2016).

a/r/tography (Wiebe, 2008, 2010; Wiebe & Morrison-Robinson, 2013), we drew on this experience in our planning. A/r/tography provided a language for talking about including art and research in teaching. Additionally, as a portmanteau of art and graphy, a/r/tography provided a concise and understandable means for Claire to describe to her students the kinds of additional emphases their learning would include. As creators of art, understood in this context as their new literacies projects, students also took up the identity of an a/r/tographer, confirming previous research that a/r/tography can reorient teacher education through role reconceptualization, whereby the contiguous processes of art, research, and teaching are embodied, shared, and distributed across and amongst communities that value research and/or art-making as part of advancing education (Irwin, Beer, Springgay, & Grauer, 2006; Wiebe, Sameshima, Irwin, Leggo, Grauer, & Gouzouasis, 2007). This is a critical point and underscores the value of frameworks and languages that would enhance teachers and teacher educators' professional possibilities within what Richardson (2000) called creative analytical practices.

It was our working hypothesis that if Claire and her students could (1) identify as a/r/tographers (broadly understood); (2) could learn a/r/tographic processes where they could clearly describe their art-making; (3) and could incorporate an artistic way of being and thinking into their learning, then, we felt, the three difficulties of previous DERT research would be addressed. We reasoned that when identifying as a/r/tographers, the focus of student and teacher thinking would be better concentrated on isolating the conceptual thinking underneath literacies, thus helping students transfer one form of thinking to another. In the 21st century, what is needed are better frameworks and language for assessing literacy success, and if the threshold concept map assisted in identifying the underlying thinking involved in new literacies practices, then teacher education programs could consider role reconceptualization as a legitimate means for addressing literacy challenges of the future. We were both eager to find out if this new literacies unit would be viable for Claire to repeat the following year, and, hopefully, be one that she could share with her colleagues. A confirmed hypothesis would remove many of the barriers that prevent students from being able using MCDs as part of their official coursework. Conversely, a negative result would give us an important critique of teacher role reconceptualization as part of multiliteracies theory. In either case, we moved forward, confident that our a/r/tographic research project would advance practical applications of digital and multiliteracies theory.

Literature review

With the digital economy growing in Western nations, Brown, Lauder and Ashton's (2008) significant literature review has affirmed the need for new approaches to education. While the majority of research is focusing on reinventing the school, less attention has been given to reconceptualizing the role of the teacher. The fundamental problem with the conventional understanding of the teacher's role in society is that it is still largely conceived as information delivery to prepare students to meet curriculum outcomes that can be accessed via provincial-wide or national testing (McKnight, 2006). When knowledge is reduced and commodified in such ways, the creative aspects of teaching are moved to the periphery as non-essential. In contrast to the predominant view, our reconceptualization of the teacher's role highlights her/his artistic creation and agency (Biesta, 2012; Wiebe, 2013).

In addition to how the teacher's role is normally conceived, there is a second barrier to creative lesson design, one that is particular to English language arts (ELA) teachers. In order to prepare students for the tested curriculum, ELA teachers are primarily devoted to discrete, text-based literacy outcomes (Crook & Bennett, 2007), for, as of yet, trustworthy conclusions about how digital literacies are taught and measured holistically have yet to gain sway (Senior, 2010). While effective for increasing students' grades on tests, Dutro, Selland, and Bien's (2013) research has shown that explicit instruction with a narrowed focus is not effective for improving students' creative and critical competences in a broad curricular sense (p. 99). Combined with a lack of research that explores students' literacies' holistically (MacArthur, Graham, & Fitzgerald, 2008), it can be argued that explicit instruction, while valuable, does not help students achieve the necessary literacies for today's digital world. This is a significant limitation given the variety of rhetorical contexts students are likely to encounter (Scardamalia & Bereiter, 1991).

A focus on discrete, single literacy competencies is also limiting to teachers who value creativity in their lives and classrooms. On Prince Edward Island, for example, when new graduates take on positions in the local school boards, they face the competing interests of testing mandates and inquiry-based learning, the latter being a pedagogical approach emphasized in their teacher preparation. With inquiry learning, by engaging students in real life contexts that require effective knowledge acquisition and application, co-learning and collaboration, and creative problem solving, students develop valuable skills for today's knowledge-based economy (Dochy, Mein, Van den Bossche, & Gijbels, 2003). Wolsey and Grisham (2007) argued that connecting students with accessible, convenient, and adaptable tools "*conveys a different set of values about what is important and who the architects of learning should be or can be*" (p. 31). These "different values" are at a critical nexus between a) literacy and how it is operationalized in knowledge commodification, and b) embodied approaches to learning that integrate competency within the individual. With the kinds of social and economic implications that follow from these contrasting ontologies, it is difficult to overstate the difference.

Outlining the trends of an increasingly globalized knowledge economy, Brown, et al. (2008) explained how the digital variable is creating new approaches to knowledge and the social systems that produce it. They have identified a digital Taylorism that will reduce "*autonomy and discretion*" and "*segment talent in ways that reserve the permission to think to a small proportion of employees responsible for driving the business forward*" (p. 139). Williamson (2013) followed the same argumentative lines, casting skepticism on the education gospel that with new technology and better teaching comes higher skilled and higher waged employees. He noted a disturbing trend in educational reform that he called 'CompPsy,' a portmanteau of computer science and psychology.

ComPsy is the reduction of complex human behaviour to simplified techniques that can be standardized. Similar to the work of articulating and mapping literacies, the phenomenon of ComPsy reduces the complexity of human behaviour. Just as an English language arts teacher might break down literacies so they can be recognized, learned, measured, and then repeated, the objective in ComPsy is to isolate variables so they can be controlled and measured. What follows are calculations from these measurements and a systematizing of the calculations into a recursive function (i.e., an algorithm). The link between new literacies and the digital economy is in the application of these algorithms that strategically organizes and employs human skills in standardized ways to reduce the cost of labour, including highly skilled labour. Brown et al. (2008) wrote,

> *The communication technologies that we have today . . . have created the realistic possibility of developing global standards that reduce technical complexity and diversity. Business processes . . . can be broken down into their component parts, which include the unbundling of occupational roles so that job tasks can be simplified and sourced in different ways. In other words, an increasing proportion of managerial and professional jobs, that were previously sheltered because they were not tradable, are being redesigned.* (p. 138)

As they look toward the future, for teacher education programs, these broad social and economic perspectives on new literacies are crucial, lest they narrowly, and mistakenly, assume that new literacies are the individual skills of the future. New literacies also describe social and economic dynamics of a digital knowledge economy where skilled labour, operationalized as key literacies, is systematized and standardized.

By contrast, what a/r/tography offers for the creative teacher is a recognition of the value of sustaining her/his own creative practices and an invitation that these practices are valuable to pedagogical success (Wiebe, 2013). Valuing creativity a/r/tographically expands the teacher's role holistically without losing the explicit embedded instruction typical of artists who combine their creative and analytical practices (Richardson, 2000; Wiebe, 2013). Not surprisingly, this artful expansion of the teacher's role is consistent with constructivist learning theory which positions teacher and learner as co-architects in the curriculum experience, not just to increase students' ownership of the process, but also because knowledge is socially constructed through lived experience and collaboration, both at the micro and macro levels of society (Pegrum, 2009; Senior, 2010). Within this framework, teachers and students as well as students with one another, co-create knowledge, with learning focused "*on the learners' experiences, needs, interests and aspirations*" (Senior, 2010, p. 138). This student-centered approach was the foundation of the research project, which challenged students to create three persuasive pieces. Students followed typical inquiry protocols, with the exception that they used the threshold concept map to guide their processes and to think about their own thinking. Each of the threshold concepts of perspective, data, innovation, genre, audience, and agency were emphasized as students incorporated and applied information, communicated and collaborated with each other, and encouraged in one another their autonomy, flexibility and innovative expression (Pegrum, 2009; Struyven, Dochy, Janssens, & Gielen, 2006).

Methodology and methods

A/r/tography is research that is undertaken by practitioners (i.e., teachers) for the purpose of developing their own artistic practices (Irwin & Springgay, 2008). With the intention of developing our art, research, and teaching, the Skype conversations Claire and I had together became a way of focusing on the 'behind the scenes' work of teaching creativity, of trying something new, uncomfortable, and different from our colleagues. Our conversations were a chance to consider the time-consuming, life-altering, and deeply challenging personal nature of such curriculum work. Important to an artist's way of thinking and being are the ways curriculum work lives in the relational, messy world beyond the simple, transactional process of knowledge delivery and acquisition.

As a/r/tographers working together, it was our connections (Irvin & O'Donaghue, 2012) and complicated conversation (Pinar, 2004) through six Skype conversations that generated our findings. Because Claire was following an inquiry-based approach in her new literacies unit, by working collaboratively in our planning sessions, we were able to find and document solutions to everyday issues that arose during implementation. As a follow-up to her directed study, this hands-on, in situ teacher education was able to provide reflection time on the varia that a teacher encounters in the-day-to-day of pedagogical decision making. Together, our conversation provided both Claire and me an opportunity to develop professionally as artists, researchers, and teachers.

As can be expected in dialogically-based methods, complexity and depth was collaboratively generated. During our conversations, we questioned and provoked one another, we took notes on our impressions, our memories, our plans, and our discoveries. As a key part of our project was to gather insight on the educational possibilities embedded within becoming a/r/tographers (Irwin et al., 2006), we did, in our first conversation, discuss Norris' (2011) curriculum heuristic for arts-based research, where he has interrelated pedagogy, poiesis, politics, and public positioning. Norris' article was chosen because of how his framework opens possibilities for teacher educators to reflect on the multiple contexts of their being creative, and how that might affect their professional growth, not simply as artists but as teachers and public intellectuals. Our discussion of Norris' framework was not structured as we wanted to proceed naturally, feeling free to develop our relationship as a/r/tographers, and in so doing, contribute to the conversation anecdotes, interpretations, questions, memories of past teaching moments, and comments about our own lives; we wove all of these together, bouncing ideas back and forth in juxtaposition, creating that open third space of possibility.

Proceeding in this way enabled us to articulate some of the less visible challenges of shifting our thinking through an a/r/tographic lens. The convenience of Skype conversation allowed us to meet multiple times during the unit, often at the end of a teaching day. This immediacy of our sharing was an advantage in that Claire could draw on her lived experience, and yet, even after the passing of a few hours, and sometimes a few days, our dialogical process enabled deeper reflection and reinterpretation. Having both immediacy and distance, it was through the act of conversation that the complex layers and challenges of a/r/tography became part of our co-construction of findings. Some of what we shared in our conversations could not be included in a public text for ethical or professional reasons. Because 21st century teacher education is situated within the larger audit culture of K-12 and university education, Claire and I felt that certain critiques of the system would need to go unvoiced. Educational institutions do all they can to market quality education, and this means keeping a tight rein on what teachers can share. By not including these in the public text, we simply hope that silence will also speak.

The last part of our methods that ought to be noted is how we chose to write up this article. While we had hoped to engage in the profound challenge of narrating this complex story as two voices, we encountered the difficulty implicit in our roles. In the K-12 school system, Claire is not afforded the same time, status, or reward for conducting research. Given that she had already committed so much time to the Skype conversations, her role in the writing began after a draft of the paper had been written. She reviewed the entirety of this text so that it would reflect her sense of our conversations.

Findings and discussion

From their predominance in our six conversations, four important findings emerged. These also passed our applicability test in that each of them was significant in Claire's decision-making process of whether to teach the unit again. For these reasons, we feel that it is fair to represent these themes as our findings.

Finding one: Students need to be taught how to use MCDs as productivity devices

Student enthusiasm, heightened by the presence of technology and the opportunity to create multiliteracies projects, was linked to good pedagogy but limited by the school context. Undoubtedly, students were excited by the opportunity to use MCDs as part of their learning. Part of this enthusiasm was enhanced by the presence of additional technology in their classroom. Claire made her personal laptop available; she created better access to the desktop computer in the classroom, and the University of Prince Edward Island provided six additional laptops. Claire noted that this would be the first time many of her middle-school-aged students would be using MCDs in the classroom to perform official school work. While school policies, informally, were becoming less restrictive, the general school policy and social practice was that students were not allowed to have MCDs in class. This exclusion from the classroom contributes to the cultural ethos that MCDs are not productivity devices; thus, part of Claire's pedagogy included demonstrations of video creation apps, moving video data from an MCD to a laptop, storing files in the cloud, and using collaborative editing software. While young people are often positioned as technologically savvy, it was our experience that the MCD became a foreign and unfamiliar tool when it needed to be used for creative or critical use.

One of Claire's most important strategies was to solve the technical issues before the new literacies unit began. Each group needed a cloud account, an app for editing video, and a system for working together—and this included transferring files from their MCDs to the laptop that they would be sharing. An important choice early in the planning was that video editing on an MCD would be inferior to video editing on a laptop or desktop. Factors included screen size, processing power, and ease of collaboration. That said, MCDs were critical. They provided not just the affordability and familiarity of 'bring[ing] your own device' (BYOD), but they gave students the freedom to collect video data anywhere and anytime. Students understood that as part of their research unit, they were doing more than filming, and that their collection of video data was equivalent to doing a Google search with keywords or going to the library to research a topic, two of the most common ways that students had been taught to do research in previous grades.

When considering different foci for teacher education in the 21st century, Claire and I discussed school limitations for her specifically, but also for schools generally. One significant school limitation, and not particular to Claire's school, is that after completion of the unit, the learning focus quickly moves on to whatever else is planned. Sustained artistic attention is difficult to achieve in a school setting. Later in the year, students had an opportunity to enter their work in a competition specific for young people. The low response suggested that, in this case, students did not take on the identity of artists or a/r/tographers beyond the scope of the new literacies unit. Thinking about how teacher education might change, in our conversations, we wondered if the identity outcomes might have been different if teacher education programs could enculturate alternative ontologies with respect to recognition, agency, authentic learning, and portfolio style assessment. Schoolwork is largely unrecognized beyond the feedback a teacher gives in formative assessment or beyond the grade awarded as part of summative assessment. Student agency is also limited, constrained to the acquisition of competencies, with the normative assumption being that students can apply skills toward employment contexts later in life. Missing is the inspiration and aspiration of becoming an artist, of being a creative person, as seeing oneself acting and participating in creative and critical ways beyond the scope of the classroom. What if, for example, instead of school-wide testing, assessment focused on students developing a portfolio of work? While teacher education programs have little power in changing K-12 policies, they can consider more deeply the ontologies underneath normalized school practices.

Finding two: Transmediation is the promise and power of multiliteracies' theory

Following on from the threshold concept map, linking analysis and creativity was an effective pedagogical strategy. Claire's classroom experience was another confirmation of the practical value of what Richardson (2000) has called creative analytical practices. To begin their new literacies unit students were tasked with gathering their favourite, short YouTube videos. Most chose commercials and the central questions before them were to ascertain what made these videos popular and to identify what artistic techniques were employed. At this point, students had minimal photography or videography experience. Despite this, after students gathered their data, they were able to successfully sort it, derive principles of success, critique individual samples according to these principles, and then create their own content in reference to these principles. In reference to the threshold concept map (see Figure 8.4.1), it was at the intersection of genre / data / innovation that students were successfully advancing their research competencies. Combined with content knowledge available on the Internet, students were able to discover a variety of sophisticated shot types (such as over-the-shoulder) and utilize them in their own filmmaking.

In our conversations, as we talked about the implications for teacher education, Claire and I felt that these discoveries were concrete and material examples of new ways to represent critical thinking regardless of the literacy focus, and it is a significant reason for why Claire will repeat this unit in the future. Already having a basic facility with reading, middle and secondary students face the challenge of becoming critical readers. Text-only environments are comparatively abstract; for example, concepts such as point of view, framing, bias, and so forth, require students to imagine what is not in the text or to think beyond the text. However, when the text becomes visible through the materiality of film, these concepts are concrete and physical. A third person point of view, where the narrator looks over the shoulder of a character, is a very physical representation when one is holding an MCD behind the shoulders of another person. Similarly, when students learn to exclude undesirable information from the frame, to use either a wider or narrower angle, they learn that what is deliberately excluded from the text is a choice based on the overall strategy or intention of the director. This transmediation from one genre to the next, or from one rhetorical context to the next, is the promise and power of multiliteracies' theory and ought to be a mainstay in literacies across the curriculum courses in teacher education programs.

Finding two also resonated with finding one. As students shared data, they hardly noticed their own complex and rich conversations. Claire observed students prompting one another with questions such as: Did you see this one? How did they do that? Where would the cameraman be standing? What's that transition? In Claire's words, "students had bought into the unit and hardly noticed that they were doing the hard and serious work of research."

Finding three: Metaphor and story are pedagogically rich concepts for multiliteracies theory

Metaphor and story are two concepts that have a high degree of transferability. In English language arts courses, the concept of metaphor needs to move beyond the poetry unit and to help create cross-curricular applications of metaphor, I have developed a series of digital and multiliteracies lessons that involve working with haiku. Claire had her students do one of my haiku activities, where, initiated into an authentic literary problem, her students learned that the Western definition of haiku (5-7-5) was formulaic, missing a key tension between the speaker and what the speaker was observing in the landscape.

John McManus' (2013) haiku is particularly illustrative of the key tension in contemporary haiku: "*swans on the lake / my daughter fidgets / with her tutu,*" and this haiku, along with four similar ones, provided a reference point for students to create their own definitions of how haiku worked. After some class discussion, with their MCDs, students collected visual landscape data (line one) and visual portrait data (line two). Data analysis came alive when students had to write a third line that brought a landscape photo and a portrait photo into metaphoric relationship. As a mini activity taking only a few classes, students were initiated into the process of selecting, arranging, patterning, deriving, and creating. Writing a high quality third line was a creative act, but it was an act dependent on a great deal of analysis and understanding of what merged in the tensional space between landscape and portrait, objective and subjective, physical and emotional, symbolic and interpretive. In pursuing a pedagogical language to convey the power of the work that students were doing, we foregrounded metaphor, not only because it was a word students had heard before, but because it carried enough flexibility to be useful across genres. Students understood that whether working in poetry, prose, or film that metaphor was a means to explain, clarify, and extend an idea.

Similarly, story is another concept that has a high degree of transferability. In creating their new literacies projects, students asked the following kinds of questions: what is our idea? What is the premise? Who are the characters? What are they feeling? These kinds of questions emerged particularly in the editing phase of the project when students were blending music, narration (if there was a narrative track), and the photographic and/or videographic shots. Oftentimes, digital literacy is defined by text, sound, image, and movement, but it became clear in our work with Claire's students that it is the concept of story that undergirds each of these discrete units. In their new literacies' projects, students understood that the story of the music needed to work with the story of the message; that the story of the images (whether moving or still, whether long or short) also needed to work with the music and the message. While separate story layers, each track was an integral part of the entire story.

In our conversations, Claire and I felt that the new literacies unit conveyed the complexity of metaphor and story in ways that make these concepts of import to teacher education courses, particularly English language arts methods. It is not without some irony that these concepts still persist in a time when there is much focus on 21st century learning. A focus on metaphor and story questions the education gospel that students need more technical skills in order to flourish in a knowledge economy. From our perspective, the simplistic equation of new device equals new learning does not hold water.

Finding four: Multigenre instructional design increases motivation to revise

Student openness to revision is a key habit of mind developed in multiliteracies units. At the end of the new literacies unit, Claire worked with her students on writing paragraphs. Perhaps unfairly, especially given how communication is changing, an important marker of success for this unit was whether students could transfer what they had learned in their new literacy projects to text-only rhetorical contexts. In line with the recent district focus on writing, Claire emphasized that the newly introduced district test now required her middle school students to produce a single, well-developed paragraph with few errors in conventions. In addition to teacher-led instruction (two classes), students were given three classes to work independently on their summative paragraphs in the computer lab. Success criteria were the typical six traits of writing, and, given the anticipated competencies that students would learn / practice in their new literacies projects, students were given a rubric that emphasized ideas, organization, and word choice.

There was no control group as part of this study design, so when Claire assessed the student paragraphs, she was comparing the results to previous years of students. In our Skype conversation, Claire felt that as a class, her students did make the kind of text-only gains that she had hoped for. Students used metaphors to develop ideas, they experimented more with colorful word choice, and they enhanced their arguments with persuasive tones of voice. Importantly, Claire emphasized that this unit created the intellectual room for her more motivated students to experiment and grow through self-direction.

After the text-only assessment, Claire gave her students the opportunity to revision their text piece into another form, whether it be a short haiku, a poem, or a rant. Having experienced student resistance to re-vision in her previous years of teaching, especially to any major or structural changes (such as changing the point of view or changing the way an argument is framed), Claire was anticipating that this group of students would also resist this potential "extra" work. Instead, students embraced the opportunity to be creative, and in a discussion circle where they had to select and briefly share what genre most represented their message, Claire noted that students demonstrated a deep understanding of the value of multiple text forms and that when creating a new form, there was an opportunity to re-vision a piece.

Multiliteracies theory is complex, especially when working with film, as it combines so many elements. Not only are there multiple combinations of elements, but regardless of the genre produced, the resulting production is always located in a particular place in a particular time. Contextual variables are always there even when it appears they are not. Thus, when working in concert with sound and narrative, an image, whether moving or still, records something real,—and then story comes alive—that is when someone or something comes into an existence that compels a response from the audience.

Students could not come to this complex understanding independently. Claire drew on her own experience as a developing a/r/tographer to guide them. In her informal conversations with students, she had them shift perspectives, trade data, change their stance, imagine new narrators or characters. She told them to not just use the lens to capture something but to find the hidden or unknown. She challenged them to look inward to their own motivations and feelings that drove actions. And she had them experiment with multiple genres and create new hybrid genres (some students created video haiku using the Vine social media platform while others created Rick-Mercer-styled rants that had the ethos of a music video). Once students understood that any of the elements of the threshold concepts could be manipulated as variables as a way for them to create new content, they had a way to be innovative without being formulaic. Just as important, once students understood the elements of metaphor and story, they were able to create films full of questions, suppositions, and wonder. As a/r/tographers (and we are including students in this naming), if we are creating art to understand life and not just to depict it, then we must imagine our way into the material—whether working with the individual medium of text, image, sound, or movement, or whether working with some combination of all of them, it is our imagination that is crucial to the endeavor.

This call to an a/r/tographic imagination is significant to the study. In the short term, reinventing the teacher's role as an a/r/tographer, as we have seen with Claire, better enables teachers to introduce, connect, and embed unconnected skills in a holistic learning environment. In the long term, our proposal to reconceptualize the teacher's role presents teacher education programs with an effective means to imagine pedagogy as imbued with both art and research. With a/r/tography, literacies are learned holistically, and holistic instruction depends on teachers' understanding the theory of how individual skills transfer in multiple domains, the very essence of multiliteracies theory.

References

Biesta, G. (2012). Receiving the gift of teaching: From "learning from" to "being taught by." Studies in *Philosophy and Education, 32*(5), 449-461.

Brown, P., Lauder, H., & Ashton, D. (2008). Education, globalization and the future of the knowledge economy. *European Educational Research Journal, 7*(2), 131-156.

Crook, C., & Bennett, L. (2007). Does using a computer disturb the organization of children's writing? *British Journal of Developmental Psychology, 25*(2), 313-321.

Dochy, F., Mien, S., Van den Bossche, P., & Gijbels, D. (2003). Effects of problem-based learning: A meta-analysis. *Learning and Instruction, 13*(1), 533-568.

Dutro, E., Selland, M. K., & Bien, A. C. (2013). Revealing writing, concealing writers: High-stakes assessment in an urban elementary classroom. *Journal of Literacy Research, 45*(2), 99-141. doi:10.1177/1086296X13475621

Irwin, R. L., Beer, R., Springgay, S., & Grauer, K. (2006). The rhizomatic relations of A/r/tography. *Studies in Art Education, 48*(1), 70-88.

Irwin, R. L., & O'Donoghue, D. (2012). Encountering pedagogy through relational art practices. *International Journal of Art and Design Education, 31*(3), 221-236.

Irwin, R. L., & Springgay, S. (2008). A/r/tography as practice based research. In S. Springgay, R. L. Irwin, C. Leggo, & P. Gouzouasis (Eds.), *Being with A/r/tography* (pp. xiii-xxvii). Rotterdam, Netherlands: Sense.

MacArthur, C. A., Graham, S., & Fitzgerald, J. (2008). *Handbook of writing research.* New York, NY: Guilford Press.

McKnight, D. (2006). The gift of curriculum method. *Curriculum and Teaching Dialogue, 8*(2), 171-183.

McManus, J. (2013, March 1). Untitled [poem]. Daily Haiku. Retrieved from http://www.dailyhaiku. org/haiku/2013-march-01

New London Group. (1996). A pedagogy of multiliteracies: Designing social futures. *Harvard Educational Review, 66*(1), 60-92.

Norris, J. (2011). Towards the use of the 'Great Wheel' as a model in determining the quality and merit of arts-based projects (research and instruction). *International Journal of Education & the Arts, 12,* 1-24. Retrieved from http://www.ijea.org/v12si1/index.html

Pegrum, M. (2009). *From blogs to bombs: The future of digital technologies in education.* Crawley, Australia: UWA.

Pinar, W. F. (2004). *What is curriculum theory?* Mahwah, NJ: Erlbaum.

Richardson, L. (2000). Writing: a method of inquiry. In N. Denzin & Y. Lincoln (Eds), *The handbook of qualitative research.* (2nd ed., pp. 923-948). Thousand Oaks, CA: Sage.

Scardamalia, M., & Bereiter, C. (1991). Literate expertise. In K. A. Ericsson & J. Smith (Eds.), *Toward a general theory of expertise: Prospects and limits* (pp. 172-194). Cambridge, United Kingdom: Cambridge University Press.

Senior, R. (2010). Connectivity: A framework for understanding effective language teaching in face-to-face and online learning communities. *RELC Journal, 41*(2), 137-147.

Struyven, K., Dochy, F., Janssens, S., & Gielen, S. (2006). On the dynamics of students' approaches to learning: The effects of the teaching / learning environment. *Learning and Instruction, 16*(1), 279-294.

Wiebe, S. (2008). Resonation in writing. In S. Springgay, R. Irwin, C. Leggo, & P. Gouzouasis (Eds.), *Being with a/r/tography* (pp. 95-107). Rotterdam, Netherlands: Sense.

Wiebe, S. (2010). A poet's journey as a/r/togrpher: Teaching poetry to create a community of practice with junior high school students. *Learning Landscapes, 4*(1), 239-255.

Wiebe, S. (2013). How do I teach writing in a digital and global world? In K. James, T. Dobson, & C. Leggo (Eds.), *English in middle and secondary classrooms* (pp. 223-227). Toronto, ON: Pearson.

Wiebe, S., & Caseley Smith, C. (2016). Teacher and student a/r/tographers creating cellphilms. In C. Burkholder, K. MacEntee, & Jo. Schwab (Eds.), *What's a Cellphilm?: Integrating mobile phone technology into participatory arts based research and activism* (pp. 87-103). Rotterdam, Netherlands: Sense.

Wiebe, S., & Morrison-Robinson, D. (2013). Becoming a/r/tographers while contesting rationalist discourses of work. *Multi-Disciplinary Research in the Arts, 3*(2), 1-18.

Wiebe, S., Sameshima, P., Irwin, R., Leggo, C., Grauer, K., & Gouzouasis, P. (2007). Re-imagining arts integration: Rhizomatic relations to the everyday. *Journal of Educational Thought, 41*(3), 263-280.

Williamson, B. (2013). The future of curriculum. School knowledge in a digital age. Cambridge, MA: MIT Press.

Wolsey, T. D., & Grisham, D. L. (2007). Adolescents and the new literacies: Writing engagement. *Action in Teacher Education, 29*(2), 29-38.

Example 7.7: Sympathizing with Social Justice

Poetry of Invitation and Generation[8]

By Sean Wiebe & Pauline Sameshima

Abstract

In this paper, we use Sameshima's Parallaxic Praxis Model to create collaborative poetry. The model invites juxtaposing articulations to generate alternative thinking. Similar to Daignault's (1992) notion of a 'thinking maybe' space, we invite readers into what we call a liminal studio to theorize new understandings of social justice. In the data phases for this project, Viet Thanh Nguyen's (2015) The Sympathizer served as a play object: The narrator, the sympathizer, is a captured communist spy in the aftermath of the Vietnam war, and his confession (the novel) considers a critical question for understanding social justice: "*What is more important than independence and freedom?" Nguyen refuses simplistic overtures of social justice. Instead, readers are confronted with questions: "What do those who struggle against power do when they seize power? What does the revolutionary do when the revolution triumphs? Why do those who call for independence and freedom take away the independence and freedom of others*?" (p. 178). These questions lead us to the frame of our own ten-part poem, the modern scholar under interrogation. Our poetry reframes social justice as the art of being/nothing, the something of nothingness being a language of resistance for a reimagined politics.

Keywords

social justice; poetry; politics; imagination; liminal studio

This poetic inquiry has four parts. Part one begins with a description of our poetic methodology, an explanation of what we mean by the liminal studio and the methodological perspectives that poets might hold when creating in such a studio. Part two sets out to understand how social justice might be interrogated through our methodology, namely, the challenge of understanding social justice

---

[8] Reprint. Wiebe, S., & Sameshima, P. (2018, January). Sympathizing with social justice, poetry of invitation and generation. *Art/Research International, 3*(1)7-29.

outside the typical knowledge binary of subjective/objective. In Part two there is also the invitation to the reader to join us in this poetic inquiry, described as a critical phenomenological exploration. Part three is a poetic response to the challenge of social justice. Using Viet Thanh Nguyen's (2015) Pulitzer prize-winning book, *The Sympathizer*, to set the motif and frame of confession, the hero of our poetry, a scholar (like Nguyen's narrator), must discover what it is that needs to be confessed. The question is age-old, and it serves to illuminate the theoretical challenge of social justice: "*What is more important than independence and freedom?*" (Nguyen, 2015, p. 178). Part four offers a denouement. Drawing on Bruner's (2002) notion of canon and breach, and Schubert's (2010) notion of curriculum as a synoptic and expansive text, we suggest that poets operate as political agents when they imagine breaches in the social canon of knowledge.

Inhabiting the Liminal Studio, a Poetic Methodology

In reviewing our poetic writing, we have come to see that rather than bridging, reconciling, or bringing disparate ideas into coherence, we have instead positioned our projects between perspectives, navigating the liminal space. We draw from Daignault's (1983) work in staging and performing "*knowledge through a passageway*" (see pp. 7-13; also see Sameshima & Irwin, 2008). Through material thinking we imagine a studio space for the poet, a space that has the accessories of thought, a composer's creative "*thinking maybe*" space (Daignault, 1992, p. 202). When we take on projects such as this one, our collaborative liminal space is a studio space, and we find it helpful to imagine this abstract, theoretical space as more tangible than it really is. Come into my studio, create with me. A critical part of this methodology is the invitation.

Creation in the liminal studio depends on tensionality; where two or more ideas are held productively to reorient a situation, rethink an issue, allowing something new to emerge. When the creatives are poets, the poetic shapes the inquiry so that it is exploratory, often ambiguous, depending on the careful use of language to inform generative processes. While careful use of language is not unique to poetic inquiry, it is an aspect of its specialization. By careful we do not mean precise or exact, where definition is a pursuit of clarification. In the way that words convey, and do not convey, ideas, possibilities to draw out new meaning, our carefulness is not being content in singular meaning, in wrapping up the work too soon. Our carefulness means playing with signs and signifiers to seek new orderings and alignments (Sameshima, Wiebe, & Hayes, in press); it is a continual twisting and reframing, turning and returning, revisioning, recycling. Within a world that is not easily understood, taking care is the ongoing pursuit of new meaning, and it is our commitment to research. The Parallaxic Praxis Model (Sameshima &

Vandermause, 2008) offers a useful means of framing the tensionality of creativity in the studio space. The model invites juxtaposing articulations to exist together simultaneously as imaginative generators. Theoretically grounded in coding and encoding frameworks (Hall, 1973) and polysemic readings of texts (Barthes, 1996), this studio space is dynamic, relational, experiential, and meaningful while preemptively incomplete.

There are three organizational phases in the model. The Data Phase consists of the raw building blocks of the poetic play—data, words, ideas, play objects—in our case, Nguyen's (2015) The Sympathizer. In the Analyses Phase, we create articulations and compositions through playful analysis of the data (writing alone or building interchangeably from a draft). The analyses phase is a place of fractalling the boundaries of the original data. As our different perspectives engage and become entangled in the meaning-making of the data, we open larger semantic fields by mapping them onto the existing relations of the other's semantic field (Stern, 2000). The meanings we each attribute to the words we use in the poem expand the ambiguity of the possible meanings of our translations of the data. In this Phase, where the data is translated to another modality (poetry), the data can be viewed metaphorically; and it is in the personally constructed links between the data and the metaphor that newness arises. The aim, then, is to use multiple interpretations as a means to complexify, to open the spaces between the non-fitting pieces of interpretation through collaborative dialogic or construction processes in order to generate interpretive possibilities. In the Rendering Phase, the ideas are materialized to provoke further discussions in public venues. In this instance, the renderings are the poems.

Troubling Social Justice in the Liminal Studio

Writing poetry in the liminal studio, we have attempted to understand the productive tension of social justice. Like any ideological concept embraced in earnest, social justice can be put forward as a non-problematic objective. But as Pinar (2010) points out, objectives, no matter how lovely, still have a means-ends orientation. That is, wherever objectives can be defined, there are ideas about the best, or most efficient, or most viable, or most cost-effective means by which to reach them. Whatever the foremost constraints, whether it be saving taxpayer dollars or making decisions based on research findings, the pursuit of ideologically-oriented ends, particularly those ends that are future situated just beyond our current reach, is a foreclosure on present concerns, such that the social energies of today are made valuable only in the future when whatever it is that we have set down as our objective is realized. Beginning with the end in mind is a Westernized style of pragmatism of splitting knowledge into objective and subjective. What results is an empty knowledge on both counts: a false objectivity that masquerades as value-free, and an empty subjectivity purporting to support difference—both positions are ungrounded, that is, they are dislocated from history and time and cannot sustain a single point of view. In the former view of knowledge, critical theorists have emphasized the need for ongoing critique; and in the latter view, they have argued that there is no value-neutral position.

Taking critical theory seriously, does this mean that any growth-oriented position is necessarily unjust? Is it possible to have progress, transformation, improvement? The fear, we suppose, is that the pursuit of social justice may become an unquestioned social good, a value-free neutrality. We have found Heidegger (1977) helpful for stepping into these aporic arguments. He encourages us to be playful and poetic in our philosophic pursuits, and so, through generative play, we have approached the social justice knowledge binary with the curiosity of what else the phrase might be asking from us; it is an intentional moving into the foreground of our thinking that we do not yet know, that what we have known up to this point is insufficient. Heidegger calls this practice enframing, which is not simply the reversal of meaning, such as the Socratic pretence of not knowing, rather, it is additionally a playful tension of juxtaposition. To paraphrase Heidegger, when we set out "*to reveal the real,*" if we were to change "*our mode of ordering,*" the real reveals itself to us (Heidegger, 1977, p. 20). The openness to revelation is simply the acknowledgment that there are possibilities that exist beyond our current frameworks. Such acknowledgment is the basis of research, that there is knowledge yet to be discovered, that we do not and cannot yet completely and fully understand. We add, too, that this aporic view leaves all revelations, findings, and knowings perpetually incomplete.

Heidegger (1977) was decidedly holistic in his explanation of revelation, bringing together techne, poiesis, episteme, which for us provides philosophical grounding of poetic inquiry in the social sciences: techne is an acknowledgment that methods, tools, and techniques belong with poiesis, and together an intention can be made to create and generate possibilities that are beyond what is already known. With poiesis we stretch to imagine the world as it might yet be, reconstructed in that moment. The interplay of such a poetic imagination with episteme suggests that our processes of knowledge are both objective and subjective at once, that ontology and epistemology are co-implicated, neither being a priori. We hold this perspective because it allows us to stand in the middle of our lives without disavowing our experience. It is a phenomenological position, but a critical phenomenological position, where our standing in the midst is held in reserve, a curiosity that pushes us to yet another explanation.

Having named the challenge before us, we invite you into our liminal studio to create with us: we seek to understand social justice outside of means-ends frameworks. While the poetry below has already been written, the studio door remains open. Remembering the phases of the Parallaxic Praxis Model, the rendering phase is meant to provoke further discussion: thus, the poetry below is meant only to draw out multiple perspectives, exploring social justice phenomenologically, post-structurally, pragmatically, culturally, and critically. Our hope is that the creative process remains ongoing, bringing us into the very details of lived experience, while still asking what if, what might be, how can we imagine it otherwise?

Sympathizing with Social, Justice

In the Data Phase for this project we used Viet Thanh Nguyen's (2015) *The Sympathizer* as a play object. The narrator, the sympathizer, is a captured communist spy in the aftermath of the Vietnam War. Of particular interest for us was how the framing of this novel, told as an ironic confession, did not follow the traditional form of confession; the confessor-narrator, being of two minds, could sympathize with both sides, both the communists (his interrogators) and the nationals (those he was spying on). Through our collaborative dialogue on the novel we discovered that the narrator's insights would be a means to generate new ideas around social justice.

Over a series of interrogations, the narrator is tormented with the question, 'What is more important than independence and freedom?' The answer his interrogators desire is 'nothing.' Like the narrator, we too, understood ourselves as resisting the obvious answer; in our poetry-making we sought (and interrogated) those moments in our lived experiences when the need for normative answers pressed on us. The process led us to the frame of our own ten-part poem, the modern scholar under interrogation. At the climax of *The Sympathizer*, Nguyen's narrator discovers the paradox of nothing; the very confession his interrogators desired all along, i.e., there is "nothing" more important than independence and freedom. But in his articulation, the narrator understands nothing as something. He finds it possible to hold nothingness in objective space; a somethingness that can be played out in the tradition of existentialist philosophy. In Nguyen's poetic play on nothingness, we found inspiration for our poetic experiment with social justice as the art of being/nothing.

Moving to the Analyses Phase, we tried to understand the historical and social voices of our being/nothing resistance. We both identified ourselves as sympathizing with the cause of social justice, but we also knew, with Nguyen, that "those who insist on their innocence believe anything they do is just" (p. 103). We needed to trouble our own positions, so, in the next phase of our poetic making, we individually created poetic compositions as a playful analysis. In this case, it was a two-week period of fractalling the borders of the data. We used our contrasting draft poems and ideas as a means to complexify, and then, mapping our poems onto one another; we sought ways to bring them into productive tension and surface new historical and social voices in our own positioning. This autobiographical turn was a response to Nguyen's (2015) troubling questions, questions that refuse simplistic overtures of social justice: "*What do those who struggle against power do when they seize power? What does the revolutionary do when the revolution triumphs? Why do those who call for independence and freedom take away the independence and freedom of others*? (p. 178). Taking the provocation of these questions seriously/playfully, what if we were the 'those' Nguyen (2015) was referring to? It is an important historical shift. Is this not what Paul Beatty (2015) is suggesting in The Sellout when he says scholars are "*all spit and no polish*" (p. 97). He describes them as "*wereniggers . . . By day, erudite and urbane, but with every lunar cycle, fiscal quarter, and tenure review their hackles rise . . . and they schlep down from their ivory towers and corporate boardrooms to prowl the inner cities*" (p. 96).

If You Want, Justice

The two most important days in your life
are the day you are born
and the day you find out why.

-Anonymous

i. "*We wake, work, eat, and sleep according to what the landlord, the owner, the banker, the politician, and the schoolmaster command . . . but in truth [time] belongs to us.*" (Nguyen, 2015, p. 160)

Awaken paper tiger
the rooster is calling

awaken public intellectuals
you conference goers, funding magnets

creatives lost in history
you need a respite from it

your own capital investments
stolen from your integrity

awaken bankrupt scholar
steal back your time

remember the pleasure
of a lawn chair, a book,

a circuitous walk, sword fern
shoulder high, a path overgrown

remember cherry blossom air
warmth through your feet

carrying firewood
arranging your words like kindling

first the twigs, fanning
the flames, poetry burning

bright symmetry
in the forests of the sky

ii. "*Fixed on his mattress, the prisoner—no, the pupil—understood . . . to be a revolutionary subject he must be a historical subject who remembered all, which he could do so only by being fully awake, even if being fully awake would, eventually, kill him.*" (Nguyen, 2015, p. 161)

Awaken paper tiger
this is your examination

your torture, first question
who are you?

your initials a post script
in history, your last name

doesn't belong to you
not even your father's father

who traded his cow
for magic beans,

you are a nursery rhyme
a jack that went up the hill

because your father could not
leave his cloister

the water to be blessed
seeps back into the ground

iii. "*You think I'm a traitor! . . . A bastard who belongs nowhere, not to be trusted by anyone! The rage subsided just as suddenly into despair, and he wept. Would his sacrifices never be honored? Would no one ever understand him? Would he always be alone?*" (Nguyen, 2015, p. 163)

You are gimp, from falling,
from bullet wounds, think with a limp

askew, off-center, speak with a lisp
hybrid language, con-lib, neolib, glib,

seeing both sides, the sympathizer
a white iron poker in the eye

what do you know of light
freedom that is your torture,

that slides down the walls
and over your skin

keeps you from sleep
a gangrene growing in the mind,

memory, perception, deception
the interrogator speaks to you

in the soft tones of your mother
sweet boy, you are here, you are mine

iv. "*He was the man with a plan, the spy with an eye, the mole in the hole, but his tongue had inflated itself to fill his entire mouth.*" (Nguyen, 2015, p. 162)

Speak, sympathetic scholar
sound your yawp

open your eyes
your office is white

the floors, walls, paper
even paperless paper

electric white, wattage
hallways plastered

in posters, save the bottom
line, white ceiling tiles,

doors painted white, budgets
whitened like teeth,

zeroes grinning wickedly,
scholar, where is your bite?

v. "*He will never see, not with all the light in the world. He's been underground too long. He's fundamentally blind . . . all we can do is help the patient see his own mind by keeping him awake, until he can observe himself as someone else.*" (Nguyen, 2015, p. 164)

It is impossible to tell,
subject of a comic experiment

pupil and patient, open
body exam, open book

scholar etherized on a table
subject to devices of self

design, Rip Van Winkle
Sleepy Beauty

second question,
what are you waiting for?

Alice? The wolf?
Someone to love you,

pluck your brows, take
your confession, and say,

how beautiful your words,
let me enclose them

in quotations, and add
you to a list of references.

If only you could see yourself
a simple matter of division.

vi. "*I saw myself admit it then. I heard myself acknowledge that I was not being punished or reeducated for the things I had done, but for the thing I had not done. I wept and cried without shame for the shame I felt. I was guilty of the crime of doing nothing.*" (Nguyen, 2015, p. 168)

Poor scholar, a stuttering subject
of re-re-re-re-education,

afraid his-her-zir words
will be taken without form

without class, from an unauthorized
biographer, their proper

height and breadth
marked simply, and only,

on the door jamb, painted
over with an exodus

and their own histories.
Poor scholar, passed over

a copyright agreement
a citation, a patent,

an assistant to collect the bones
these hands, your hands

must not come in contact
with the earth.

vii. "*If you could see that I have nothing left to confess, if history's ship had taken a different tack, if I had become an accountant, if I had fallen in love with the right woman.*" (Nguyen, 2015, p. 167)

If they could see
if you had a mentor

shaping you in the ways
of class and form

if there were another school
that hadn't been closed down

if there weren't an ideology
to flee from, or soldiers,

if fire were only used
for boiling water,

if gunpowder hadn't been invented
or riffling, or combustion engines

or orthodoxy, if Henry
hadn't been a king

or if the pope's arms
were shorter,

or if there were years
of jubilee,

or if you had a land
that could not be taken

if there were a law
that could make it so

if there were no need
for such a law

viii. "*Looking down on myself, I could still see the child in the man and the man in the child. I was ever always divided, although it was only partially my fault. While I chose to live two lives and be a man of two minds, it was hard not to, given how people had always called me a bastard.*" (Nguyen, 2015, p. 169).

Lovesick scholar
chasing wildfire

ideologies, flying
across borders

of all kinds, a trans
professional, transnational

transitional, between homes
afraid to unpack

freightphobia,
boxes and boxes

circling the globe
unopened, bags packed

waiting, each affair
ending childless

curses and crying
echoing in a windowless

panel van, the salesman
said could be converted

when the time came.
Is there ever a good time

to convert? Endings
in beginnings, both as inevitable

as the nothingness
you carry within you

to trade on something
more. If they could see

ix. "*What's so funny? The commandant demanded. Nothing! I cried. I was, at last, broken. I had, at last, spoken. Don't you get it? I cried. The answer is nothing! Nothing, nothing, nothing!*" (Nguyen, 2015, p. 172)

Third question
why are you here?

you know they want something
more, let the truth serum,

take hold, let the buried
be resurrected, speak:

you want justice, and, and, and
each desire a brick

stacked in the sand,
build a monument

to your new gods
and the winds and the wars

of sibling rivalry still come,
you need a new history,

and I will give you one:
for billions of years

in the nothingness
was nothing, that nothing

came of nothing
was an insentient logic

unappreciated in its elegant
acquiescence to nothing,

the refusal to become
something even as words

were spelled out to describe
the nothingness to make it

understandable to no one.
Out of the nothingness

was the perfection of a circle
that was infinitely expanding

beyond knowledge of its boundary,
there was only perpetual center.

x. "*But what was this meaning? What had I intuited at last? Namely this: while nothing is more precious than independence and freedom, nothing is also more precious than independence and freedom! These two slogans are almost the same, but not quite.*" (Nguyen, 2015, p. 175)

The teacher reads
from their genealogies:

the first act of creation
murdered perfection,

put a something in the heart
of nothing.

Putting up their hands
the good students

know this is mockery
the class clown, too,

hand up so far
into the rarified air

the teacher wonders
who to call on,

or if it matters
who is mocking who.

She wonders why
she's kept a diary

of their genealogies
keeping them alive

with the morning reading,
her mother's smile

also hanging outside
the principal's office

a lifeline of prayers
squeezed into an eight by ten,

a hallway long
ready for renovation.

What is the point
of these memories

she digs up, a coffin
cannot be turned

into a museum,
letters, lovers, books,

childhood itself
turned into an artifact

of her care?
She cannot find you,

scholar, the desk you sat in
crushed, burned

and deposited in a heap
10 miles outside

the city, the purgatory,
the I love you

of your past a nothingness
so small it is a ghost,

a shiver up the spine
mistaken for the flu.

Perhaps that is the point
of her profession,

to give these ghosts
a chance to haunt her,

to syphon off whatever hope
is left in her heart.

A Denouement

In the lead up to the climactic rant of chapter 21, the prisoner pleads with his interrogators, saying he has nothing left to confess. At a point when he knows himself as completely emptied, his interrogators still want something more, and it prompts the following monologue:

> *If you could see that I have nothing left to confess, if history's ship had taken a different tack, if I had become an accountant, if I had fallen in love with the right woman, if I had been a more virtuous lover, if my mother had been less of a mother, if my father had gone to save souls in Algeria instead of here, . . . if we forgot our resentment, if we forgot revenge, if we acknowledged that we are all puppets in someone else's play, . . . if some of us had not called ourselves nationalists or communists or capitalists or realists, . . . if the Americans hadn't come to save us from ourselves, . . . if the Bible had never been written.* (Nguyen, 2015, p. 167)

In this ludicrous arrangement of the players in history, the prisoner realizes that justice is impossible, but for it to exist in this world, a completely different world would need to exist, and so begins a rant imagining an alternative history. His imagination of an alternative is a nothing/something, the first critical step in generating an alternative future. To do so the prisoner/narrator experiences a split; seeing his body as an object, as if from above, able to comment on his thoughts and feelings from a new narrative space. This necessary subjective/objective split creates liminal space, a studio space, if you will, that invites the possibility of alternatives to exist beside ideologies. What is created in this liminal studio space is a new recognition that "*nothing is, indeed, something*" (Nguyen, 2015, p. 167). The prisoner discovers the possibilities of holding nothingness in objective space; a somethingness that can be played out in the tradition of existentialist philosophy. This discovery refuses simplistic overtures of social justice.

Because it is possible, indeed more than likely, that the struggle for "*independence and freedom [can] make those things worth less than nothing*" (Nguyen, 2015, p. 169), what Viet Thanh Nguyen advises is the humour, paradox, ambiguity, and/or irony of being/nothing. To take one's ideology too seriously is dangerous, he says, "people who do not get the joke are dangerous people indeed. They are the ones who say nothing with great piousness, who ask everyone else to die for nothing" (p. 169). Nguyen asks, "*Why do those who call for independence and freedom take away the independence and freedom of others?*" (p. 171). And he answers his own question:

> *I understood, at last, how our revolution had gone from being the vanguard of political change to the rearguard hoarding power. In this transformation, we were not unusual. Hadn't the French and the Americans done exactly the same? Once revolutionaries themselves, they had become imperialists, colonizing and occupying our defiant little land, taking away our freedom in the name of saving us.* (p. 170)

We propose the something of nothingness as a language of resistance for a reimagined politics of creativity and generation. We write poetry to generate alternative networks of social relationships: in poetry these exist imaginatively; nevertheless, ideas remain powerful, and in so being, there is a resistance of a nothing/something. The liminal paradox is important, lest an articulation become too zealous, too invested in outcomes that can be applied broadly. Attributed to Aristotle is the maxim that the general is always unjust. To derive rules, policy, or laws that can be applied generally as a means to convey order, make decisions, or refine practices has been at the very core of human knowledge making activities. Given this rulemaking propensity in human beings, what Aristotle realized is that the general, when applied to the particular, is always unjust. There is always an exception to the rule. This is the heart of justice, to seek ways to value rule-creation for the general good while simultaneously recognizing that these rules will always fall short and that in this gap is the further work of modifying the general for the particular, the social for the individual.

Narrative scholar, Jerome Bruner (2002), called the collection of social laws canon. Canon represents the social accumulation of knowledge that is valued. Through historical and cultural influences, certain knowledge is assembled and represented as normative, as real, true, best, or good. Corollary to canon is what he called breach. The breach is an exception. It is a discovery, the generation of something new that cannot be categorized based on current frames of understanding. Bruner characterized the breach as inevitable, that, most often, societies will eventually incorporate the breach as part of the canon. Breaches occur at the margins of society, at the edges of what is perceived to be normal; it is at the margins of the world that we might expect the most fecund ideas, where the imagination is primed. Canon without breach is a techno-rationalism that supposes social justice is simply a matter of asking, 'what is it that we want to achieve?' and, 'what is the best way to achieve it?' Metaphors of commerce, with the efficiency of the assembly line and management practices that ensure everyone is working toward the same goal, understanding things from the same perspective, have been the primary means of politics for centuries.

Operationalized in education, this techno-rationalism, say den Heyer and Conrad (2011), creates a privileged ignorance. Reporting on bachelor of education students' beliefs about their competence, after having taken extensive training in Indigenous perspectives, these new teachers still reported that they were not prepared to teach junior high curriculum on Indigenous histories and knowledges. Why? Conrad and den Heyer (2011) speculate that students had positioned themselves outside these issues as if it were possible to be an effective teacher in Canada and have a history that did not include Indigenous peoples. What mattered for students was simply the literacies of knowledge disciplines, a technorational knowledge without history or politics. Insightfully, Conrad and den Heyer argue that such a positioning comes from privilege, the ability to choose one's place in history, or, more accurately, to not include others' histories as co-implicated in your own. They had hoped this bachelor of education course would create a breach in normative knowledge, that students might, in our words, enter the liminal studio.

Working with Bruner's (2002) terminology, we imagine poets as political agents when they imagine breaches. We are not arguing that poets take on a particular ideology of social justice, but that they work in a social justice studio of liminal space. Creation in the liminal studio depends on tensionality where two or more ideas are held productively to reorient a situation, rethink an issue, allowing something new to emerge. Canon and breach. In the liminal studio, the inquiry is exploratory, ambiguous, the poet using language in myriad ways to generate breaches.

In the Western history of knowledge, the human energy empowering the canonic drive has been a synoptic one (Schubert, 2010). In synopsis is the desire for clarity, refinement, prioritization. It is the pursuit to define so that concepts can be distinguished and recognized, enough so that they can be passed on to the next generation, a process called education (Aoki, 2000). Despite this, Einstein urges us that while knowledge can be made as simple as possible, it should be no simpler (Yale book of quotations, 2006, p. 231). In other words, synoptic processes need a complement of expansive ones. Knowledge assemblage processes need to be both synoptic and expansive. With every rule there is an exception. With every and, there is a but. In early Hebraic language, the sign wav, could signify either and or but. As a coordinating conjunction the sign wav had multiple, even oppositional meanings, and it was up to the reader to understand meaning through context and tradition. And, in the way that paradox often operates as a poetic trope, there is always the possibility that oppositional meanings were meant to both be true at the same time. Social justice is both expansive and synoptic. Communities are both individual and social. Justice is comprised of rules and exceptions to them. As poets, we work with these productive tensions in a liminal studio.

References

Aoki, D. S. (2000). The thing never speaks for itself: Lacan and the politics of clarity. *Harvard Educational Review, 70*(3), 347-369. Retrieved from https://doi.org/10.17763/haer.70.3.83729226065nxq27

Barthes, R. (1996). From work to text. In P. Rice & P. Waugh (Eds.), *Modern literary theory*. New York, NY: Arnold.

Beatty, P. (2015). *The sellout*. New York, NY: Farrar, Straus, and Giroux.

Bruner, J. (2002). Life as narrative. *Social Research, 71*(3), 691-710. Retrieved from http://www.jstor.org/stable/40970444

Daignault, J. (1983). Curriculum and action-research: An artistic activity in a perverse way. *Journal of Curriculum Theorizing, 5*(3), 4-28.

Daignault, J. (1992, October). Serenity. Paper presented at the Bergamo Conference, Dayton, OH.

den Heyer, K., & Conrad, D. (2011). Using Alain Badiou's ethic of truths to support an 'eventful' social justice teacher education program. *Journal of Curriculum Theorizing, 27*(1), 7-19. Retrieved from http://journal.jctonline.org/index.php/jct/article/view/302

Hall, S. (1973). *Encoding and decoding in the television discourse*. Birmingham, England: Centre for Contemporary Cultural Studies.

Heidegger, M. (1977). *The question concerning technology, and other essays*. New York, NY: Garland.

Nguyen, V. T. (2015). The sympathizer. New York, NY: Grove Press. Pinar, W. F. (2010). Notes on a blue guitar. *Journal of Educational Controversy, 5*(1), 1-9. Retrieved from http://cedar.wwu.edu/jec/vol5/iss1/18

Sameshima, P., & Irwin, R. (2008). Rendering dimensions of a liminal currere. Transnational *Curriculum Inquiry, 5*(2), 1-15. Retrieved from http://ojs.library.ubc.ca/index.php/tci/article/view/28

Sameshima, P., & Vandermause, R. (2008). Parallaxic praxis: An artful interdisciplinary collaborative research methodology. In B. Kožuh, R. Kahn & A. Kozlowska (Eds.), *The practical science of society* (pp. 141-152). Grand Forks, Nottingham, Krakow: The College of Education and Human Development & Slovenian Research Agency (AARS).

Sameshima, P., Wiebe, S., & Hayes, M. (in press). Imagination: The generation of possibility. In B. Andrews (Ed.), *Perspectives on arts education research in Canada*.

Schubert, W. (2010). Journeys of expansion and synopsis: Tensions in books that shaped curriculum inquiry, 1968–present. *Curriculum Inquiry, 40*(1), 17–94. doi: 10.1111/j. 1467-873X.2009.00468.x

Stern, J. (2000). *Metaphor in context.* Cambridge, MA: MIT Press.

Yale book of quotations (2006). New Haven, CT: Yale University Press.

Example 7.8: Climbing the Ladder with Gabriel

Poetic Inquiry of a Methamphetamine Addict in Recovery[9]

By Pauline Sameshima, Roxanne Vandermause,
Stephen Chalmers & Gabriel

Abstract

Climbing the Ladder with Gabriel demonstrates the power of photography and poetry to render the experience of methamphetamine addiction and recovery through the art of an interdisciplinary research methodology. Instructors, students, recovering addicts, and prevention/recovery advocates will find this a valuable resource. There are many ways to "know the world." The authors of this remarkable text have adopted an eclectic mix of methodologies from the arts and sciences to portray the experience of methamphetamine addiction. While it may never be possible to fully "know" another's experience, this book provides readers with one of the most intimate portraits of a methamphetamine addict ever assembled. The reader will be touched by the juxtaposition of everyday joy and the hopelessness and regret so poignantly portrayed by these authors. The book is also hopeful, documenting that, even in the throes of terrible addiction, unique humanness survives and recovery is always possible.

Keywords

parallaxic praxis; addiction and recovery; interdisciplinary research; arts integrated research; research methodology

Introduction

How do we address the larger questions of society, those that threaten or diminish the well being of individuals and communities? How do we solve the big problems, find answers for hardship, inequity, suffering, and loss? Such issues overwhelm, raise concern, and puzzle. Which method of inquiry clarifies complex issues? Which method can explain drug addiction, for example, or why a woman with children uses and sells methamphetamine? In

---

[9] Reprint. Sameshima, P., Vandermause, R., Chalmers, S., & Gabriel. (2009). Introduction. *Climbing the ladder with Gabriel: Poetic inquiry of a methamphetamine addict in recovery* (pp. 3-16). Rotterdam, The Netherlands: Sense.

the health care disciplines, various quantitative and qualitative research methods are used to ask and answer such questions; but methods fall short when a deeper understanding of complex issues is desired. For this reason, we assert that multiple methods, media, and disciplines provide broader, deeper understandings of questions of meaning. Further, the blending of science and the humanities, the infusion of arts into research inquiry, offers a reach into the paradoxical and the mysterious, a move toward knowing better that which is important to know.

Gabriel, a recovering methamphetamine addict and dealer, became the subject and participant of a research study that tells her story in multiple ways, not the least of which is through the poems and pictures of this volume. Originating in the field of nursing as a means to address the health care problems associated with addiction, this study grew from a need to expand upon traditional scientific research methods. The questions inherent in the problem of addiction cross disciplinary boundaries and cannot be contained by the methods and media of a single means of inquiry. To delve into a deeper understanding of experience, one that cannot be categorized or constrained, it was necessary to reach for multiple perspectives and be open to a confluence of ideas and ideology. Further, in applying the tools of scientific and scholarly inquiry and by inviting the interpretations of scholars in the humanities, what emerged from the data in this study were findings unexpected and revealing. Through the poetry and art of this volume, the meaning of Gabriel's experiences offers the scientific community valuable insights for health care practice that yield new understandings. This introduction describes the study from which these artistic representations arose.

Researching the Problem of Methamphetamine Addiction and Recovery

The problem of methamphetamine addiction prompted the initiation of this research project. The intent to stimulate a broader understanding of the experience of addiction and recovery was to advance clinical, methodological, and social changes.

Methamphetamine addiction has stormed the culture and threatens the health of individuals, families, and communities. In 2007, U.S. national surveys identified methamphetamine as the *primary* drug of abuse in 142,955 treatment facility admissions, 7.5% of all admissions for substance use; these numbers represent a rising proportion of women (SAMHSA, 2008). It is a pernicious, and devastating form of chemical addiction that has severe psychological, physical, social, and environmental effects (Gettig, Grady, & Nowosadzka, 2006; Lineberry & Bostwick, 2006; Tanne, 2006). The expanding popularity of the drug across the country and exponential increases in methamphetamine related healthcare admissions (Lineberry & Bostwick, 2006) have rallied stakeholders in healthcare, law, politics, education, social work, environmental services, and in the public domain. Researchers have become attentive to studying the short and long term cognitive effects of the drug (Johanson et al., 2006) and there is progressive work in the area of treatment for methamphetamine users, including pharmacological and behavioral interventions (Heinzerling et al., 2006; Roll, 2007; Shoptaw et al., 2006). This promising research, necessary to build a science base for addictions treatment, unfortunately, omits the detailed and in depth analyses of the *experience* of addiction and recovery, thereby raising the possibility of a disconnect between current clinical practices and the real life struggles of people with addictions.

The question that is commonly asked and for which our team was concerned with was, 'What does it mean to experience methamphetamine addiction? What does it mean to recover?' Answers to these social questions were sorely desired. Many of the faculty members at our university expressed consternation that a clear answer could not be readily appropriated. An in depth examination, through multiple lenses, of one woman's story might give way to an understanding that has eluded science and society. Our study was designed to move deeper into methodological technique while, at the same time, opening possibilities for interpretive representation of meaning.

Scholarly approaches to examine life story make it possible to illuminate patterns and processes that have gone unnoticed or, in the case of methamphetamine addiction, have been elided by the incendiary media coverage of the trauma to children and the environmental impact of methamphetamine laboratories. These community concerns are glaring and important to address, yet the initiation and experience of using this drug are often unexamined, leaving a vacuum in our understanding of the complex and fundamental problems that accompany this addiction.

Due to the complexity of substance use disorders and high rates of treatment failure, multiple venues for drug dependency assessment, diagnosis, and treatment are needed. Substance use is associated with serious social problems, including violence, poverty, homelessness, incarceration, theft, and property damage. These problems contribute to suffering, social injustice, and tax burdens on citizens. Compounding the problem are funding limitations for addictions research, socio-political factors that impede community action, and financial challenges in public schools. Therefore, new and innovative approaches to addressing addictions in our communities are needed so that professional and public groups create and sustain fresh opportunities for education, prevention and treatment. For these reasons, along with an academic challenge to improve methods that address the serious social problems of our time, a study examining Gabriel's story was undertaken.

Gathering a Research Team

The use of collaborative, interpretive research methods to convey meaning and enrich understanding is growing. Such methods are innovative because the various personal, epistemological, and philosophical orientations that contribute to group work create a unique alchemy that opens thinking and expands possibilities for understanding. In considering the need for interpretive methods to study addiction and recognizing the limits of a single approach, multiple perspectives, as well as multiple representational media, were sought. A call to scholars in the sciences and humanities at Washington State University resulted in the response of 20 interested scholars, all from humanities disciplines. Eager to explore this complex topic using literary and artistic forms, many of these scholars, though intrigued, could not continue with a new project in light of their current obligations. Ultimately, six scholars (See Table 1) joined the inquiry and continue to participate in analyzing, interpreting and representing findings from this research study as well as a subsequent study, funded by the American Nurses' Foundation, which examines the experiences of additional participants in recovery. The scholars and artists' commitment was driven by their own interests in answering the compelling questions described, an interest grounded in their concerns for students and community members at risk for chemical addiction. This sincerity of purpose may be a key factor for success in implementing this transmethodological study.

Scholars	**Position**	**Academic Discipline**	**Foci in this project**
Stephen Chalmers	Independent Photographer	Fine Arts	Photographs significant addiction and recovery locations
Sheila Kearney Converse	Clinical Assistant Professor	Music	Studies the intersection between songs of childhood, addiction, and recovery life periods
Laurilyn Harris	Professor and Chair	Theatre & Dance	Interprets transcripts leading to screenplays
Linda Kittell	Clinical Associate Professor	English	Develops poetry from the transcripts with English undergraduate students
Pauline Sameshima	Assistant Professor	Teaching and Learning	Develops research methodology, art, and educational materials
Roxanne Vandermause	Assistant Professor	Nursing	Leads project and develops hermeneutic explication of patterns and themes

Table 7.8.1. Contributing Scholars. P. Sameshima, 2009.

Collecting Data

In our study of Gabriel's experience, we established research aims and procedural steps to collect data. The aims were to: 1) better understand methamphetamine addiction struggles and uncover prevention and recovery possibilities; 2) develop thought provoking information for educational programs in schools and public venues; and 3) design collaborative methodologies that could inform research and practice in new ways. Following approval by our institutional Office of Research Compliance, in depth interviews were conducted, audiotaped, and transcribed verbatim. De-identified transcripts were made available to all members of the team for analysis.

Considering Methods

Multiple methodological approaches contributed to the conception of this study, but the methods themselves evolved as the study progressed. The infusion of art in the interpretive effort led us not only to deeper understandings about Gabriel's experience but also to methodological discovery. In interpreting the phenomenon of interest, via our respective attempts to make meaning, we were compelled to examine our methodological orientations in the process. Looking at our respective analytic processes alongside the artistic renderings or interpretive results required a focus that raised our awareness and allowed us to develop a research comportment that transcends traditional methods.

In organizing the study as part of an effort to answer the question of meaning, a Heideggerian hermeneutic approach was initially used to ground the study philosophically (Benner, 1985; Diekelmann, Allen, & Tanner, 1989; Diekelmann & Magnussen Ironside, 1998; Leonard, 1994; Nehls & Sallmann, 2005; Rice, 2005; Vandermause, 2007). Using this approach, common practices are identified to uncover meaning. Such practices are revealed contextually through stories that are analyzed carefully in their textual form. The interpretation of these texts requires a particular open stance that is cultivated for the interpretive project. There is not a specific guiding theory, nor is there a specific expected outcome. Rather, it is a philosophical approach to inquiry and analysis that permeates all aspects of the study. Results stimulate new, previously unattended thinking that generates questions and recognizes the hidden or overlooked. This approach is valuable when the intention is to see deeply into a phenomenon that is complex and puzzling and when questions of meaning are entertained.

A single case study was chosen, through which questions of meaning could be explored and from which a method and methodology could be launched. We used the in-depth portrayal of the experience of one woman, through various interpretive representations of her life story, as the vehicle by which understanding was sought. Gabriel (self chosen pseudonym), in her fifties and in recovery for a decade from methamphetamine addiction, centered the activity by providing intimate interviews of her addiction and recovery experience. From the audiotaped interviews, we re-interpreted and represented her experience through our own lenses via narrative description, photography, poetry, music, and theatre arts. As representations, these translations are not intended to be literal or personal but interpretive and evocative, available to the academy and the public in the form of scholarly publications, presentations at conferences, fine arts gallery presentations, and community based presentations to lay audiences.

To establish a guiding frame that would address the question of meaning, include a social action component, and also incorporate multiple methods, Roxanne Vandermause, the primary investigator and nurse, found it useful to identify an overarching framework that would include the multiple methods and methodologies that would influence the data collection and analysis. At first, *Portraiture* (Lawrence-Lightfoot & Davis, 1997; Dixson, Chapman, & Hill, 2005) was identified as a reasonable approach because, as a method, it could be useful alone or in concert with empirical/analytical and other interpretive methodologies. Portraiture is a way of thinking about and also producing rich representations of phenomena; it aims to "bridge the realms of science and art" (p. 4). Further, its purpose to appeal to professional, as well as lay audiences, was considered to be highly relevant in an attempt to inspire social change. The attempt is to move beyond academy's inner circle, to speak in a language that is not coded or exclusive, and to develop new literacies that will entice readers to think more deeply about issues that concern social wellbeing. Portraitists write to inform and inspire readers (see p. 10).

Portraitists in various disciplines have illuminated ideas and understandings that complement and extend other methods of inquiry, describing artistic representations as well as best practices in education (Appenzeller, Amm, & Jones, 2004; Davis, Soep, Maira, Remba, & Putnoi, 1993; Harding, 2005; Lawrence-Lightfoot, 1983, 1994; Newton, 2005). Thus, a central frame for thinking about the goals and objectives of this project provided an early touchstone intended to give the project some cohesion and allow us to reorient during critical periods as our unique methodology developed.

Underlying the entire project is a participatory research approach (Small, 1995; Reason, 1994), which incorporates the key participant's (Gabriel's) role in the research. Gabriel is integral to decision turns regarding data collection, analysis, and dissemination. This means that there are ongoing modifications made in the study and, consequently, the consent and protocol. Such movement affects each step of the research process. Our commitment to participatory research required us to inform Gabriel of the analytic steps and the creative project plans. She was welcome to participate in the research discussions; however, she chose to limit her personal contact to the interviewer and photographer to maintain as much anonymity as possible. Interpretations, therefore, were derived from textual analysis of interview transcriptions (reported in other venues) and the synthesis of artful representations.

It is in the infusion of artful representations and the synthesis of these analyses that we are able to generate the understandings we seek. The methodological framework, informed by various interpretive traditions (hermeneutics, portraiture, participatory research) gave way to an approach described by Pauline Sameshima, an educational researcher that expanded the original structure of this work, taking it outside the boundaries of traditional research methodologies, even those used in the realm of interpretive research. Sameshima's work in curriculum theory and research paradigms incorporates the work of various qualitative research methods including narrative inquiry (Clandinin, 2007; Connelly & Clandinin 1990, 1994; Leggo, 2008; Richardson & St. Pierre, 2005), arts-informed research (Cole & Knowles, 2001a, 2001b; Sameshima, 2007), a/r/tography (Irwin, 2004; Springgay, Irwin, Leggo & Gouzouasis, 2008, Sameshima, 2007), and poetic inquiry (Prendergast, Leggo & Sameshima, 2009a, 2009b).

Through this project with Gabriel, the methodological and pedagogical model of *Parallaxic Praxis* has been developing. The model has since been incorporated as a tool to query teacher education engagement issues (Sameshima & Sinner, 2009), contemporary technology integration (Marino, Sameshima & Beecher, 2009) and other educational research inquiries. This model rests in the investigators' authority, integrity, experience, and commitment to guide their interpretations, reconceptualizations, and research. As mentioned earlier, one of the critical factors to the success of this transmethodological work is a genuine sincerity and focus on the team goals or mission. In this case, *"What does it mean to experience methamphetamine addiction? What does it mean to recover?"*

In juxtaposing and re-presenting artful interpretations in tension and in tandem, the team's belief is that new, greater, and deeper understandings can be surfaced. By studying the hybrid spaces of coupled interpretive systems, complex patterns are revealed which are not evident when researched separately. These ways of thinking rest in the vein of conceptual models followed by archaeologists such as Timothy Kohler, Washington State University's Regents Professor, who studies the interactions between natural and human systems. Kohler's work focuses on understanding the causes for changes in settlement systems in southwestern Colorado by looking at changes in the environment and how these changes may have affected human settlement behavior. Without looking at the systems side by side, understandings of "why" settlement behavior changed over time is not possible.

Compare the following two models of research design. The first (Figure 7.8.1) closes with an answer. The second (Figure 7.8.2), is the Parallaxic Praxis paradigm model. The research is initiated with questions. Data is collected and interpreted by a collaborative team with the focus on analysis of the nexus spaces between researchers' interpretations and systems for meaning-making. The confluence of interpretations creates novel understandings, provokes new questions, generates new knowledge, and presses new thinking. This model has grown out of a number of research models but is specifically grounded by a pedagogy of parallax (Sameshima, 2007)—that all knowledge, learning, and understanding is incomplete and that only through multi-perspectives, and in this case, multi-researcher discourse and varied systems of representation, can fuller personal understanding be had.

Figure 7.8.1. Traditional Research Design. P. Sameshima, 2009.

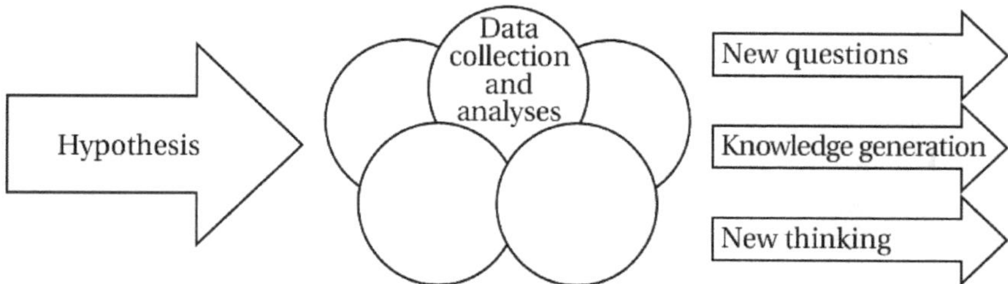

Figure 7.8.2. Parallaxic Praxis Paradigm Design.

Curricular Perspectives

This project employs perspectives supported by the *Interdisciplinary Studies Project* based at Harvard Graduate School of Education which includes the work of Boix Mansilla (2004), Dillon (2001), Nikitina (2002), and Miller (2005). Specifically, researchers utilize the approaches of a *Pedagogy of Parallax* (Sameshima, 2007, 2008) which support Bakhtin's (1986) notion of *heteroglossia* which refers to the inclusion of all conflicting voices as having value. This type of research further validates Denzin's (1997) view that postmodern ethnography "values and privileges the authority and voice of the reader and thus changes the role and authority of the researcher as meaning maker and theorizer" (p. 36).

The team supports the understanding that curriculum is "the site on which the generations struggle to define themselves and the world, [that] curriculum is an extraordinarily complicated conversation" (Pinar et al., 1995, p. 848), and that curriculum [refers] to educational courses of action that facilitate human 'growth' [that are] so complex that [they] cannot be studied through any particular theoretical perspective" (Henderson & Slattery, 2004, p. 3).

In "playing" out the hermeneutic interview transcripts or engaging with the participant's texts through arts practices, multi-genre narrative texts and visual art, or music, performance, or movement; a complicated and complex conversation is created; and through this shifting and sifting (Aoki, 1996) and agitation of reciprocality, reversibility, resonance, reverberation, and echo, within and between forms and mediums, the unarticulated becomes articulated, seen, marked, and visible (see Springgay, Irwin, & Wilson Kind, 2005; Jones, 1998; Pollock, 1998; Sumara & Luce-Kapler, 1993). Artful research like this, is the act of focusing the camera lens to still a moment in time for others to "see" an iteration, to make the consciousness visible for others to interrogate, judge, and edit (see Sameshima, 2007a).

It is important to note that the visual model shown cannot be reinstituted by any research team for any research project. The design must be specifically created for each project based on the expertise of the team members. Also, note that data collection sources may not necessarily be interview transcripts. The data could be multiple types of content. The researchers promote a model which is always contextualized to the particular team and project.

Parallaxic Praxis

Parallaxic Praxis is a researching, teaching and learning design model which is grounded in holistic arts-integrated inquiry. Parallaxic Praxis supports personal meaning-making as knowledge production. In this case, researchers work with content through various avenues utilizing mediums such as video production, art making, poetry, plays, and other artful endeavours. They utilize the arts in order to create renderings of understanding. The product then becomes a medium to share, engage, and provoke further learning through Socratic conversation. The model encourages the researcher to not only engage with the content in a personal artful or representative way but to think more critically about the content from a relational meaning-making perspective.

The Parallaxic Praxis method of meaning-generation produces an artifact, which can then spur further learning in others. Figure 7.8.3 illustrates the progression of content fractalled through artful knowledge generation. This space facilitates dialogue and the juxtaposition of the interstices of research discourses as described in the research paradigm design in Figure 7.8.2.

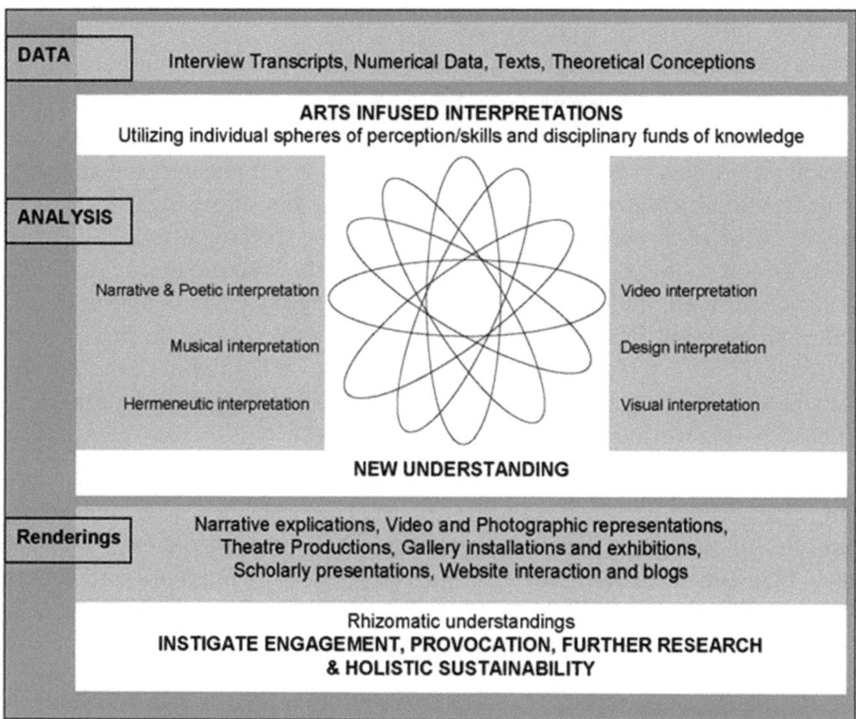

Figure 7.8.3. Parallaxic Praxis for a Portrait of Methamphetamine Addiction and Recovery.

The complexity of voice, experience, and interpretation can be distilled using innovative and thoughtful interpretive approaches to inquiry. It is via such methods that issues often held in shadow are examined and new approaches to matters of suffering are conceptualized. In examining the complex, unappealing and consequential phenomenon of addiction, methods such as those described here are necessary to explore those aspects that cannot be fully addressed by empirical/ analytic methods alone.

Poetic Inquiry

> *Nothing speaks for itself. Interpretation is as necessary to human life as breathing. Authors can be hidden, but nothing in actuality can be done without them. Distancing oneself through reporting that avoids first-person constructions and other overtly personal appearances in the text usually comes with the posture of being "objective." It has a long-established place in social science research, despite its fictional nature—a useful one, to be sure, but a fiction nonetheless because all research necessarily starts with an observer moving through the world as a personally-situated sensuous and intellectual being.* (Brady, 2009, p. 5)

In a Canadian federally-funded postdoctoral research project on poetry in qualitative research, Monica Prendergast (2009) found 182 citations of poems published in peer-reviewed social science journals within the preceding decade and noted the increasing use of poetry in academic research. The term *poetic inquiry* is an umbrella phrase for the multiple ways scholars name poetry in research. The term covers a variety of labels such as: research poetry (Cannon Poindexter, 2002), data poems (Commeyras & Montsi, 2000), poetic representation (Richardson, 1994), poetic transcription (Glesne, 1997), found poetry (Butler-Kisber, 2002), anthropological poetry (Brady 2000), ethnopoetics (Rothenberg, 1994), field note poems (Cahnmann, 2003), and more. Prendergast (2009) found that poetic inquiry spans multiple areas of the social sciences including "*psychology, sociology, anthropology, nursing, social work, geography, women's/feminist studies and education*" (p. 14).

The work of Laurel Richardson (1992a, 1992b, 1994, 1997, 1998), Corinne Glesnes (1997), and Carl Leggo (1999, 2002, 2004, 2005) provide seminal work in the field of poetry in inquiry. Other defining works in this area include the University of British Columbia's journal, *Educational Insights,* which hosts a special issue (2009) on poetic inquiry guest edited by Monica Prendergast, Carl Leggo, and Pauline Sameshima (www.educationalinsights.ca). There is also a book by these guest editors titled *Poetic Inquiry: Vibrant Voices in the Social Sciences* (2009) which includes reprints of select defining works and examples of the varied uses of poetic inquiry around the world and across disciplines.

Glesnes (1997) describes well the process used to write the Gabriel section of this book. The first approach is a typical qualitative analysis involving coding and categorizing by themes. The transcripts are then approached from the beginning and although "chronologically and linguistically faithful to the transcript" (p. 207), the resulting poems draw from recognition of the themes and "takes more license with words" (p. 207). Ely et al. (1997) suggest that "*one joyful thing about writing poetry is that, given the same data, different people create differing versions*" (p. 136). Prendergast (2009) posits, "Creating poetic inquiry is a performative act, revealing researcher/participants as both masked and unmasked, costumed and bared, liars and truth-tellers, actors and audience, offstage and onstage in the creation of research" (p. 16).

Transmethodological Results

The results of our study, emerging from Gabriel's story, continue to evolve. This volume includes some of the interpretive products of our analysis and a description of a dynamic methodology that cannot be delineated or contained, only explicated and experienced.

The data, which began as transcribed interviews, has developed into artistic representations that can be analyzed alongside one another and against the original text (interview transcripts). In this way, interpretations are modified, understood better and differently, perhaps even validated. For instance, as initial hermeneutic interpretations and poetic pieces were simultaneously rendered, the photographs shown in this volume were being created as well. Each of these mediums conveyed an interpretation that answered to the initial research inquiry. Yet, when Vandermause saw the photographs and poems, she understood better the themes she had generated in the hermeneutic analysis. Sameshima moved beyond an explanatory approach, conveying meaning through poetic renderings that "made sense" of the story as told, while keeping the question alive. Chalmers presented the "facts" of the story, told via snapshots of real life locations, those places that make up pieces of Gabriel's story, yet tell a story of paradox, one that is incomprehensible even in its everydayness.

We understand that the experience of addiction is not self-contained. The addiction and recovery experience is integrally meshed within the very everydayness of Chalmers' photos. In our project, we understand that Gabriel had all the preventative knowledge available. She started methamphetamine use as the anecdote to an already spirally-out-of-control context. If we think of the drug as the anecdote, then the next question of our study may be, in terms of recovery, "*What is the anecdote for the anecdote?*" The products are data that relate to one another, giving answers and raising new questions that add to our understandings while propelling us to question more. Thus, the methodology leading to this volume is unique and the results ever-changing.

We conclude this introduction with Chalmers describing his experience visiting key locations Gabriel circled on map printouts. He obtained the latitude and longitude of thirty of Gabriel's critical addiction locations and used this information to generate aerial maps. At these sites, Chalmers experienced a clear sense of tension. As he set up his tripod and medium-format camera, he noticed curtains in windows move as unseen persons watched him. Vehicles slowed down as they drove past, before looping around for another drive-by. The images included in this volume deny the viewer any visual evidence of the historical use of these sites. Studying addiction and recovery without looking at the experience is perfectly framed by Chalmers when he says, "*without the context of the handwritten text, as provided by Gabriel, the empty stillness of the images conveys the inaccessibility of another's experience.*"

References

Aoki, T. T. (1996, Fall). Spinning inspirited images in the midst of planned and live(d) curricula. *Fine, 96*, 7-14.

Appenzeller, O., Amm, M., & Jones, H. (2004). A brief exploration of neurological art history. *Journal of the History of the Neurosciences, 13*(4), 345-350.

Bakhtin, M. (1986). *Speech genres and other late essays.* Austin, TX: University Press.

Benner, P. (1985). Quality of life: A phenomenological perspective on explanation, prediction, and understanding in nursing science. *Advances in Nursing Science, 8*(1), 1-14.

Boix Mansilla, V. (2004). Interdisciplinary work at the frontier; An empirical examination of expert interdisciplinary epistemologies. *Issues in Interdisciplinary Studies, 24*, 1-31.

Brady, I. (2000). Three jaguar/Mayan intertexts: Poetry and prose fiction. *Qualitative Inquiry, 6*(1), 58–64.

Brady, I. (2009). Foreword. In M. Prendergast, C. Leggo, & P. Sameshima (Eds.), *Poetic inquiry: Vibrant voices in the social sciences* (pp. xi - xvi). Rotterdam, the Netherlands: Sense.

Butler-Kisber, L. (2002). Artful portrayals in qualitative inquiry: The road to found poetry and beyond. *The Alberta Journal of Educational Research, XLVIII* (3), 229-239.

Cahnmann, M. (2003). The craft, practice, and possibility of poetry in educational research. *Educational Researcher, 32*(3), 29-36.

Cannon Poindexter, C. (2002). Research as poetry: A couple experiences HIV. *Qualitative Inquiry, 8*(6), 707-714.

Clandinin, D. J. (2007). *Handbook of narrative inquiry: Mapping a methodology.* Thousand Oaks, CA: Sage.

Cole, A. L., & Knowles, J. G. (2001a). *Lives in context: The art of life history research.* Walnut Creek, CA: Alta Mira Press.

Cole, A. L., & Knowles, J. G. (2001b). Qualities of inquiry. In L. Neilsen, A. Cole, & J. G. Knowles (Eds.), *The art of writing inquiry* (Vol. 1, Arts-informed Research Series, pp. 211-219). Halifax, NS & Toronto, ON: Backalong Books & Centre for Arts-Informed Research.

Connelly, F. M., & Clandinin, D. J. (1990). Stories of experience and narrative inquiry. *Educational Researcher, 19*(5), 2-14.

Connelly, F. M., & Clandinin, D. J. (1994). Telling teaching stories. *Teacher Education Quarterly, 21*(2), 145-158.

Commeyras, M., & Montsi, M. (2000). What if I woke up as the other sex? Botswana youth perspectives on gender. *Gender & Education, 12*(3), 327-347.

Davis, J., Soep, E., Maira, S., Remba, N., & Putnoi, D. (1993). *Safe havens: Portraits of educational effectiveness in community art centers that focus on education in economically disadvantaged communities.* Cambridge, MA: Harvard Project Zero, Harvard University.

Denzin, N. K. (1997). *Interpretive ethnography: Ethnographic practices for the 21st century.* Thousand Oaks, CA: Sage.

Diekelmann, N., Allen, D., & Tanner, C. (1989). *The NLN Criteria for appraisal of baccalaureate programs: A critical hermeneutic analysis* (No. 15-2253). New York: National League for Nursing.

Diekelmann, N., & Magnussen Ironside, P. (1998). Hermeneutics. In J. Fitzpatrick (Ed.), *Encyclopedia of nursing research* (pp. 243-245). New York: Springer.

Dillon, D. (2001). *Interdisciplinary research and education: Preliminary perspectives from the MIT media laboratory.* Retrieved March 27, 2009, from http://www.pz.harvard.edu/interdisciplinary/ pubone.html

Dixson, A. D., Chapman, T. K., & Hill, D. A. (2005). Research as an aesthetic process: Extending the portraiture methodology. *Qualitative Inquiry, 11*(1), 16–26.

Ely, M., Vinz, R., Downing, M., & Anzul, M. (1997). *On writing qualitative research: Living by words.* London: The Falmer Press.

Gettig, J., Grady, S., & Nowosadzka, I. (2006). Methamphetamine: Putting the brakes on speed. *Journal of School Nursing, 22*(2), 66-73.

Glesne, C. (1997). That rare feeling: Re-presenting research through poetic transcription. *Qualitative Inquiry, 3*(2), 202-221.

Harding, H. A. (2005). "City girl": A portrait of a successful white urban teacher. *Qualitative Inquiry, 11*(1), 52-80.

Heinzerling, K. G., Shoptaw, S., Peck, J. A., Yang, X., Liu, J., Roll, J., et al. (2006). Randomized, placebo-controlled trial of baclofen and gabapentin for the treatment of methamphetamine dependence. *Drug and Alcohol Dependence, 85*(3), 177-184.

Henderson, J. G., & Slattery, P. (2004). Editors' introduction: The arts create synergy for curriculum and pedagogy. *Journal of curriculum and pedagogy, 1*(2), 1-8.

Irwin, R. L. (2004). A/r/tography: A metonymic métissage. In R. L. Irwin & A. de Cosson (Eds.), *A/r/tography: Rendering self through arts-based living inquiry* (pp. 27–38). Vancouver, BC: Pacific Educational Press.

Israel, B. A., Eng, E., Schulz, A. J., & Parker, E. A. (Eds.). (2005). *Methods in community-based participatory research for health.* San Francisco: Jossey-Bass.

Johanson, C.-E., Frey, K. A., Lundahl, L. H., Keenan, P., Lockhart, N., Roll, J., et al. (2006). Cognitive function and nigrostriatal markers in abstinent methamphetamine abusers. *Psychopharmacology, 186*(4), 620.

Jones, A. (1998). *Body art/performing the subject.* Minneapolis, MN: University of Minnesota.

Lawrence-Lightfoot, S. (1983). *The good high school: Portraits of character and culture.* New York: Basic Books.

Lawrence-Lightfoot, S. (1994). *I've known rivers: Lives of loss and liberation.* Reading, MA: Addison-Wesley, Jossey-Bass.

Lawrence-Lightfoot, S., & Davis, J. H. (1997). *The art and science of portraiture.* San Francisco, CA.

Leggo, C. (1999). Research as poetic rumination: Twenty-six ways of listening to light. In L. Neilsen, A. L. Cole, & J. G. Knowles (Eds.), *The art of writing inquiry* (pp. 173–195). Halifax, NS: Backalong Books.

Leggo, C. (2002). A calling of circles: Ruminations on living the research in everyday practice. *Networks: Online Journal for Teacher Research, 5*(1). Retrieved from http://www.oise.utoronto.ca/~ctd/ networks/journal/Vol%205(1). 2002march/ index.html

Leggo, C. (2004). The poet's corpus: Nine speculations. *JCT: Journal of Curriculum Theorizing, 20*(2), 65-85.

Leggo, C. (2005). Pedagogy of the heart: Ruminations on living poetically. *The Journal of Educational Thought, 39*(2), 175-195.

Leggo, C. (2008). Autobiography: Researching our lives and living our research. In S. Springgay, R. Irwin, C. Leggo, & P. Gouzouasis (Eds.), *Being with a/r/tography* (pp. 3-24). Rotterdam, The Netherlands: Sense.

Leonard, V. (1994). A heideggerian phenomenological perspective on the concept of person. In P. Benner (Ed.), *Interpretive phenomenology: Embodiment, caring, and ethics in health and illness.* Thousand Oaks, CA: Sage.

Lineberry, T. W., & Bostwick, J. (2006, January). Methamphetamine abuse: A perfect storm of complications. *Mayo Clinic Proceedings, 81*(1), 77-84.

Marino, M. T., Sameshima, P., & Beecher, C. C. (2009). Enhancing TPACK with assistive technology: Promoting inclusive practices in preservice teacher education. *Contemporary Issues in Technology and Teacher Education, 9*(2). Retrieved from http://www.citejournal.org/vol9/iss2/general/article1.cfm

Miller, J. (2005). *Educating for wisdom and compassion: Creating conditions for timeless learning.* Thousand Oaks, CA: Corwin Press.

Nehls, N., & Sallmann, J. (2005). Living with a history of physical and/or sexual abuse, substance use, and mental health problems: The perspectives of women. *Qualitative Health Research, 15*(3), 1-17.

Newton, R. M. (2005). Learning to teach in the shadow of 9/11: A portrait of two Arab American preservice Teachers. *Qualitative Inquiry, 11*(1), 81-94.

Nikitina, S. (2002). *Three strategies for interdisciplinary teaching: Contextualizing, conceptualizing, and problem-solving.* Retrieved March 25, 2009, from http://www.pz.harvard.edu/interdisciplinary/ pubtwo.html

Pinar, W., Reynolds, W. M., Slattery, P., & Taubman, P. M. (1995). *Understanding curriculum: An introduction to the study of historical and contemporary curriculum discourses.* New York: Peter Lang.

Pollock, D. (1998). Performative writing. In Phelan, Peggy, & Lane (Eds.), T*he ends of performance* (pp. 73-103). New York: University Press.

Prendergast, M. (2009). Introduction. In M. Prendergast, C. Leggo, & P. Sameshima (Eds.), *Poetic inquiry: Vibrant voices in the social sciences* (pp. xix-xlii). Rotterdam, the Netherlands: Sense.

Prendergast, M., Leggo, C., & Sameshima, P. (Eds.). (2009a). *Poetic inquiry: Vibrant voices in the social sciences.* Rotterdam, the Netherlands: Sense.

Prendergast, M., Leggo, C., & Sameshima, P. (Guest Eds.). (2009b). Poetic inquiry. *Educational Insights, 13*(3). Retrieved from http://www.ccfi.educ.ubc.ca/publication/insights/index.html

Reason, P. (1994). Three approaches to participative inquiry. In N. K. Denzin & Y. S. Lincoln (Eds.), *Handbook of qualitative research* (pp. 324–329). Thousand Oaks, CA.

Rice, E. (2005). *Schizophrenia and violence: The perspectives of women and case managers.* Madison, WI: University of Wisconsin-Madison.

Richardson, L. (1992a). The poetic representation of lives: Writing a postmodern sociology. *Studies in Symbolic Interaction, 13,* 19-29.

Richardson, L. (1992b). The consequences of poetic representation: Writing the other, rewriting the self. In C. Ellis & M. G. Flaherty (Eds.), *Investigating subjectivity: Research on lived experience* (pp. 125–140). Newbury Park, CA: Sage.

Richardson, L. (1994). Nine poems. *Journal of Contemporary Ethnography, 23*(1), 3-13.

Richardson, L. (1997). *Fields of play: Constructing an academic life.* New Brunswick, NJ: Rutgers University Press.

Richardson, M. (1998). Poetics in the field and on the page. *Qualitative Inquiry, 4*(4), 451-462.

Richardson, L., & St. Pierre, E. (2005). Writing: A method of inquiry. In N. K. Denzin & Y. S. Lincoln (Eds.), *Handbook of qualitative research* (3rd ed., pp. 959–978). Thousand Oaks, CA: Sage.

Roll, J. M. (2007). Contingency management: An evidence-based component of methamphetamine use disorder treatments. *Addiction, 102*(Suppl. 1), 114-120.

Rothenberg, J. (1994). Je est un autre: Ethnopoetics and the poet as other. *American Anthropologist, 96*(3), 523-524.

SAMHSA (Substance Abuse and Mental Health Services Administration). (2008). Office of applied studies. *Treatment Episode Data Set (TEDS).* Retrieved May 6, 2009, from http://oas.samhsa.gov/TEDS2k7highlights/TEDSHigh12k7Tbl2a.htm

Sameshima, P. (2007a). *Seeing red—a pedagogy of parallax: An epistolary bildungsroman on artful scholarly inquiry.* Amherst, NY: Cambria Press.

Sameshima, P. (2008). AutoethnoGRAPHIC relationality through paradox, parallax, and metaphor. In S. Springgay, R. Irwin, C. Leggo, & P. Gouzouasis (Eds.), *Being with a/r/tography* (pp. 45-56). Rotterdam, The Netherlands: Sense.

Sameshima, P., & Sinner, A. (2009). Awakening to soma heliakon: Encountering teacher-researcher-learning in the 21st Century. *Canadian Journal of Education, 32*(2), 271-284.

Shoptaw, S., Huber, A., Peck, J., Yang, X., Liu, J., Dang, J., et al. (2006). Randomized, placebo-controlled trial of sertraline and contingency management for the treatment of methamphetamine dependence. *Drug and Alcohol Dependence, 85*(1), 12-18.

Small, S. A. (1995). Action-oriented research: Models and methods. *Journal of Marriage and the Family, 57,* 941-955.

Springgay, S., Irwin, R., & Wilson Kind, S. (2005). A/r/tography as living inquiry through art and text. *Qualitative Inquiry, 11*(6), 897-912.

Springgay, S., Irwin, R., Leggo, C., & Gouzouasis, P. (Eds.). (2008). *Being with a/r/tography.* Rotterdam, The Netherlands: Sense.

Sumara, D., & Luce-Kapler, R. (1993). Action research as writerly text: Locating co-labouring in collaboration. *Educational Action Research, 1*(3), 387-395.

Tanne, J. H. (2006, February). Methamphetamine epidemic hits middle America. *BMJ, 332*(7538), 382.

Vandermause, R. K. (2007). Assessing for alcohol use disorders in women: Experiences of advanced practice nurses in primary care settings. *Journal of Addictions Nursing, 18*(4), 187-198.

Volkow, N. D., Chang, L., & Wang, G. J. (2003). Low level of brain dopamine D2 receptors in methamphetamine abusers: Association with metabolism in the orbitofrontal cortex. *Year Book of Psychiatry & Applied Mental Health,* 305-306.

Master References

Adorno, T. W. (1962). *Commitment.* (Francis McDonagh, Trans.). Retrieved from http://ada.evergreen.edu/~arunc/texts/frankfurt/commitment/commitment.pdf

Agamben, G. (1999). *Remnants of Auschwitz: The witness and the archive.* NY: Zone Books.

Akesson, B., D'Amico, M., Denov, M., Khan, F., Linds, W., & Mitchell, C. (2014). '"*Stepping back*" as researchers: Addressing ethics in arts-based approaches to working with war-affected children in school and community settings', *Educational Research for Social Change, 3*(1), 75-89.

Antiphon. (2014). *Encyclopedia Britannica.* Retrieved from http://dictionary.reference.com/browse/antiphon

Antiphon. (2016). *Oxford English Dictionary online.* Retrieved from http://www. oed. com/ view/ Entr y/8760?redirected From=antiphon&

Antiphona. (2018). Online Liddell-Scott-Jones Greek-English Lexicon (LSJ). Retrieved from http://stephanus.tlg.uci.edu/lsj/#eid=11022&context=search

Aoki, D. S. (2000). The thing never speaks for itself: Lacan and the politics of clarity. *Harvard Educational Review, 70*(3), 347-369. Retrieved from https://doi.org/10.17763/haer.70.3.83729226065nxq27

Aoki, T. T. (1996, Fall). Spinning inspirited images in the midst of planned and live(d) curricula. *Fine, 96,* 7-14.

Aoki, T. T. (2005). Toward Curriculum Inquiry in a New Key (1978/1980). In W. F. Pinar & R. L. Irwin (Eds.), *Studies in curriculum theory. Curriculum in a new key: The collected works of Ted T. Aoki* (pp. 89-110). Mahwah, NJ, US: Lawrence Erlbaum Associates Publishers.

Aporia. (2018). *Collins English dictionary.* Dictionary.com. Retrieved from http://dictionary.reference.com/browse/aporia

Aporia. (2018). Online Liddell-Scott-Jones Greek-English Lexicon (LSJ). Retrieved from http://stephanus.tlg.uci.edu/lsj/#eid=13926&context=lsj&action=from-searchAppenzeller, O., Amm, M., & Jones, H. (2004). A brief exploration of neurological art history. *Journal of the History of the Neurosciences, 13*(4), 345-350.

Applebaum, D. (1995). *The stop.* Albany, NY: University Press & SUNY.

Arendt, H. (1963/2006). *Eichmann in Jerusalem: A report on the banality of evil.* New York, NY: Penguin.

Arendt, H. (1978). *Life of the mind: Thinking.* San Diego, CA: Harcourt Brace Jovanovich.

Bakhtin, M. (1919/1990). Art and answerability. In M. Holquist & V. Liapunov (Eds.), *Art and answerability: Early philosophical essays by M. M. Bakhtin.* (pp. 1-3). (V. Liapunov & K. Brostrom, Trans.). Austin, TX: University of Texas press.

Bakhtin, M. (1981). *The dialogic imagination: Four essays.* M. Holquist (Trans.). Austin, Texas: University Press.

Bakhtin, M. (1984) *Rabelais and his world* (H. Iswolsky, Trans.). Bloomington, IN: Indiana University Press.

Bakhtin, M. (1986). *Speech genres and other late essays.* Austin, TX: University Press.

Bakhtin, M. (1993). *Toward the philosophy of the act.* (V. Liapunov & M. Holquist, Eds.). (V. Liapunov, Trans.). Austin, TX: University of Texas Press.

Barbezat, D. P., & Bush, M. (2013). *Contemplative practices in higher education: Powerful methods to transform teaching and learning.* San Francisco, CA: Jossey-Bass.

Barad, K. (2007). *Meeting the universe halfway: Quantum physics and the entanglement of matter and meaning.* Durham, NC: Duke University Press.

Barnes, G., Crowe, E., & Schaefer, B. (2007). The cost of teacher turnover in five school districts: A pilot study. *National Council on Teaching and America's Future.* Retrieved from http:// nctaf.org/wp-content/uploads/2012/01/ NCTAF-Cost-of-Teacher-Turnover-2007-full-report.pdf.

Barthes, R. (1977). *Roland Barthes by Roland Barthes.* R. Howard (Trans.). New York, NY: Hill and Wang.

Barthes, R. (1996). From work to text. In P. Rice & P. Waugh (Eds.), *Modern literary theory.* New York, NY: Arnold.

Barthes, R. (1980), *Camera lucida: Reflections on photography* (R. Howard, Trans.). New York, NY: Hill and Wang.

Barone, T., & Eisner, E. (1997). Arts-based educational research. In R. M. Jaeger (Ed.), *Complementary methods for research in education,* 2nd ed. (pp.72-116). Washington, DC: American Educational Research Association.

Barone, T., & Eisner, E., (2012). *Arts-based research.* Thousand Oaks, CA: Sage.

Beattie, M. (1997). Fostering reflective practice in teacher education: Inquiry as a frame-work for the construction of a professional knowledge in teaching. *Asia-Pacific Journal of Teacher Education, 25*(2), 111-128. doi:10.1080/1359866970250202

Beatty, P. (2015). *The sellout.* New York, NY: Farrar, Straus, and Giroux.

Beittel, J. S. (2013, April). *Mexico's Drug Trafficking Organizations: Source and Scope of the Violence.* Congressional Research Service. (Report – R41576). Retrieved from http://globalinitiative.net/wp-content/uploads/2017/01/ crs-mexicos-drug-trafficking-organizations-source-and-scope-of-the-violence-2013.pdf

Beltman, S., Glass, C., Dinham, J., Chalk, B., & Nguyen, B. (2015). Drawing identity: Beginning pre-service teachers' professional identities. *Issues in Educational Research, 25*(3), 225-245.

Benjamin, W. (1968/2007). *Illuminations: Essays and reflections.* (English trans.). H. Arendt (Ed.). New York, NY: Random House.Benner, P. (1985). Quality of life: A phenomenological perspective on explanation, prediction, and understanding in nursing science. *Advances in Nursing Science, 8*(1), 1-14.

Binder, M. (2016). Review. Arts-Based and Contemplative Practices in Research and Teaching: Honouring Presence. *International Journal of Education through Art, 12*(2), Volume 12 doi: 10.1386/eta.12.2.227_5

Boe, E., Cook, L., & Sunderland, R. (2008). Teacher turnover: Examining exit attrition, teacher area transfer, and school migration. *Exceptional Children, 75(1)*, 7-31.

Boeri, M. (2013). *Women on ice: Methamphetamine use among suburban women.* New Brunswick, NJ: Rutgers University Press.

Boisvert, R. D. (1998). *John Dewey: Rethinking our time.* Albany, New York, NYY: State University of New York Press.

Boix Mansilla, V. (2004). Interdisciplinary work at the frontier; An empirical examination of expert interdisciplinary epistemologies. *Issues in Interdisciplinary Studies, 24*, 1-31.

Boulton-Funke, A. (2014). Narrative form and Yam Lau's Room: The encounter in arts based research. *International Journal of Education & the Arts, 15*(17), 1–17.

Bourriaud, N. (2002), *Relational Aesthetics.* (S. Pleasance, F. Woods & M. Copeland, Trans.). Dijon, France: Les presses du reel France.Boyce, S. (Artist, Director). (2010). *Network* [Film]. London, United Kingdom: Peckham Space, Visual and Performing Arts (VAPA).

Boydell, K. M., Solimine, C., & Siona, S. (2015), 'Visual embodiment of psychosis: Ethical concerns in performing difficult experiences', *Visual Methodologies, 3*(2), 43-52.

Boydell, K.M., Volpe, T., Cox, S., Katz, A., Dow, R., Brunger, F., Parsons, J., Belliveau, G., Gladstone, B.M., Zlotnik-Shaul, R., & Cook, S. (2012), 'Ethical challenges in arts-based health research', *International Journal of the Creative Arts in Interprofessional Practice,* 11, 1-17.

Boxall, K. K., & Ralph, S. (2009), 'Research ethics and the use of visual images in research with people with intellectual disability', *Journal of Intellectual & Developmental Disability, 34*(1), 45-54.

Brady, I. (2000). Three jaguar/Mayan intertexts: Poetry and prose fiction. *Qualitative Inquiry, 6*(1), 58-64.

Brady, I. (2009). Foreword. In M. Prendergast, C. Leggo, & P. Sameshima (Eds.), *Poetic inquiry: Vibrant voices in the social sciences* (pp. xi - xvi). Rotterdam, the Netherlands: Sense.

Branfman, S. (2001). *Raku.* Iola, WI: Krause.

Brecht, M., O'Brian, A., von Mayrhauser, C., & Anglin, D. (2004). Methamphetamine use behaviors and gender differences. *Addictive Behavior,* 29, 89-106.

Bregman, M. (Producer), De Palma, B. (directed). (1982). *Scarface* [Motion Picture]. U.S.A.: Universal.

Biesta, G. (2012). Receiving the gift of teaching: From "learning from" to "being taught by." Studies in *Philosophy and Education, 32*(5), 449-461.

Brinton, L. J. (2000). *The structure of modern English: A linguistic introduction.* Philadelphia, PA: John Benjamins.

Brown, P., Lauder, H., & Ashton, D. (2008). Education, globalization and the future of the knowledge economy. *European Educational Research Journal, 7*(2), 131-156.

Bruner, J. (2002). Life as narrative. *Social Research, 71*(3), 691-710. Retrieved from http://www.jstor.org/stable/40970444

Buchanan, J. (2015). Metaphors as two-way mirrors: Illuminating pre-service to in-service teacher identity development. *Australian Journal of Teacher Education, 40*(10), 32-50.

Burnaford, G., April, A., & Weiss, C. (Eds.). (2000). *Renaissance in the classroom: Art integration and meaningful learning.* Mahwah, NJ: Lawrence Erlbaum.

Bush, M. (2011). Mindfulness in higher education. *Contemporary Buddhism, 12*(01), 183-197.

Butler, J. (2007). Torture and the ethics of photography. *Environment and Planning: Society and Space, 25*(6), 951 – 966.

Butler-Kisber, L. (2002). Artful portrayals in qualitative inquiry: The road to found poetry and beyond. *The Alberta Journal of Educational Research, XLVIII* (3), 229-239.

Butterwick, S., & Lawrence, R. I. (2009). Creating alternate realities: Arts-based approaches to transformative learning. In J. Mezirow & E. Taylor (Eds.), *Transformative learning in practice. Insights from community, workplace and higher education* (pp. 35-45). San Francisco, CA: Jossey-Bass.

Cahnmann, M. (2003). The craft, practice, and possibility of poetry in educational research. *Educational Researcher, 32*(3), 29-36.

Camus. A. (1942). *The stranger* (Trans. M. Ward). New York, NY: Vintage International.

Camus, A. (1956). *The rebel: An essay on man in revolt.* New York, NY: Random House. Cannon Poindexter, C. (2002). Research as poetry: A couple experiences HIV. *Qualitative Inquiry, 8*(6), 707–714.

Carlyle, D., & Woods, P. (2002). *Emotions of teacher stress.* Stoke on Trent, UK: Trentham Books.

Chambers, C., Hasebe-Ludt, E., Leggo, C., & Sinner, A. (Eds.), (2012, October). *A heart of wisdom: Life writing as empathetic inquiry.* New York, NY: Peter Lang.

Cheng, M. M. H., Chan, K.W., Tang, Y. F., & Cheng, A. Y. N. (2009). Pre-service teacher education students' epistemological beliefs and their conceptions of teaching. *Teaching and Teacher Education, 25,* 319–327.Clandinin, D. J. (2007). Handbook of narrative inquiry: Mapping a methodology. Thousand Oaks, CA: Sage.

Clandinin, D. J., Schaefer, L., Long, J. S., Steeves, P., McKenzie-Robblee, S., Pinnegar, E., et al. (2012, April 30). *Early career teacher attrition: Problems, possibilities, potentials.* Centre for Research for Teacher Education and Development: University of Alberta. Retrieved from http://www.elementaryed. alberta.ca/en/Centres/CRTED/~/media/ elementaryed/Documents/Centres/CRTED/ ECA_-_FINAL_Report.pdf

Clark, A., Prosser, J., & Wiles, R. (2010), Ethical issues in image based research, *Arts & Health,* 2(1), 81-93.

Clark, R., & Antonelli, F. (2009). *Why teachers leave: Results of an Ontario survey 2006-08.* Ontario Ministry of Education. Retrieved from http:// www.otffeo.on.ca/english/media_room/ briefs/why_teachers_leave.pdf

Cliché. (2016). *Dictionary.com.* Retrieved from http://dictionary.reference.com /brow

Coetzee, J.M. (1999). *Disgrace.* London: Vintage.

Coffey, N. (Ed.). (1996-2006). *French linguistics: Site for the study of the French language.* Retrieved from http://www.french-linguistics.co.uk/dictionary/

Cohen, J., Greenberg, R., Uri, J., Halpin, M., & Zweben, J. (2007). Women with methamphetamine dependence: Research on etiology and treatment. *Journal of Psychoactive Drugs, 11*(4), 347-351.

Cole, A. L., & Knowles, J. G. (2000). *Researching Teaching: Exploring teacher development through reflexive inquiry.* New York, NY: Allyn & Bacon.

Cole, A. L., & Knowles, J. G. (2001a). *Lives in context: The art of life history research.* Walnut Creek, CA: Alta Mira Press.

Cole, A. L., & Knowles, J. G. (2001b). Qualities of inquiry. In L. Neilsen, A. Cole, & J. G. Knowles (Eds.), *The art of writing inquiry* (Vol. 1, Arts-informed Research Series, pp. 211-219). Halifax, NS & Toronto, ON: Backalong Books & Centre for Arts-Informed Research.

Cole, A. L., & Knowles, J. G. (2008). Arts-informed research. In J. G. Knowles & A. L. Cole (Eds.), *Handbook of the arts in qualitative research: Perspectives, methodologies, examples, and issues* (pp. 55-70). Thousand Oaks, CA: Sage.

Connelly, F. M., & Clandinin, D. J. (1990). Stories of experience and narrative inquiry. *Educational Researcher, 19*(5), 2-14.

Connelly, F. M., & Clandinin, D. J. (1994). Telling teaching stories. *Teacher Education Quarterly, 21*(2), 145-158.

Commeyras, M., & Montsi, M. (2000). What if I woke up as the other sex? Botswana youth perspectives on gender. *Gender & Education, 12*(3), 327-347.

Cox, S. M., Guillemin, M., Waycott, J., & Warr, D. (2015), Editorial: Visual methods and ethics: stories from the field, *Visual Methodologies, 3*(2), 1-3.

Crook, C., & Bennett, L. (2007). Does using a computer disturb the organization of children's writing? *British Journal of Developmental Psychology, 25*(2), 313-321.

Crotty, M. (2003). *The foundations of social research.* Thousand Oaks, CA: Sage.

Daignault, Jacques. (1992). Traces of work from different places. In W. Pinar & W. Reynolds (Eds.), *Understanding curriculum as phenomenological and deconstructed text* (pp. 195-215). New York, NY: Teachers College Press.

Daignault, Jacques. (1983). Curriculum and action-research: An artistic activity in a perverse way. *Journal of Curriculum Theorizing, 5*(3), 4-28.

Daignault, J. (1992, October). Serenity. Paper presented at the Bergamo Conference, Dayton, OH.

Daiute, C. (2014). *Narrative inquiry: A dynamic approach.* Los Angeles, CA: Sage.

Davis, J., Soep, E., Maira, S., Remba, N., & Putnoi, D. (1993). *Safe havens: Portraits of educational effectiveness in community art centers that focus on education in economically disadvantaged communities.* Cambridge, MA: Harvard Project Zero, Harvard University.

Davidson, R. J., & Kaszniak, A. W. (2015). Conceptual and methodological issues in research on mindfulness and meditation. *American Psychologist, 70*(7), 581-592.

Defechereux, P. (2017, March 24). The DaVinci paradigm: Arts and sciences building community. Paper presentation at the *2017 Annual Bay Area HIV Health Disparities Symposium.* San Francisco, CA.

deLanda (2006). *A new philosophy of society.* New York, NY: Continuum.

Deleuze, G., & Guattari, F. (1987). *A thousand plateaus: Capitalism and schizophrenia.* Minneapolis, MN: University Press.

DeMoss, D. (2011). Empty and extended craving: An application of the extended mind thesis to the four noble truths. *Contemporary Buddhism, 12*(2), 309-325.

den Heyer, K., & Conrad, D. (2011). Using Alain Badiou's ethic of truths to support an 'eventful' social justice teacher education program. *Journal of Curriculum Theorizing, 27*(1), 7-19. Retrieved from http://journal.jctonline.org/index.php/jct/article/view/302

Denzin, N. K. (1997). *Interpretive ethnography: Ethnographic practices for the 21st century.* Thousand Oaks, CA: Sage.

Denzin, N. K. (2002). *Interpretive interactionism.* London, UK: Sage.

Derrida, J. (1982. Différance. In J. Derrida (Ed.). *Margins of philosophy* (pp. 3-17). Chicago, IL.: University Press.

Dewey, J. (1916). Force and coercion. *International Journal of Ethics,* 26, 359-367.

Dewey, J. (1916/2011). *Democracy and education.* Hollywood, FL: Simon & Brown.

Dewey, J. (1922). *Human nature and conduct: An introduction to social psychology.* New York, NY: Henry Holt.

Dewey, J. (1927/1988). *The public and its problems: An essay in political inquiry.* Athens, OH: Ohio University Press.

Dewey, J. (1930). Conduct and experience. In Carl Murchison (Ed.), *Psychologies of 1930* (p. 409–422). Worcester, MA: Clark University Press.

Dewey, J. (1934/2005). *Art as experience.* New York, NY: Perigee.

Dewey, J. (1938/1997). *Experience and education.* New York, NY: Touchstone.

Dewey, J. (1939). *John Dewey and the promise of America.* (Progressive Education Booklet No. 14). Columbus, OH: American Education Press.

Dewey, J. (1958). *Experience and nature.* New York, NY: Dover.Diekelmann, N., Allen, D., & Tanner, C. (1989). *The NLN Criteria for appraisal of baccalaureate programs: A critical hermeneutic analysis* (No. 15-2253). New York: National League for Nursing.Diekelmann, N., & Magnussen Ironside, P. (1998). Hermeneutics. In J. Fitzpatrick (Ed.), *Encyclopedia of nursing research* (pp. 243-245). New York: Springer.

Diggins, J. P. (1994). *The promise of pragmatism: Modernism and the crisis of knowledge and authority.* Chicago, IL: University of Chicago Press.Dillon, D. (2001). *Interdisciplinary research and education: Preliminary perspectives from the MIT media laboratory.* Retrieved March 27, 2009, from http://www.pz.harvard.edu/interdisciplinary/ pubone.html

Dixson, A. D., Chapman, T. K., & Hill, D. A. (2005). Research as an aesthetic process: Extending the portraiture methodology. *Qualitative Inquiry, 11*(1), 16-26.

Djuraskovic, I., & Arthur, N. (2010). Heuristic inquiry: A personal journey of acculturation and identity reconstruction. *The Qualitative Report, 15*(6), 1569-1593. Retrieved from http://www.nova.edu/ssss/QR/QR15-6/djuraskovic.pdf

Dochy, F., Mien, S., Van den Bossche, P., & Gijbels, D. (2003). Effects of problem-based learning: A meta-analysis. *Learning and Instruction, 13*(1), 533-568.

Donovan, D., & Marlatt, G. A. (Eds.). (2005). *Assessment of Addictive Behaviors* (2nd ed.). New York, NY: Guilford Press.

Douglas, M. (Producer), Zemeckis, R. (Director). (1984). Romancing the Stone [Motion Picture]. U.S.A.: 20th Century Fox.

DPNC. (2016). *Drug Prevention Network of Canada.* Retrieved from http://dpnoc.org/drug-facts/crystal-meth/

DRS. (2017). *Drug rehab & addiction services.* Retrieved from http://www.drugrehab.ca/

Dressman, M. (2004). Dewey and Bakhtin in dialogue: From Rosenblatt to a pedagogy of literature as social, aesthetic practice. In A. F. Ball & S.W. Freedman (Eds.). *Bakhtinian perspective on language, literacy, and learning* (pp. 34-52). New York, NY: Cambridge University Press.

Droogsma, R. A. (2006). *"He might of cracked my spirit, but he never broke it": A feminist standpoint analysis of woman abuse survivors' messages in the clothesline project.* (Unpublished doctoral dissertation). Howard University, Washington, DC.

Droogsma, R. A. (2009). "I am the woman next door": The Clothesline Project as woman abuse survivors' societal critique. *Communication, Culture & Critique,* 2, 480-502.

Dutro, E., Selland, M. K., & Bien, A. C. (2013). Revealing writing, concealing writers: High-stakes assessment in an urban elementary classroom. *Journal of Literacy Research, 45*(2), 99-141. doi:10.1177/1086296X13475621

Eaton, M., & Moore, R. (2002). Aesthetic experience: its revival and its relevance to aesthetic education. *Journal of Aesthetic Education, 36*(2), 9-23.

Ecstatic. (2018). *Collins English dictionary.* Retrieved from https://www.collinsdictionary.com/dictionary/english/ecstatic

Eisner, E. W. (1991). *Enlightened eye: Qualitative inquiry and the enhancement of educational practice.* New York, NY: Macmillan.

Eisner, E. W. (2002). *The arts and the creation of mind.* Harrisonburg, VA: R.R. Donnelly & Sons.

Eisner, E. W. (2008). Art and knowledge. In G. Knowles & A. L. Cole (Eds.), *Handbook of the arts in qualitative research* (pp. 3-12). Thousand Oaks: Sage.

Ekphrasis. (2018). Wikipedia. Retrieved from https://en.wikipedia.org/wiki/EkphrasisEly, M., Vinz, R., Downing, M., & Anzul, M. (1997). *On writing qualitative research: Living by words.* London: The Falmer Press.

Emerson, C. (1993). Preface to Mikhail K. Ryklin, "Bodies of terror", *New Literary History, 24*(1), 45-49.

Ensler, E. (2008). *The vagina monologues.* New York: NY: Random House.

Eren, A., & Tekinarslan, E. (2013). Prospective teachers' metaphors: Teacher, teaching, learning, instructional material and evaluation courses. *International Journal of Social Sciences and Education, 3*(2), 345-445.

Ergas, O., & Todd, S. (2016). *Philosophy East/West: Exploring intersections between educational and contemplative practices.* Hoboken, NJ: Wiley-Blackwell.

Ericson, T., Kjønstad, B. G., & Barstad, A. (2014). Mindfulness and sustainability. *Ecological Economics*, 104, 73-79.

Evanagnostos. (2018). Online Liddell-Scott-Jones Greek-English Lexicon (LSJ). Retrieved from http://stephanus.tlg.uci.edu/lsj/#eid=44570&context=lsj&action=from-search

Evanagnostos. (2018). Wordreference. com. Retrieved from http://www.wordreference.com/gren/evanagnostos

Fels, L. (2010). Coming into presence: The unfolding of a moment. *Journal of Educational Controversy, 5*(10). Available at: http://cedar.wwu.edu/jec/vol5/iss1/8

Fesmire, S. (2003). *John Dewey & moral imagination: Pragmatism in ethics.* Bloomington, IN: Indiana University Press.

Ferretti, A. (2014, June 30). A beginner's guide to the Chakras. *Yoga Journal. R*etrieved from http://www.yogajournal.com/article/chakras-yoga-for-beginners/beginners-guide-chakras/

Finegan, E. (2012). *Language: Its structure and use* (6th ed). Boston, MA: Wadsworth.

Fishman, S., & McCarthy L. (1998). *John Dewey and the challenge of classroom practice.* NY: Teachers College Press.Forbes. (2015). *Forbe's America's largest private companies.* Retrieved from http://www. forbes.com/companies/amway/

Foucault, M. (1969). *The archeology of knowledge and the discourse on language.* (A. M. S. Smith, Trans. New York, NY: Pantheon Books.

Frost, R. (1972/1930). Education by poetry. In E. Lathem & L. Thompson (Eds.). *Robert Frost: poetry and prose.* (pp. 329-340). New York, NY: Holt, Rinehart & Winston.

Frye, N. (1968). *The educated imagination.* Toronto, ON: Anansi.

Gadamer, H. G. (1975/2004). *Truth and method.* (D. Marshall & J. Weinsheimer, Trans.). (2nd revised ed.). New York, NY: Continuum. (Original work published 1960)

Gadamer, H. G. (1980). *Dialogue and dialectic: Eight hermeneutical studies on Plato* (P. C. Smith, Trans.). New Haven, CT: Yale University Press.

Gallop, J. (1988). *Thinking through the body.* New York Chichester, West Sussex: Columbia University Press.

Gambhir, M., Broad, K., Evans, M., & Gaskell, J. (2008, September). *Characterizing initial teacher education in Canada: Themes and issues.* International Alliance of Leading Education Institutes. University of Toronto. Retrieved from http://www.oise.utoronto. ca/ite/UserFiles/File/CharacterizingITE.pdf

Gay, G., & Neftali Kirkland, K. (2003). Developing cultural critical consciousness and self-reflection in preservice teacher education. *Theory into Practice, 42*(3), 181-187.

Gee, J. P. (2000). Identity as an analytic lens for research in education. *Review of Research in Education, 25,* 99-125. doi:10.3102/0091732 X025001099

Geijsel, F., & Meijers, F. (2005). Identity learning: The core process of educational change. *Educational Studies, 31*(4), 419-430. doi:10.1080/03055690500237488

Gelineau, P. R. (2004). *Integrating the arts across the elementary school curriculum.* Belmont, CA: Wadsworth, Cengage Learning.

Gettig, J., Grady, S., & Nowosadzka, I. (2006). Methamphetamine: Putting the brakes on speed. *Journal of School Nursing, 22*(2), 66-73.

Glesne, C. (1997). That rare feeling: Re-presenting research through poetic transcription. *Qualitative Inquiry, 3*(2), 202-221.

Green, R. (2002). Survival: Ruminations on archival lacunae. In *Interarchive: Archival practices in the contemporary art field* (pp. 147-153). Köln, Germany: Walther König.

Greene, M. (2006, February). Prologue: From jagged landscapes to possibility. *Journal of Educational Controversy, 1*(1). Retrieved from http://www.wce.wwu.edu/Resources/CEP/eJournal/v001n001/a005.shtml

Gregory, J., Lewton, A., Schmidt, S., & Mattern, M. (2002). Body politics with feeling: The power of the Clothesline Project. *New Political Science, 24*(3), 433-448.

Guiney Yallop, J. (2016). A book review of Arts-based and contemplative practices in research and teaching: Honoring presence. *Art/Research International, 1*(1), 283-291.

Haidet, P. (2007). Jazz and the 'art' of medicine: Improvisation in the medical encounter. *Annals of Family Medicine, 5*(2), 164-169. Retrieved from: www.annfammed.org

Haiven, M., & Khasnabish, A. (2014). The radical imagination. Winnipeg, MB: Fernwood.

Hall, S. (1997). The work of representation & spectacle of the 'other'. In S. Hall (Ed.). *Representation: Cultural representations and signifying practices* (pp. 1-75, 223-291). London: Sage.

Hall, S. (2007/1973). Encoding, decoding. In S. During (Ed.). *The cultural studies reader* (3rd ed., pp. 477-487). New York, NY: Routledge.

Hall, S. (1973). *Encoding and decoding in the television discourse.* Birmingham, England: Centre for Contemporary Cultural Studies.

Harding, H. A. (2005). "City girl": A portrait of a successful white urban teacher. *Qualitative Inquiry, 11*(1), 52-80.

Harrison, T. M., & Barthel, B. (2009). Wielding new media in Web 2.0: Exploring the history of engagement with the collaborative construction of media products. *New Media Society,* 11, 155-178.

Hasebe-Ludt, E., Chambers, C., & Leggo, C. (2009). *Life writing and literary métissage as an ethos for our times.* New York, NY: Peter Lang.

Hasebe-Ludt, E., & Leggo, C. (2018). (Eds.), *Canadian curriculum studies: A métissage of inspiration/ imagination/ interconnection.* Toronto, ON: Canadian Scholars' Press.

Hayes, M. T., Sameshima, P., & Watson, F. (2015, February). Imagination as method. *International Journal of Qualitative Methods, 14*(1), 36-52.

Head, F. (1992). Student teaching as initiation into the teaching profession. *Anthropology & Education Quarterly, 23*(2), 89-107.

Heidegger, M. (1933-34/2010). *Being and truth* (G. Fried & R. Polt, Trans.). Bloomington, IN: Indiana University Press.

Heidegger, M. (1977). *The question concerning technology, and other essays.* New York, NY: Garland.

Heidegger, M. (1996). *Being and time* (J. Stambaugh, Trans.). New York: State University of New York Press. (Original work published in 1953)

Heinzerling, K. G., Shoptaw, S., Peck, J. A., Yang, X., Liu, J., Roll, J., et al. (2006). Randomized, placebo-controlled trial of baclofen and gabapentin for the treatment of methamphetamine dependence. *Drug and Alcohol Dependence, 85*(3), 177-184.

Henderson, J. G., & Slattery, P. (2004). Editors' introduction: The arts create synergy for curriculum and pedagogy. *Journal of curriculum and pedagogy, 1*(2), 1–8.

Hess, Ed. (2011, Feb. 24). The business revolution that's destroying the American Dream. *Forbes.* Retrieved from http://www.forbes.com/2011/02/24/destroy-american-dream-leadership-leaders-financialism.html

Hickman, L. A. (1992). *John Dewey's pragmatic technology* (First Midland Book Ed.). Bloomington, IN: Indiana University Press.

Hickman, L. A., Neubert, S., & Reich, K. (2009). *John Dewey between pragmatism & constructivism.* New York, NY: Fordham University Press.

Higgins, L. A., & Silver, B. R. (Eds.). (1991). *Rape and representation.* New York, NY: Columbia University Press.

Hipple, P. C. (1998). *Hegemonic disguise in resistance to domination: The Clothesline Project's response to violence against women.* (Unpublished Ph.D. dissertation). Iowa State University.

Hipple, P. C. (2000). Clothing their resistance in hegemonic dress: The Clothesline Project's response to violence against women. *Clothing and Textiles Research Journal, 18*(3), 163-177.

Hoban, P. (2008), 'How far is too far?', *Art News.* Retrieved from http://www.artnews.com/2008/07/01/how-far-is-too-far/

Hollis, H. (2001). The other side of carnival: Romola and Bakhtin. *Papers on Language & Literature, 37*(3), p. 227-254.

Holquist, M. (2004). *Dialogism: Bakhtin and his world* (2nd ed.). New York, NY: Routledge.

Holquist, M., & Liapunov, V. (Eds.). (1990). *Art and answerability: Early philosophical essays by M. M. Bakhtin.* (V. Liapunov & K. Brostrom, Trans.). Austin, TX: University of Texas press.

hooks, b. (1994). What's passion go to do with it? In b. hooks (Ed.), *Outlaw culture: Resisting representations* (pp 43-60). New York, NY: Routledge.

hooks, b. (2010). *Teaching critical thinking: Practical wisdom.* New York: Routledge.

Hong, J. Y. (2010). Pre-service and beginning teachers' professional identity and its relation to dropping out of the profession. *Teaching and Teacher Education, 26*(8), 1530-1543.

Hughes, J. (Producer), Columbus, C. (Director). (1990). *Home Alone* [Motion Picture]. U.S.A.: 20th Century Fox.

Hwu, Wen-Song. (1993). Toward understanding poststructuralism and curriculum. Unpublished doctoral dissertation. Louisiana State University, Baton Rouge, LA.

Hyland, T. (2015). The commodification of spirituality: Education, mindfulness and the marketisation of the present moment. *Prospero, 21*(2). 11-17.

Ingalls Vanada, D. (2017). Teaching for the ambiguous, creative, and practical: Daring to be A/R/Tography. *Art/Research International: A Transdisciplinary Journal, 2*(10), 110-135.

Intertextuality. (2018). Perseus Tufts Latin Dictionary. Retrieved from http://www.perseus.tufts.edu/hopper/resolveform?type=exact&lookup=textum&lang=la

Irwin, R. L. (2004). A/r/tography: A metonymic métissage. In R. L. Irwin & A. de Cosson (Eds.), *A/r/tography: Rendering self through arts based living inquiry* (pp. 27-38). Vancouver, BC: Pacific Educational Press.

Irwin, R. L., Beer, R., Springgay, S., & Grauer, K. (2006). The rhizomatic relations of A/r/tography. *Studies in Art Education, 48*(1), 70-88.

Irwin, R. L., & O'Donoghue, D. (2012). Encountering pedagogy through relational art practices. *International Journal of Art and Design Education, 31*(3), 221-236.

Irwin, R. L., & Springgay, S. (2008). A/r/tography as practice based research. In S. Springgay, R. L. Irwin, C. Leggo, & P. Gouzouasis (Eds.), *Being with A/r/tography* (pp. xiii-xxvii). Rotterdam, Netherlands: Sense.

Israel, B. A., Eng, E., Schulz, A. J., & Parker, E. A. (Eds.). (2005). *Methods in community-based participatory research for health.* San Francisco: Jossey-Bass.

Izadinia, M. (2013). A review of research on student teachers' professional identity. *British Educational Research Journal, 39*(4), 694-713. doi:10.1080/01411926.2012.679614

Jackson, P. W. (1998). *John Dewey and the lessons of art.* New Haven, CT: Yale University Press.

Jacobs, J. (1890). Jack and the beanstalk. *English fairy tales* (pp. 59-67). London, UK: David Nutt.

Johanson, C.-E., Frey, K. A., Lundahl, L. H., Keenan, P., Lockhart, N., Roll, J., et al. (2006). Cognitive function and nigrostriatal markers in abstinent methamphetamine abusers. *Psychopharmacology, 186*(4), 620.

Johnston, J. S. (2001). Authority, social change, and education: A response to Dewey's critics. *Education and Culture, 17*(2), 1-10.

Jones, A. (1998). *Body art/performing the subject.* Minneapolis, MN: University of Minnesota.

Jones, R. (2009). The aesthetics of protest: Using image to change discourse. Enculturation: *Journal of Rhetoric, Writing, and Culture, 6*(2) 1-12. Retrieved from http://www.enculturation.net/6.2/jones

Kabat-Zinn, J. (2003). Mindfulness-based interventions in context: past, present, and future. *Clinical Psychology: Science and Practice, 10*(2), 144-156.

Kabat-Zinn, J. (2011). Some reflections on the origins of MBSR, skillful means, and the trouble with maps. *Contemporary Buddhism, 12*(1). 281-306.

Kester, G. H., & Strayer, J. (2005). *Groundworks: Environmental Collaboration in Contemporary Art.* Pittsburgh, PA: Carnegie Mellon University.

Khong, B. S. L. (2009). Expanding the understanding of mindfulness: Seeing the tree and the forest. *The Humanistic Psychologist, 37*(2), 117-136.

King, T. (2003). *The truth about stories, a Native narrative.* Toronto, ON: House of Anansi Press.

Kittay, E. (1990). *Metaphor: Its cognitive force and linguistic structure.* NY: Oxford University Press.

Knowles, J. G., & Cole, A. L. (Eds.). (2008). *Handbook of the arts in qualitative research: Perspectives, methodologies, examples, and issues.* Thousand Oaks, CA: Sage.

Knowles, G., Luciani, T., Cole, A., & Neilsen, L. (Eds.). (2007). *The art of visual inquiry.* (Vol. 3, Arts-informed inquiry series). Halifax, Canada: Backalong Books.

Knowles, J. G., Promislow, S., & Cole, A. L. (Eds.). (2008). *Creating scholartistry: Imagining the arts-informed thesis or dissertation* (Vol. 4, Arts-informed inquiry series). Halifax, Nova Scotia, Canada: Backalong Books.

Kristeva, J. (2003). *Intimate revolt: The powers and limits of psychoanalysis.* New York, NY: Columbia University Press.

Kristeva, J. (1980). *Desire in language: A semiotic approach to literature and art* (T. Gora, A. Jardine & L. S. Roudiez, Trans,). New York, NY: Columbia University Press.

Kumar, A. (2011). *Understanding curriculum as meditative inquiry: A study of the ideas of Jiddu Krishnamurti and James MacDonald.* Unpublished dissertation. University of British Columbia, Canada. Available at https://open.library.ubc.ca/cIRcle/collections/ubctheses/24/items/1.0055327

Kwon, M. (1997). One place after another: Notes on site specificity. *October, 80*(1), p. 85-110.

Laclau, E., & Mouffe, C. (2014). *Hegemony and socialist strategy: Towards a radical democratic politics* (2nd ed.). New York, NY: Routledge.

Lash, S., & Lury, C. (2007). *Global culture industry.* Malden, MA: Polity Press.

Latour, B. (2005). *Reassembling the social.* New York, NY: Oxford University Press.

Lawrence-Lightfoot, S. (1983). *The good high school: Portraits of character and culture.* New York: Basic Books.

Lawrence-Lightfoot, S. (1994). *I've known rivers: Lives of loss and liberation.* Reading, MA: Addison-Wesley, Jossey-Bass.

Lawrence-Lightfoot, S. (2005). Reflections on portraiture: A dialogue between art and science. *Qualitative Inquiry, 11*(1), 3-15.

Lawrence-Lightfoot, S., & Davis, J. H. (1997). *The art and science of portraiture.* San Francisco, CA.

Lavrakas, P. J. (2008) Intercoder reliability. *Encyclopedia of survey research methods.* doi: http://dx.doi.org/10.4135/9781412963947.n228

Lee, A., & Denshire, S. (2013). Conceptualizing autoethnography as assemblage: Accounts of occupational therapy practice. *International Journal of Qualitative Methods, 12,* 221-236.

Leggo, C. (1999). Research as poetic rumination: Twenty-six ways of listening to light. In L. Neilsen, A. L. Cole, & J. G. Knowles (Eds.), *The art of writing inquiry* (pp. 173–195). Halifax, NS: Backalong Books.

Leggo, C. (2002). A calling of circles: Ruminations on living the research in everyday practice. *Networks: Online Journal for Teacher Research, 5*(1). Retrieved from http://www.oise.utoronto.ca/~ctd/networks/journal/Vol%205(1). 2002march/ index.html

Leggo, C. (2004). The poet's corpus: Nine speculations. *JCT: Journal of Curriculum Theorizing, 20*(2), 65-85.

Leggo, C. (2005). Pedagogy of the heart: Ruminations on living poetically. *The Journal of Educational Thought, 39*(2), 175–195.

Leggo, C. (2008). Autobiography: Researching our lives and living our research. In S. Springgay, R. Irwin, C. Leggo, & P. Gouzouasis (Eds.), *Being with a/r/tography* (pp. 3–24). Rotterdam, The Netherlands: Sense.

Leggo, C. (2008). The ecology of personal and professional experience: A poet's view. In M. Cahnmann-Taylor & R. Siegesmund (Eds.) *Arts-based research in education: Foundations for practice* (pp. 89-97). New York: Routledge.

Leggo, C. (2011), Living lve: Confessions of a fearful teacher, *Journal of the Canadian Association for Curriculum Studies,* 9(1), 115-144.

Leonard, V. (1994). A Heideggerian phenomenological perspective on the concept of person. In P. Benner (Ed.), *Interpretive phenomenology: Embodiment, caring, and ethics in health and illness.* Thousand Oaks, CA: Sage.

Levinas, E. (2008). *Totality and Infinity. An Essay on Exteriority.* (A. Lingis, Trans.) Pittsburgh, PA: Duquesne University Press.

Levinas, E. (1981). Otherwise than being or beyond essence. Norwell, MA: Kluwer.

Levine, S.K. (2009). *Trauma, tragedy, therapy: The arts and human suffering.* Philadelphia: Jessica Kingsley.

Levinson, B. (2000). The symbolic animal: Foundations of education in cultural transmission and acquisition. In Bradley A. Levinson, K. Borman, & M. Eisenhart (Eds.), *Schooling the symbolic animal: Social and cultural dimensions of education* (pp. 15-24). Lanham, Md: Rowman & Littlefield.

Lidchi, H. (1997). The poetics and the politics of exhibiting other cultures. In S. Hall (Ed.). *Representation: Cultural representations and signifying practices* (pp. 151-222). London: Sage.

Lifton, R. J. (1989). *Thought reform and the psychology of totalism: A study of brainwashing in China.* Chapel Hill, NC: UNC Press.

Lineberry, T. W., & Bostwick, J. (2006, January). Methamphetamine abuse: A perfect storm of complications. *Mayo Clinic Proceedings, 81*(1), 77-84.

Liu, X., & Ramsey, J. (2008). Teachers' job satisfaction: Analyses of the teacher follow-up survey in the United States for 2000-01. *Teaching and Teacher Education, 24,* 1173-1184.

Lotz, C. (2012). Distant presence: Representation, painting and photography in Gerhard Richter's reader. *Symposium: Canadian Journal for Continental Philosophy*, 1, p. 87-111.

Maarhuis, P. (2013, May). *Collaborative writing as a method of inquiry.* Panelist: *9th International Congress of Qualitative Inquiry (ICQI).* University of Illinois at Urbana Champaign. Urbana, IL.

Maarhuis, P. (2016). Replies to wounds: *Meaning across multiple ekphrasic interpretations of interpersonal violence and the clothesline project* (Doctoral dissertation) Proquest, #11770. Retrieved from Washington State University Research Libraries: https://research.libraries.wsu.edu:8443/xmlui/bit stream/handle/2376/12049/Maarhuis_wsu_0251E_11770.pdf?sequence=1

Maarhuis, P., & Sameshima, P. (2012, May). Material echoes: A hermeneutic phenomenological and arts-informed study of a Clothesline Project. Paper presentation. *Canadian Society for the Study of Education (CSSE). Arts, Researchers, Teachers Society.* Waterloo, ON, Canada.

Maarhuis, P., & Sameshima, P. (2013a, March). Place of agitation, place of learning: The narrative canvasses of a Clothesline Project. Paper presentation. *National Art Educators Association (NAEA) Conference.* Fort Worth, TX.

Maarhuis, P., & Sameshima, P. (2013b, June). Pedagogy and parallax: Paper presentation. *Canadian Society for the Study of Education (CSSE). Arts, Researchers, Teachers Society.* Victoria, BC, Canada.

Maarhuis, P., & Sameshima, P. (2015, Nov). Materializing the punctum: A poetic study of the Washington State University Clothesline Project. In K. Galvin & M. Prendergast (Eds.), *Poetic inquiry II: Seeing, understanding and caring* (pp. 279-302). Rotterdam, The Netherlands: Sense.

Maarhuis, P., Sameshima, P., & Chalykoff, J. P. (2014, May 25). Research-antiphona: One transcript, four responses, and five catechizations. *Arts, Researchers & Teachers Society, Canadian Society for the Study of Education,* St. Catharines, Ontario.

Macintyre Latta, M. (2015). Book review. Arts-based and contemplative practices in research and teaching: Honoring presence. *Canadian Journal of Education, 38*(3), 1-3.

MacLure, M. (2013). Researching without representation? Language and materiality in post-qualitative methodology. *International Journal of Qualitative Studies in Education, 26*(6), pp. 658-667. doi: 10.1080/09518398.2013.788755

Magritte, R. (1988). Modern and contemporary paintings. In S. F. Rossen, R. V. Sharp, E. Stepina & S. Weidemeyer (Eds.), *Master paintings.* The Art Institute of Chicago. Chicago, IL.

MacArthur, C. A., Graham, S., & Fitzgerald, J. (2008). *Handbook of writing research.* New York, NY: Guilford Press.

MacLaren, K., & Becker, C. (2018, May 28). The benefits of classroom libraries. Poster session at the Canadian Society for the Study of Education, Regina, SK.

MacLure, M. (2013). Researching without representation? Language and materiality in post-qualitative methodology. *International Journal of Qualitative Studies in Education, 26*(6), 658-667. doi: 10.1080/09518398.2013.788755

McClelland, K. (2005). John Dewey: Aesthetic experience and artful conduct. *Education and Culture, 21*(2), 44-62.

McKay, D. (2001). *Vis à vis: Field notes on poetry and wilderness.* Kentville, NS: Gaspereau Press.

Makiguchi, T. (2002). *A geography of human life* (Katsusuke Hori et al., Trans.). San Francisco, CA: Caddo Gap.

Mandoki, K. (2007). *Everyday aesthetics: Prosaics, the play of culture and social identities.* Hampshire, UK: Ashgate.

Marais, M. (2006). J. M. Coetzee's disgrace and the task of the imagination. *Journal of Modern Literature 29*(2) 75-93.

Marino, M. T., Sameshima, P., & Beecher, C. C. (2009). Enhancing TPACK with assistive technology: Promoting inclusive practices in preservice teacher education. *Contemporary Issues in Technology and Teacher Education, 9*(2).

Marino, M. T., Sameshima, P., & Beecher, C. C. (2009). Enhancing TPACK with assistive technology: Promoting inclusive practices in preservice teacher education. *Contemporary Issues in Technology and Teacher Education, 9*(2). Retrieved from http://www.citejournal.org/vol9/iss2/general/article1.cfm

Marx, R. (2015). Accessibility versus integrity in secular mindfulness: A Buddhist commentary. *Mindfulness, 6*(5), 1153-1160.

Mattern, M. (1999). John Dewey, art and public life. *The Journal of Politics, 61*(1), 54–75.

Matus, J. (1998). *Toni Morrison: Contemporary world writers.* Manchester: Manchester University Press.

McKnight, D. (2006). The gift of curriculum method. *Curriculum and Teaching Dialogue, 8*(2), 171-183.

McManus, J. (2013, March 1). Untitled [poem]. Daily Haiku. Retrieved from http://www.dailyhaiku. org/haiku/2013-march-01

Merriam-Webster. (2018). Catechize. Available from: https://www.merriam-webster.com/dictionary/catechize

Merriam-Webster. (2016). Danger Available from http://www.merriam-webster.com/dictionary/dangerous.

Meth Project Foundation, Inc. (2012). *Meth - not even once campaign* [Videos]. Retrieved from http://www.methproject.org/ads/tv/

Meyer, J. (1996). The functional site. *Documents, 7*(Fall), 20-29.

Mezirow, J. (2012). Learning to think like an adult: Core concepts of transformation theory. In E. W. Taylor & P. Cranton (Eds.). *The handbook of transformative learning: Theory, research, and practice* (pp. 73-95). San Francisco, CA: Jossey–Bass.

Miller, J. (2005). *Educating for wisdom and compassion: Creating conditions for timeless learning.* Thousand Oaks, CA: Corwin Press.

Mimesis. (2018). Mimesis (2018). Online Liddell-Scott-Jones Greek-English Lexicon (LSJ). Retrieved from http://stephanus.tlg.uci.edu/lsj/#eid=70053&context=lsj&action=from-search

Mitchell, W. J. T. (1994). *Picture theory: Essays on verbal and visual representations.* Chicago, IL: University of Chicago Press.

Morrill, J., & Stancill, N. (1995, March 20). Yager motivational tapes reel in cash. The Charlotte Observer. Retrieved from http://www.ex-cult.org/Groups/Amway/dexter-yager-2.txt

Morris, P. (Ed). (1994). *The Bakhtin reader: Selected writings of Bakhtin, Medvedev, Voloshinov.* New York, NY: Routledge, Chapman, & Hall.

Morrison, T. (1970). *The bluest eye.* London: Vintage Books.

Morson, G. S., & Emerson, C. (1990). *Mikhail Bakhtin: Creation of a prosaics.* Stanford, CA: Stanford University Press.

Mouffe, C. (2007). Artistic activism and agonistic spaces. *Art and Research: A Journal of Ideas, Contexts and Methods, 1*(2), 1-5. Retrieved from http://www.artandresearch.org.uk/v1n2/mouffe.html

Mouffe, C. (1999). Deliberative democracy or agonistic pluralism? *Social Research, 66*(3), 745-758. Retrieved from http://www.jstor.org/stable/40971349

Mouffe, C. (2005). *On the political.* New York, NY: Verso.

Mouffe, C. (2007). Artistic activism and agonistic spaces. *Art and Research: A Journal of Ideas, Contexts and Methods, 1*(2), 1–5. Retrieved from http://www.artandresearch.org.uk/v1n2/mouffe.html

Mouffe, C. (2008). Art and democracy: Art as an agonistic intervention in public space. *Open,* 14, 6-15. Retrieved from www.skor.nl/_files/Files/OPEN14_P6-15(1).pdf

Mouffe, C. (2013). *Agonistics: Thinking the world politically.* NY: Verso.

Nardi, S. D. (2014). An embodied approach to Second World War storytelling mementoes: Probing beyond the archival into the corporeality of memories of the resistance. *Journal of Material Culture, 19*(4), 443-464.

National Institute on Drug Abuse (NIDA). Cocaine (2016, May) National Institutes of Health; U.S. Department of Health and Human Services Retrieved from: https://d14rmgtrwzf5a.cloudfront.net/sites/default/files/1141-cocaine.pdf

National Network Website for the Clothesline Project (n.d.). Retrieved from http://www.clotheslineproject.org/index.htm

NCES (National Center for Education Statistics). (2011, September). *Beginning teacher attrition and mobility: Results from the first through third waves of the 20007-08 beginning teacher longitudinal study.* Retrieved from http://nces.ed.gov/pubs2011/ 2011318/

Nehls, N., & Sallmann, J. (2005). Living with a history of physical and/or sexual abuse, substance use, and mental health problems: The perspectives of women. *Qualitative Health Research, 15*(3), 1-17.

Neumiller, J., Corbett, C., Gates, B., & Vandermause, R. (2015). *Preserving self: Empowering older persons with multiple chronic medical conditions.* Patient Centered Outcomes Research Institute. Washington State University. Retrieved from https://nursing.wsu.edu/research/funded-projects/preserving-self-empowering-older-persons-with-multiple-chronic-medical-conditions/

New London Group. (1996). A pedagogy of multiliteracies: Designing social futures. *Harvard Educational Review, 66*(1), 60-92.

Newton, R. M. (2005). Learning to teach in the shadow of 9/11: A portrait of two Arab American preservice Teachers. *Qualitative Inquiry, 11*(1), 81–94.

Nguyen, V. T. (2015). *The sympathizer.* New York, NY: Grove Press.

Nikitina, S. (2002). *Three strategies for interdisciplinary teaching: Contextualizing, conceptualizing, and problem-solving.* Retrieved March 25, 2009, from http://www.pz.harvard.edu/interdisciplinary/ pubtwo.html

Nilan, P. (2002), "Dangerous fieldwork" Re-examined: The question of researcher subject position, *Qualitative Research,* 2(3), 363-386.

Northcote, M., & Featherstone, T. (2006). New metaphors for teaching and learning in a university context. In *Critical visions: Proceedings of the 29th Annual HERDSA Conference,* Perth, WA, 10-12 July (pp. 251-258). Retrieved from http://www.herdsa.org.au/publications/conference-proceedings/research-and-development-higher-education-critical-visions-33

Norris, J. (2011). Towards the use of the 'Great Wheel' as a model in determining the quality and merit of arts-based projects (research and instruction). *International Journal of Education & the Arts, 12,* 1-24. Retrieved from http://www.ijea.org/v12si1/index.html

Norris, J., & Sawyer, R. D. (2016). (Eds.). *Theorizing curriculum studies, teacher education and research through duoethnographic pedagogy.* New York, NY: Palgrave Macmillan.

Norris, J., Sawyer, R. D., & Lund, D. (Eds.). (2012). *Duoethnography: Promoting personal and societal change within dialogic self-study.* Walnut Creek, CA: Left Coast.

Norris, J., Sawyer, R. D., & Wiebe, S. (2016). Teaching through duoethnography in teacher education and graduate curriculum theory courses. In J. Norris & R. D. Sawyer (Eds.), *Theorizing curriculum studies, teacher education and research through duoethnographic pedagogy* (pp. 15-38). New York, NY: Palgrave Macmillan.

Nutbrown, C. (2010). Naked by the pool? Blurring the image? Ethical issues in the portrayal of young children in arts-based educational research, *Qualitative Inquiry, 17*(1), 3-14.

Oman, D., Shapiro, S. L., Thoresen, C. E., Plante, T. G., & Flinders, T. (2008). Meditation lowers stress and supports forgiveness among college students: A randomized controlled trial. *Journal of American College Health, 56*(5), 569-578.

Orr, D. (2014). In a mindful moral voice: Mindful compassion, the ethic of care and education. *Philosophical Inquiry in Education, 21*(2), 42-54.

Ortega, M. (2008). Wounds of self: Experience, word, image, and identity. *Journal of Speculative Philosophy, 22*(4), 235-247. Retrieved from http://johncarroll.academia.edu/MarianaOrtega/Papers/245527/Wounds_of_Self_Experience_Word_Image_and_Identity

O'Sullivan, S. (2006). *Art encounters Deleuze and Guattari: Thought beyond representation.* New York, NY: Palgrave Macmillan.

Palimpsest. (2018). Online Liddell-Scott-Jones Greek-English Lexicon (LSJ). Retrieved from http://stephanus.tlg.uci.edu/lsj/#eid=79327&context=search&action=from-search

Parallax. (2018). Dictionary.com. Retrieved from http://www.dictionary.com/browse/parallax

Paulson, S., Davidson, R., Jha, A., & Kabat-Zinn, J. (2013). Becoming conscious: The science of mindfulness. *Annals of the New York Academy of Sciences, 1303*(1), 87-104.

Peckham Space (2011, August). *Network: Sonia Boyce* [Press release]. Retrieved from http://www.peckhamplatform.com/system/files/062013/51b491af7d63685384000002/original/Network_Press_Release.pdf?137078827

Pegrum, M., (2009). *From blogs to bombs: The future of digital technologies in education.* Crawley, Australia: UWA.

Pilgrim, R. B. (1986). Intervals (*ma*) in space and time: Foundations for a religio-aesthetic paradigm in Japan. *History of Religions, 25*(3), 255-277. Retrieved from http://www.jstor.org.ezproxy.lakeheadu.ca/stable/1062515?seq=1#page_scan_tab_contents

Pinar, W. (1988). Autobiography and the architecture of self. *JCT, 8*(1), 7-36.

Pinar, W. F. (2004). *What is curriculum theory?* Mahwah, NJ: Erlbaum.

Pinar, W. F. (2010). Notes on a blue guitar. *Journal of Educational Controversy, 5*(1), 1-9. Retrieved from http://cedar.wwu.edu/jec/vol5/iss1/18

Pinar, W., & Grumet, M. (1976). *Toward a poor curriculum.* Dubuque, IA: Kendall/Hunt.

Pinar, W., Reynolds, W. M., Slattery, P., & Taubman, P. M. (1995). *Understanding curriculum: An introduction to the study of historical and contemporary curriculum discourses.* New York: Peter Lang.

Pink, S. (2007). *Doing visual ethnography.* (2nd Edition). Thousand Oaks, CA: Sage.

Pinnegar, S., Mangelson, J., Reed, M., & Groves, S. (2011). Exploring preservice teachers' metaphor plotlines. *Teaching and Teacher Education, 27,* 639–647. doi:10.1016/j. tate.2010.11.002

Poiesis. (2018). Online Liddell-Scott-Jones Greek-English Lexicon (LSJ). Retrieved from http://stephanus.tlg.uci.edu/lsj/#eid=86774&context=lsj&action=from-search

Pollock, D. (1998). Performative writing. In Phelan, Peggy, & Lane (Eds.), *The ends of performance* (pp. 73–103). New York: University Press.

Polysemy. (2018). *Collins English dictionary.* Dictionary.com. Retrieved from http://dictionary.reference.com/browse/Polysemy

Pope, D., Brown, M., & Miles, S. (2015). *Overloaded and underprepared: Strategies for stronger schools and healthy, successful kids.* San Francisco: Jossey-Bass.

Prendergast, M. (2004). Ekphrasis and inquiry: Artful writing on arts-based topics in educational research. *Proceedings from Imaginative Education Research Group Annual Meeting.* Retrieved from http://ierg.net/confs/2004/Proceedings/Prendergast_Monica.pdf

Prendergast, M. (2009). Introduction: The phenomena of poetry in research. In M. Prendergast, C. Leggo, & P. Sameshima (Eds.), *Poetic inquiry: Vibrant voices in the social sciences* (pp. xix-xiii). Rotterdam, the Netherlands: Sense.

Prendergast, M., Leggo, C., & Sameshima, P. (Eds.). (2009a). *Poetic inquiry: Vibrant voices in the social sciences.* Rotterdam, The Netherlands: Sense.

Prendergast, M., Leggo, C., & Sameshima, P. (Guest Eds.). (2009b). Poetic inquiry. *Educational Insights, 13*(3). Retrieved from http://www.ccfi.educ.ubc.ca/publication/insights/index.html

Punter, D. (2007). *Metaphor.* New York, NY: Routledge.

Purser, R., & Loy, D. (2013, July 1). Beyond McMindfulness. *Huffington Post.* Retrieved from: http://www.huffingtonpost.com/ron-purser/beyond-mcmindfulness_b_3519289.html

Puurveen, G., Phinney, A., Cox, S., & Purvest, B. (2015), Ethical issues in the use of video observations with people with advanced dementia and their caregivers in nursing home environments'. *Visual Methodologies, 3*(2), 16-24.

Rancière, J. (1991). *The ignorant schoolmaster* (K. Ross, Trans.). Stanford, CA: Stanford University Press. Reason, P. (1994). Three approaches to participative inquiry. In N. K. Denzin & Y. S. Lincoln (Eds.), *Handbook of qualitative research* (pp. 324-329). Thousand Oaks, CA.

Renfrew, A. (2015). *Mikhail Bakhtin.* New York, NY: Routledge.Rice, E. (2005). *Schizophrenia and violence: The perspectives of women and case managers.* Madison, WI: University of Wisconsin-Madison.

Richardson, L. (1992a). The poetic representation of lives: Writing a postmodern sociology. *Studies in Symbolic Interaction, 13,* 19-29.

Richardson, L. (1992b). The consequences of poetic representation: Writing the other, rewriting the self. In C. Ellis & M. G. Flaherty (Eds.), *Investigating subjectivity: Research on lived experience* (pp. 125-140). Newbury Park, CA: Sage.

Richardson, L. (1994). Nine poems. *Journal of Contemporary Ethnography, 23*(1), 3-13.

Richardson, L. (1997). *Fields of play: Constructing an academic life.* New Brunswick, NJ: Rutgers University Press.

Richardson, M. (1998). Poetics in the field and on the page. *Qualitative Inquiry, 4*(4), 451-462.

Richardson, L. (2000). Writing: a method of inquiry. In N. Denzin & Y. Lincoln (Eds), *The handbook of qualitative research.* (2nd ed., pp. 923-948). Thousand Oaks, CA: Sage.

Richardson, L., & St. Pierre, E. (2005). Writing: A method of inquiry. In N. K. Denzin & Y. S. Lincoln (Eds.), *Handbook of qualitative research* (3rd ed., pp. 959–978). Thousand Oaks, CA: Sage.

Ritchie, L. (2013), Photographs of the ageing body in a nursing journal: A profession's response', *Nursing Inquiry, 20*(2), 101-110. Roll, J. M. (2007). Contingency management: An evidence-based component of methamphetamine use disorder treatments. *Addiction, 102*(Suppl. 1), 114-120.

Rosenblatt, L. (1978). *The Reader the text, the poem: The transactional theory of the literary work.* Carbondale, IL: Southern Illinois University Press. Rothenberg, J. (1994). Je est un autre: Ethnopoetics and the poet as other. *American Anthropologist, 96*(3), 523-524.

Rud, A. G., Garrison, J., & Stone, L. (Eds.). (2009). *John Dewey at 150: Reflections for a new century.* West Lafayette, IN: Purdue University Press.

Ryklin, M. K. (1993). Bodies of terror: Theses toward a logic of violence. *New Literary History, 24*(1), 51-74.

Saito, N. (2009). Reconstruction in Dewey's pragmatism: Home, neighborhood, and otherness. In A. G. Rud, J. Garrison, & L. Stone (Eds.), *John Dewey at 150: Reflections for a new century* (p. 84-95). West Lafayette, IN: Purdue University Press.

Sameshima, P. (2007a). *Seeing red: A pedagogy of parallax.* Amherst, NY: Cambria Press.

Sameshima, P. (2007b). Seeing shadows in new light: A procatalepsis on narrative inquiry as professional development. (Special issue: Creativity and education: An international perspective), *New Horizons in Education, 55*(3), 10-21.

Sameshima, P. (2008a). Letters to a new teacher: A curriculum of embodied aesthetic awareness. *Teacher Education Quarterly, 35*(2), 29-44.

Sameshima, P. (2008b). AutoethnoGRAPHIC relationality through paradox, parallax, and metaphor. In S. Springgay, R. Irwin, C. Leggo, & P. Gouzouasis (Eds.), *Being with a/r/tography* (pp. 45-56). Rotterdam, The Netherlands: Sense.

Sameshima, P. (2009). Stop teaching! Hosting an ethical responsibility through a pedagogy of parallax. Journal of Curriculum and Pedagogy, 6(1), 11-18. doi:10.1080/15505170.2009.10411719

Sameshima, P. (2013). Review of Duoethnography: Understanding qualitative research & Duoethnography: Promoting personal and societal change within dialogic self-study. *Journal of the Canadian Association for Curriculum Studies, 11*(1), 174-190.

Sameshima, P. (2019). I'm thinking about nothing. In P. Sameshima, B. White & A. Sinner (Eds.), *Ma: Materiality in teaching and Learning* (pp. 3-16). New York, NY: Peter Lang.

Sameshima, P. (in review). Designing imaginative processes: Making the world.

Sameshima, P., & Irwin, R. (2008). Rendering dimensions of a liminal currere. *Transnational Curriculum Inquiry, 5*(2), 1-15.

Sameshima, P., & Knowles, G. (2008). Into artfulness: Being grounded but not bounded. In J. G. Knowles, S. Promislow, and A. Cole (Eds.), *Creating scholartistry: Imaging the arts-informed thesis or dissertation* (pp. 107-120). Halifax, Nova Scotia, Canada: Backalong Books.

Sameshima, P., & Maarhuis, P. (2013, March). *Deepening and widening semantic fields through arts integrated inquiry.* Paper presentation. National Art Educators Association Conference (NAEA). Fort Worth, TX.

Sameshima, P., & Maarhuis, P. (2013, June 5). *Ekphrastic catechization: Arts-integrated, collaborative, and multimodal research techniques.* Presentation for the Canadian Society for the Study of Women in Education, Canadian Society for the Study of Education, Victoria, BC

Sameshima, P., Miyakawa, M., & Lockett, M. (2017, Dec.). Scholarly engagement through making: A response to Arts-Based and Contemplative Practices in Research and Teaching. *Revista VIS, 16*(2), 45-67. Accessed at: http://periodicos.unb.br/index.php/revistavis/article/view/25466

Sameshima, P., & Sinner, A. (2009). Awakening to soma heliakon: Encountering teacher-researcher-learning in the 21st Century. *Canadian Journal of Education, 32*(2), 271-284.

Sameshima P., & Slingerland, D. (2015, Aug.). Reparative pedagogy: Empathic aesthetic learning. *Canadian Review of Art Education, 42*(1), 1-21

Sameshima, P., & Slingerland, D. (2016, July 22-28). Dandelion hopes [Sewing and needle felting penny rug]. *The Alzheimer Society in Conjunction with the Alzheimer's Association International Conference: Visual Art Exhibition.* Toronto, ON.

Sameshima, P., Slingerland, D., Wakewich, P., Morrisseau, K., & Zehbe, I. (2017, February). Growing wellbeing through community participatory arts: The Anishinaabek cervical cancer screening study (ACCSS). In G. Barton & M. Baguley (Eds.), *The Palgrave handbook of global arts education* (pp. 399-416). Brisbane, Australia: Palgrave. doi: 10.1057/978-1-137-55585-4

Sameshima, P., & Vandermause, R. (2008). Parallaxic praxis: An artful interdisciplinary collaborative research methodology. In B. Kožuh, R. Kahn & A Kozlowska (Eds.), *The practical science of society* (pp. 141-152). Grand Forks, Nottingham, Krakow: The College of Education and Human Development & Slovenian Research Agency (AARS).

Sameshima, P., & Vandermause, R. (2009). Methamphetamine addiction and recovery: Poetic inquiry to feel. In M. Prendergast, C. Leggo & P. Sameshima (Eds.), *Poetic inquiry: Vibrant voices in the social sciences* (pp. 275-286). Rotterdam, The Netherlands: Sense.

Sameshima, P., Vandermause, R., Chalmers, S., & Gabriel. (2009). *Introduction. Climbing the ladder with Gabriel: Poetic inquiry of a methamphetamine addict in recovery* (pp. 3-16). Rotterdam, The Netherlands: Brill.

Sameshima, P., Vandermause, R., Chalmers, S., & Gabriel. (2009). *Climbing the ladder with Gabriel: Poetic inquiry of a methamphetamine addict in recovery.* Rotterdam, The Netherlands: Sense.

Sameshima, P., Vandermause, R., & Santucci, C. (2012). Motherhood and meth: Ekphrasic intervention. In S. Thomas, A. Cole, & S. Steward (Eds.), *The art of poetic inquiry* (Vol. 5, Arts-Informed Inquiry Series). Halifax, NS & Toronto, ON, Canada: Backalong Books & Centre for Arts-Informed Research.

Sameshima, P., Wiebe, S., & Becker, C. (2019, July. Submitted). leaves evergreen / she walks / down the street: dialogic meaning from making. *International Society for Education through Art (InSEA) World Congress.* Vancouver, BC.

Sameshima, P., Wiebe, S., & Hayes, M. (in review). Imagination: The generation of possibility. In B. Andrews (Ed.), *Perspectives on arts education research in Canada. Vol. 1. Surveying the landscape.* Rotterdam, The Netherlands: Brill.

SAMHSA (Substance Abuse and Mental Health Services Administration). (2008). Office of applied studies. *Treatment Episode Data Set (TEDS).* Retrieved May 6, 2009, from http://oas.samhsa.gov/TEDS2k7highlights/TEDSHigh12k7Tbl2a.htm

Sartre, J. P. (1946). *Existentialism is a humanism* (C. Macomber, Trans.). New Haven, CT: Yale University Press.

Saunders, V. (2014, October). "*If you knew the end of a story would you still want to hear it?*" PhD Pre-Completion Seminar, Cairns Institute, JCU, Cairns.

Saunders, V (2015) *". . .": Using a non-bracketed narrative to story recovery in Aboriginal mental health care.* Unpublished thesis. Townsville, Australia: Nursing, Midwifery & Nutrition, College of Healthcare Sciences, Division of Tropical Health and Medicine, James Cook University.

Sawyer, R. D., & Norris, J. (2013). *Duoethnography: Understanding qualitative research.* New York: NY: Oxford University Press.

Scardamalia, M., & Bereiter, C. (1991). Literate expertise. In K. A. Ericsson & J. Smith (Eds.), *Toward a general theory of expertise: Prospects and limits* (pp. 172-194). Cambridge, United Kingdom: Cambridge University Press.

Schafer, L. (2013). Beginning teacher attrition: A question of identity making and identity shifting. *Teachers and Teaching: Theory and Practice. 19*(3), 260–274.

Schubert, W. (2010). Journeys of expansion and synopsis: Tensions in books that shaped curriculum inquiry, 1968–present. *Curriculum Inquiry, 40*(1), 17–94. doi: 10.1111/j. 1467-873X.2009.00468.x

Sedgwick, E. (1997). Paranoid reading and reparative reading; Or, you're so paranoid, you probably think this introduction is about you. In E. Sedgwick (Ed.), *Navel gazing: Queer readings in fiction* (pp. 1-40). Durham and London: Duke University Press.

Seigfried, C. H. (Ed.). (2002a). *Feminist interpretations of John Dewey.* University Park, PA: University of Pennsylvania Press.

Seigfried, C. H. (2002b). Shedding skins. *Hypatia, 17*(4) 173-186. Retrieved from http://onlinelibrary.wiley.com/doi/10.1111/hypa.2002.17.issue-4/issuetoc

Semple, S., Grant, I., & Patterson, T. L. (2004). Female methamphetamine users: social characteristics and sexual risk behavior. *Women's Health, 40*(3), 35-50.

Semple, S., Strathdee, S., Zians, J., & Patterson, T. (2011). Methamphetamine-using parents. *Journal of Studies on Alcohol and Drugs,* 72, 954-964.

Senior, R. (2010). Connectivity: A framework for understanding effective language teaching in face-to-face and online learning communities. *RELC Journal, 41*(2), 137-147.

Simon, R. (2000). The paradoxical practice of Zakhor. In Simon, R., Rosenberg, S., & Eppert, C. (Eds.), *Between hope & despair: Pedagogy and the remembrance of historical trauma.* NY: Rowman & Littlefield.

Simon, R. (2014). *A pedagogy of witnessing: Curatorial practice and the pursuit of social justice.* Albany, NY: State University of New York.

Sinclair, M. (2006). *Heidegger, Aristotle and the work of art: poiesis in being.* New York, NY: Palgrave Macmillan.

Sinner, A., Wicks, J., & Rak, S. (2015). Minding the gap: Exploring the potential of the teaching portfolios as curricular innovation. *Visual Arts Research, 41*(1), 16-26. doi:10.5406/ visuartsrese.41.1.0016

Shapiro, S., Brown, K. W., & Astin, J. A. (2008, October). *Toward the integration of meditation into higher education: A review of research.* Northampton, MA: Contemplative Mind in Society. Retrieved from http://prsinstitute.org/

downloads/related/spiritual-sciences/meditation/TowardtheIntegrationof MeditationintoHigherEducation.pdf

Shoptaw, S., Huber, A., Peck, J., Yang, X., Liu, J., Dang, J., et al. (2006). Randomized, placebo-controlled trial of sertraline and contingency management for the treatment of methamphetamine dependence. *Drug and Alcohol Dependence, 85*(1), 12-18.

Shusterman, R. (2008). Body consciousness: A philosophy of mindfulness and somaesthetics. New York, NY: Cambridge University Press.

Small, S. A. (1995). Action-oriented research: Models and methods. *Journal of Marriage and the Family, 57*, 941-955.

Sontag, S. (1973). *On photography.* New York, NY: Picador.

Sontag, S. (2003). *Regarding the pain of others.* New York, NY: Picador.

Sorites. (2018). *Online Liddell-Scott-Jones Greek-English Lexicon* (LSJ). Retrieved from http://stephanus.tlg.uci.edu/lsj/#eid=104963&context=lsj&action=from-search

Sorites. (n.d.). *Collins English dictionary.* Dictionary.com. Retrieved from http://dictionary.reference.com/browse/sorites

Spivak. G. C. (2012). *An aesthetic education in the era of globalization.* Cambridge MA: Harvard University Press.

Springgay, S., Irwin, R., & Wilson Kind, S. (2005). A/r/tography as living inquiry through art and text. *Qualitative Inquiry, 11*(6), 897-912.

Springgay, S., Irwin, R., Leggo, C., & Gouzouasis, P. (Eds.). (2008). *Being with a/r/tography.* Rotterdam, The Netherlands: Sense.

St. Pierre, E. A. (1997). Methodology in the fold and the irruption of transgressive data. *International Journal of Qualitative Studies in Education, 10*(2), 175-189.

Stallybrass, P., & White, A. (1986). *The politics and poetics of transgression.* Ithaca, NY: Cornell University Press.

Stern, J. J. (2000). *Metaphor in context.* Massachusetts Institute of Technology Press: Cambridge, MA. Retrieved from http://www.sas.upenn.edu/~campe/Papers/Camp.SternMICNous.pdf

Sternberg, R. J., Kaufman, J. C., & Pretz, J. E. (2001). The propulsion model of creative contributions applied to the arts and letters. *Journal of Creative Behavior, 35*, 75 – 101.

Sternberg, R. J., Kaufman, J. C., & Pretz, J. E. (2002). *The creativity conundrum: A propulsion model of kinds of creative contributions.* New York, NY: Psychology Press.

Sternberg, R. J., Kaufman, J. C., & Pretz, J. E. (2003). A propulsion model of creative leadership. *Leadership Quarterly, 14*, 455-473.

Stock, R. V., Sameshima, P., & Slingerland, D. (2016, July). Constructing pre-service teacher identities through processes of parallax. *LEARNing Landscapes, 9*(2), 489-512. Retrieved from http://www.learninglandscapes.ca/index.php/learnland/article/view/Constructing-Pre-Service-Teacher-Identities-Through-Processes-of-Parallax

Stern, J. (2000). *Metaphor in context.* Cambridge, MA: MIT Press.

Struyven, K., Dochy, F., Janssens, S., & Gielen, S. (2006). On the dynamics of students' approaches to learning: The effects of the teaching / learning environment. *Learning and Instruction, 16*(1), 279-294.

Sullivan, G. (2005). *Art practice as research: Inquiry in the visual arts.* Thousand Oaks, CA: Sage.

Sumara, D., & Luce-Kapler, R. (1993). Action research as writerly text: Locating co-labouring in collaboration. *Educational Action Research, 1*(3), 387-395.

Tanne, J. H. (2006, February). Methamphetamine epidemic hits middle America. *BMJ, 332*(7538), 382.

Tavin, K., & Kallio-Tavin, M. (2014), The Cat, the cradle, and the silver spoon: Violence in contemporary art and the question of ethics of art education', *Studies in Art Education, 56*:1, 426-437

TCPS2 (2014), Tri-Council policy statement: Ethical conduct for research involving humans. Government of Canada. Retrieved from, http://www.pre.ethics.gc.ca/pdf/eng/tcps2-2014/TCPS_2_FINAL_Web.pdf.

The Guardian Teacher Network. (2015, October 11). *'Show us that you care': A student's view on what makes a perfect teacher.* Retrieved from http://www.theguardian.com/teacher-network/2015/oct/11/show-care-students-view-what-makes-perfect-teacher

Thomas, L., & Beauchamp, C. (2011). Understanding new teachers' professional identities through metaphor. *Teaching and Teacher Education, 27,* 762–769. doi:10.1016/j. tate.2010.12.007

Thayer-Bacon, B. J. (2003). Buddhism as an example of a holistic, relational epistemology. *Encounter: Education for Meaning and Social Justice, 16*(3), 27-38.

Todres, L. (2008). Being with that: The relevance of embodied understanding for practice. *Qualitative Health Research, 18*(11), 1566-1573.

Tsun Haggarty, H. (2015). *The epistemology of arts-integrating research methodologies: How are the arts a way of knowing?* Unpublished Masters Thesis, Lakehead University.

Universities Canada (2016, November). *Mobilizing people and ideas: Supporting the creative economy and fostering Canadian culture in the digital world.* Available from https://www.univcan.ca/wp-content/uploads/2016/12/universities-canada-submission-fed-govt-review-on-canadian-content-in-digital-world-dec-2016.pdf

Upshaw, A. (2018, February submission). *Proposal topic: Stories on veteran post-traumatic stress syndrome.* US Department of Defence. Vandermause, R. K. (2007). Assessing for alcohol use disorders in women: Experiences of advanced practice nurses in primary care settings. *Journal of Addictions Nursing, 18*(4), 187-198.

Vanderwees, C. (2015). Photographs of falling bodies and the ethics of vulnerability in Jonathan Safran Foer's extremely loud and incredibly close. *Canadian Review of American Studies', 45(2),* 174-194.

Vessey, D. (2006). Philosophical hermeneutics. In J. R. Shook & J. Margolis (Eds.), A companion to pragmatism (pp. 209-214). Malden, MA: Blackwell.

Vic, P., & Ross, T. (2003). Research report: Methamphetamine use among incarcerated women. *Journal of Substance Use, 8*(2), 69-77.

Volkow, N. D., Chang, L., & Wang, G. J. (2003). Low level of brain dopamine D2 receptors in methamphetamine abusers: Association with metabolism in the orbitofrontal cortex. *Year Book of Psychiatry & Applied Mental Health*, 305-306.

Waks, L. J. (2009). Inquiry, agency, and art: John Dewey's contribution to pragmatic cosmopolitanism. In A. G. Rud, J. Garrison, & L. Stone (Eds.), *John Dewey at 150: Reflections for a new century* (pp. 96-103). West Lafayette, IN: Purdue University Press.

Walsh, S., & Bai, H. (2014). Writing witness conscious. In S. Walsh, B. Bickel, and C. Leggo (Eds.), *Arts-based contemplative practices in research and teaching: Honoring presence.* (p. 24). New York, NY: Routledge.

Waycott, J., Guillemin, M., Warr, D. J., Cox, S., Drew, S., & Howell, C. (2015), Re/formulating ethical issues for visual research methods', *Visual Methodologies, 3(2)*, 4-15.

Weber, S. J., & Mitchell, C. (1996). Drawing ourselves into teaching: Studying the images that shape and distort teacher education. *Teaching & Teacher Education, 12*(3), 303-313.

Westbrook, R. (1991). *John Dewey and American democracy.* Ithaca NY: Cornell University Press. Whitacre, E. (2013). *Virtual choir live.* Ted Talks Conferences. Retrieved from: http://www.ted.com/talks/eric_whitacre_virtual_choir_live; http://www.amara.org/en/videos/eocjrPZZ3cU8/en/5759/

White, B. E., & Lemieux, A. (2015, Autumn). Reflecting selves: Pre-service teacher identity development explored through material culture. *LEARNing Landscapes 9*(1), 267-283.

Wiebe, S. (2008). Resonation in writing. In S. Springgay, R. Irwin, C. Leggo, & P. Gouzouasis (Eds.), *Being with a/r/tography* (pp. 95-107). Rotterdam, Netherlands: Sense.

Wiebe, S. (2010). A poet's journey as a/r/togrpher: Teaching poetry to create a community of practice with junior high school students. *Learning Landscapes, 4*(1), 239-255.

Wiebe, S. (2012). The poet and the pea: poems staged in Menippean dialogue to explore empathy in education. *Creative Approaches to Research, 5*(2), 34-47.

Wiebe, S. (2013). How do I teach writing in a digital and global world? In K. James, T. Dobson, & C. Leggo (Eds.), *English in middle and secondary classrooms* (pp. 223-227). Toronto, ON: Pearson.

Wiebe, S. (2016). Rock 'em sock 'em poetry. In M. McLarnon et al. (Authors), The school bus symposium: A poetic journey of co-created conference space. Art *Research International: A transdisciplinary Journal, 1*(1), 141-173.

Wiebe, S. (2019). Breathe with the magnificent materiality of being: Haiku, ma, and kokoro. In P. Sameshima, B. White & A. Sinner (Eds.), *Ma: Materiality in teaching and Learning* (pp. 73-82). New York, NY: Peter Lang.

Wiebe, S., & Caseley Smith, C. (2016). A/r/t/ography and teacher education in the 21st century. *McGill Journal of Education, 51*(3). 1163-1178. Retrieved from http://mje.mcgill.ca/article/view/9312

Wiebe, S., & Morrison-Robinson, D. (2013). Becoming A/r/tpgraphers whilst contesting rationalist discourses of work. *UNESCO Observatory Multi-Disciplinary Journal of the Arts*, 3(2), 1-18.

Wiebe, S., & Sameshima, P. (2017, Dec.). Generating self: Catechizations in poetry. *Revista VIS, 16*(2), 140-155. Retrieved from ttp://periodicos.unb.br/index.php/revistavis/article/view/25465

Wiebe, S., & Sameshima, P. (2018, January). Sympathizing with social justice, poetry of invitation and generation. *Art/Research International, 3*(1)7-29. Retrieved from https://journals.library.ualberta.ca/ari/index.php/ari/index

Wiebe, S., & Sameshima, P. (2018, February). Sympathizing with social justice, poetry of invitation and generation. *Art/Research International*, 3(1)7-29.

Walsh, S., Bickel, B., & Leggo, C. (2014). *Arts-based contemplative practices in research and teaching: Honoring presence.* New York, NY: Routledge.

Wiebe, S., Sameshima, P., Irwin, R., Leggo, C., Grauer, K., & Gouzouasis, P. (2007). Re-imagining arts integration: Rhizomatic relations to the everyday. *Journal of Educational Thought, 41*(3), 263-280.

Wiersma, E., Sameshima, P., Dupuis, S., Caffery, P., & Harvey, D. (2015, July 3). Visually depicting the dementia journey. *44th Annual British Society of Gerontology Conference 2015.* Newcastle Upon Tyne, England.

Wiles, R., Prosser, J., Bagnoli, A., Clark, A., Davies, K., Holland, S., & Renold, E. (2008), Visual Ethics: Ethical Issues in Visual Research, *ESRC National Centre for Research Methods. Retrieved from* http://eprints.nacrm.ac.uk/421/1/MethodsReviewPaperNCRM-011.pdf.

Williamson, B. (2013). The future of curriculum. School knowledge in a digital age. Cambridge, MA: MIT Press.

Wolsey, T. D., & Grisham, D. L. (2007). Adolescents and the new literacies: Writing engagement. *Action in Teacher Education, 29*(2), 29-38.

Yale book of quotations (2006). New Haven, CT: Yale University Press.

Zappan, J. (2000). Mikhail Bakhtin. In Michael G. Moran and Michelle Ballif (Eds.), *Twentieth-Century rhetoric and rhetoricians: Critical studies and sources* (pp. 7-20). Westport, CT: Greenwood Press.

Zapperi, G. (2013). Women's reappearance: Rethinking the archive in contemporary art–feminist perspectives. *Feminist Review, 105*(1), p. 21-47.

Ziek, B. (2004). The felt frontier: I: Polly Stirling: Contemporary feltmaker. *Surface Design Journal, 28*(4), 35-38

Zwicky, J. (2008). *Wisdom and metaphor.* Kentville, NS: Gaspereau Press.

Author Biographies

Dr. Pauline Sameshima is a Professor and Canada Research Chair in Arts Integrated Studies at Lakehead University. Her interests are in creativity, imagination, community health, and curriculum theory. As a practicing artist, poet, and designer, Sameshima's interdisciplinary projects use the arts to catalyze innovation, generate wanderings, and provoke new dialogues through creative scholarship. She is the Editor-in-Chief of *The Journal of the Canadian Association for Curriculum Studies* and curates the Lakehead Research Education Galleries. Website: solspire.com

Dr. Patricia L. Maarhuis is a researcher, educator, and artist in Health & Wellness Services at Washington State University. Her interdisciplinary research projects and artwork focus on the intersections between high-risk behavior, cultural context, the aesthetic dimensions of education, and experiential learning. She designs curricula and teaches faculty, staff, and healthcare professionals on research-based interventions and education strategies for adults with high-risk health experiences such as violence, trauma, substance abuse, and mental health concerns across multiple university departments. Website: Inbricolage.com

Dr. Sean Wiebe is an Associate Professor of Education at the University of Prince Edward Island and teaches courses in multiliteracies, curriculum theory, and critical pedagogy. He has been the principal investigator on four Canadian Social Sciences and Humanities Research Council funded projects exploring the intersections of creativity, the creative economy, language and literacies, and arts-integrated inquiries. One of his projects, based on findings generated from multiple sites across Canada and using the parallaxic praxis model, investigates how establishing a creative ethos in schools might support teachers as contributors to Canada's creative economy.

Glossary

Select terms suggested by students:

Aesthetic: the physical beauty of an object or work; the focus on the physical appearance, underlying principles

Agonism: struggle between adversaries; a philosophy where conflict is important to politics and societal change

Answerability: responsibility for explaining or justifying one's actions

Antiphona: a refrain that repeats, the ways in which the commonalities between rendered works echo one another or come together to teach the viewer/researcher something new

Artefact vs. Artifact: The use of the word artefact throughout the book is intentional. While many sources indicate that the difference in spelling is geographic with British English preferring artefact and North American English preferring artifact, the word artefact is used in this book to specifically refer to constructed objects that reference a part, a residual, or an abstract object, perceived through context. An artifact is generally considered a complete object, a whole. An artefact is an object made by a human being or is something that results from a preparation or investigation

Aporia: challenges or puzzles regarding the rendered work that challenge closure in thinking

Assemblage: a gathering, accumulation, or remixture

Bacchanalian: a drunken revelry

Bricolage: the construction of a creation from a variety of available objects

Catchization: question or examine closely or methodically; to move knowledge forward through questioning systematically or searchingly

Dissonance: tension created as a result of two clashing or disharmonious elements

Ekphrasis: a device where something is recreated in a different medium; i.e., a painting translated into a poem

Etiology: the cause or reason for something; investigation of the cause of something

Evanagnostos: the legibility of the rendered work; how well the audience can read the rendered work

Found poetry: poetry created from previously available text; i.e., creating a poem from interview transcripts by using the participant's words

Hermeneutic: methodology of interpretation of human actions, specific texts or other literary texts

Heteroglossia: the presence of multiple expressed viewpoints located in a text or an artwork; notion that all conflicting perspectives have value

Heuristic: an approach to learning where the answer is found using hands on, trial and error based inquiry processes

Intertextuality: interconnection and how different words influence interpretation; how the rendered works speak to each other, the researchers and the data they represent

Juxtaposition: the placement of objects side by side, often to create contrast or comparison between the objects

Liminal: transitional, borderline, at the edge, in progress, just beginning or forming

Mimesis: imitation or making a likeness; a mirroring or reproduction of data found in the rendered artwork

Narrative: the story created by the data collected in a study

Ontological: beliefs about what exists and how reality is categorized. An epistemological position refers to a stance the researcher adopts toward the nature of knowledge or how something is known

Palimpsest: traces of different perspectives that come through the underlayers of a work

Parallax: the change in an object/view point due to a change in perspective by the viewer

Polysemy: phrases and words that have multiple meanings

Poiesis: a moment when the rendered work has meaning added to it through discussion and interpretation; the process of a work being moved from a static object to an interpretive body

Portraiture: a method of thinking about and producing rich representations of phenomena

Post-Qualitative: inquiry that seeks to move outside the normalized structures of qualitative research methodologies and humanist epistemologies, and ontologies

Praxis: the process in which the learned is put into practice; the embodied form of engaging, realizing, and applying theory in practice

Punctum: to wound; the emotional connection that occurs when looking at a visual

Reparative: effecting repair, balance, returning

Residual research: research benefits that continue to occur without the researcher present. i.e., Similar to royalties from a book publication, permanent research art exhibitions can create reminders in communities of community involvement

Sorites: a significance found in the data or rendered works

Transactive: an object that interacts with a viewer in a reciprocal or influential manner

Index

A

B

C

D

E

K

L

M

N

O

P

R

S

T

W

CPSIA information can be obtained
at www.ICGtesting.com
Printed in the USA
BVHW021910181019
561508BV00006B/9/P